ARROWS
OF THE
ALMIGHTY

ALSO BY MICHAEL BAR-ZOHAR

The Hunt for German Scientists
Ben Gurion: The Armed Prophet
The Avengers
Embassies in Crisis
The Third Truth
Spies in the Promised Land
The Spy Who Died Twice
Ben Gurion: A Political Biography
The Deadly Document
The Quest for the Red Prince

Michael
Bar-Zohar

ARROWS
OF
THE
ALMIGHTY

The Most Extraordinary
True Spy Story of
World War II

Macmillan Publishing Company   New York

Macmillan Publishing Company
866 Third Avenue, New York, N.Y. 10022
Collier Macmillan Canada, Inc.

Library of Congress Cataloging in Publication Data
Bar-Zohar, Michael, 1938-
    Arrows of the almighty.
    Includes index.
    1. Fackenheim, Paul Ernst, 1892-   2. World
War, 1939-1945—Secret Service—Germany.   3. Spies—
Germany—Biography.   4. Jews—Germany—Biography.
I. Title.
D810.S8F317   1985   940.54′87′43   85-10643
ISBN 0-02-507610-8

Macmillan books are available at special discounts for bulk purchases
for sales promotions, premiums, fund-raising, or educational use.
For details, contact:

Special Sales Director
Macmillan Publishing Company
866 Third Avenue
New York, N.Y. 10022

10 9 8 7 6 5 4 3 2 1

Designed by Jack Meserole

Printed in the United States of America

Contents

For the arrows of the Almighty
are within me, the poison whereof
drinketh up my spirit: the terrors
of God do set themselves in array
against me.

—JOB 6: 4

Part One
PRISONER 26336

1

Miracle in Dachau

"**B**LOCK VIER, Stillgestanden! Mützen . . . ab!"

As the order echoed through the huge Appelplatz, five hundred men removed their caps and froze in attention. It was a cold and damp morning at the Dachau concentration camp in April of 1941. A sharp wind, rising from the banks of the Amper River, blew across the bleak peat bogs. The wind howled in the windows of the long wooden huts and mercilessly flogged the prisoners lined on the parade ground. They'd been standing there since 4:30 in the morning. As they faced the machine guns on the guard towers, they continued to shiver in their coarse blue-striped uniforms stamped with yellow-black, red, or green stars. The stars indicated that the men were inmates of the "Jewish block" of Camp Number Three. Some of the prisoners, skeletal, gray-skinned, barely managed to stand. Their emaciated faces bore no expression; they were the living dead, the "muselmans," whose lifespan could be counted in days, maybe hours. If they did not succumb to the strain of the work, they would probably have the base of their skull blown apart by a bullet fired at close range. Then the SS guards would enter into the block log "Auf der Flucht erschossen"—shot while trying to escape. Hermann Goering himself had established the rule when the Nazis had assumed power in 1933. "Shoot first," he had told the Gestapo," and inquire afterward, and if you make mistakes I'll protect you."

The SS guards didn't like shooting their prisoners. A bullet cost three pfennig, they would explain to their Jewish captives, and that undoubtedly was too high a price for the life of

3

a "Dreck Jude"—a shit Jew. Therefore they often murdered their prisoners by less expensive methods, such as the way they disposed of poor Schwartz, the Viennese attorney, who had been beaten to death because he refused to shout "I am a dirty Jewish lawyer." Or the manager of the "Bata" shoe factories from Prague, who was killed by some sadistic kapos, most of them former Communists. And all the other men shot, beaten, drowned, dragged naked to the crematorium with their number tags strapped to their toes, or simply left dead, their bloated cadavers decomposing alongside the barbed-wire fences surrounding the camp.

That will not happen to me, a prisoner standing in the second row kept repeating to himself. *I shall not give them any pretext. I must survive.* He was about fifty, thick-set, of medium height. He had an open face, a clear forehead, deep brown eyes, and a willful, stubborn chin. His skull was closely shaven in accordance with Dachau regulations and he clutched his prisoner's cap in his right hand. The number 26336 was stamped in brown numerals under the yellow-black star printed on his uniform.

"Block Vier," the SS guard was barking, "engetreten mit Belegschaft von vier hundert und achtzig Häftlingen"—on parade with complement of four hundred and eighty prisoners, eight are in sick block, twelve at work. . . .

He had been lucky until now, 26336 thought, and except for the traditional savage beating on the night of his arrival, he had been left unmolested. He had escaped the favorite SS punishment, the three dreadful B's. First there was the Bock, the wooden concave table where they would bind the upper part of your body and strike you twenty-five or thirty times with long bullwhips previously soaked in water. One had to count aloud the strokes while being whipped, and if the prisoner stopped or made a mistake the beating would start all over again. Then there was the Baum, an eight-foot pole studded with hooks, where they would suspend you for hours by your wrists tied behind your back. When they kicked the stool from under you, your body would plunge into the void, swinging helplessly like a gigantic pendulum. Even if they didn't flog you, the abrupt fall of your body, suddenly suspended on your twisted wrists, could tear your muscles or break your arms, and then you were good for the crematorium. And finally there was the Bunker, the sinister cave used for solitary confinement, where the tortures inflicted upon the prisoners were so cruel that they were kept secret even from the regular SS guards.

Number 26336 had been spared all that, but how could he know when his luck might turn? Every day the SS invented new games and rules to humiliate the prisoners, and if they were dissatisfied with one prisoner's performance they would inflict terrible punishments on the entire block. The previous week they had forced all the Schutzhaft-Juden to march on the parade grounds singing SS hymns and anti-Semitic songs taken from the *Sturmer*, the Nazi newspaper, describing Jews as pigs and garbage. The Jews had spent the whole of a recent Sunday moving huge piles of stones and cement from one part of the camp to another, digging pits and filling them again; then the SS, laughing, had tied their hands behind their backs and forced them to crawl on their bellies and lap their food while imitating the grunting of pigs. The inmates of the neighboring block had been ordered to smear their faces with feces, then spit in each other's eyes and slap and lick one another. New tortures were invented daily for Catholic priests, Jehovah's Witnesses, and political prisoners, while the Poles were so expendable they were shot outright. A wagonload of fifty-five intellectuals, recently arrived from Warsaw, had been herded straight to the firing range and shot.

Out of the corner of his eye, Number 26336 noticed the Oberscharführer Beck slowly approaching along the rows of prisoners. He stiffened, praying silently that Beck would not pass behind him. A few days before, a huge, purulent ulcer had formed on the back of 26336's neck. Big as the palm of his

hand, the wound, discharging blood and pus, had cancer-
ously spread over his shoulders. He had dressed it with thick
strips of dirty paper. He knew that he was supposed to report
to sick bay, of course, but they might decide that the wound
was too much of a handicap and then shoot him like a mad
dog. People were being killed for lesser reasons in Dachau,
like that boy from Munich who happened to have lice in his
hair. The SS guard had pointed at a poster hanging on the
wall bearing the inscription "Eine Laus—Dein Tod"—one
louse—your death; then he had dragged the stunned boy out
of the hut, never to be seen again. Similar fates awaited people with phlegmons on their feet, with diphtheria, tuberculosis, pneumonia, dysentery, typhoid fever, and other diseases
caused by the cold and the terrible hunger. A friend employed
at the offices of the camp had told 26336 that during the last
three months some 1,200 men had died in Dachau. 26336 had
been lucky the last two weeks: They had sent him to work at
the kennels, and he had devoured some chunks of raw meat
that he had practically yanked from the hounds' jaws.

"The Hound" was the grim nickname the prisoners had
chosen for Oberscharführer Beck, who passed before them
now, supervising the count of the block inmates. Twenty-five
years old, he was clad impeccably, wearing shining boots
and carrying a whip under his left armpit. He was tall,
blond, and handsome—and a sadistic murderer, surpassed in
bestiality only by Egon Zill, the camp commander.

Beck, however, seemed in a reasonably good mood this
morning. He didn't look at 26336, and stopped only briefly at
the end of the line to check the identity of four corpses lying in
the mud. They had died during the night, and according to
regulations had to be brought outside for the morning roll
call, counted, recorded, and duly struck from the register.
Everything had to be in perfect order at Dachau, and every
block had to prove it had the same number of "stück"—
pieces—entered in the books the previous evening.

On Beck's order, the guards and the kapos fanned among

the prisoners, waving their lists, and started forming the work squads, shouting "Tempo! Tempo! Los! Los!" The largest group was dispatched to the workshops, a second "kommando" went to the plantation, and others were sent to the swamp, the slaughterhouse, and the notorious stone quarry. A week at the quarry was equivalent to a death sentence. 26336 couldn't suppress showing a twinge of relief when the last number of the quarry squad was called and the prisoners trudged glumly on their way, escorted by four armed SS.

Another death trap was the pigsty. Many prisoners had been deliberately drowned by the SS in the stinking puddles amid the filthy, grunting swine. What a way to die. 26336 stood still, listening to the kapo call the numbers of the pigsty squad. He wasn't in that Kommando either. His spirits soared. His luck might last another day—perhaps they would send him to the kennels again. The SS living quarters were also considered a bonanza. In the garbage cans there one had a good chance of finding leftovers from the previous night's supper, sometimes even a thick slice of buttered bread left there on purpose by a kindhearted SS wife.

Or maybe they'd send him to the museum? The crazed commanders of Dachau prided themselves on a bizarre exhibition they called the camp museum. Every type of Dachau prisoner was represented in photos, wax, and plaster for the diversion of visiting SS dignitaries. The visitor could contemplate effigies of the regime's political opponents, scarred and tattooed criminals, degenerate Jews robbing honest Germans. The only exhibit the museum didn't show, 26336 bitterly thought, was how the Reich disposed of prisoners. But a day's work over there was a day of rest and calm, and that was the best a Dachau "subhuman" could dream about.

The Appelplatz was almost empty now, work Kommandos hurrying in all directions. 26336 suddenly realized that, outside of the dead corpses on his left, he was the only prisoner who hadn't been called and assigned a day's work. He stood erect, all alone, in the middle of the huge parade ground, feeling utterly defenseless in his striped pajamas and heavy wooden clogs. What was going on? A wave of fear surged in his chest. Why didn't they call his number? Why didn't they send him to work? Could they have forgotten him? Impossible. The German machine was too perfect to commit such an error. They would not forget a Dreck Jude in Dachau.

He looked around with growing apprehension. The fierce wind was flapping some badly glued posters on the outer walls of the huts. "Arbeit macht frei" said one of them in big Gothic print—work sets free. "Alles für den Endsieg"—all for final victory—said another. From where he stood he could see the huge slogan painted on the slanted roof of the administration building, the "Wirtschaftgebäude": "There is one road to freedom. Its milestones are obedience, zeal, honesty, order, cleanliness, temperance, truth, sense of sacrifice, and love for the Fatherland." He had done all that, he said to himself. He had given his beloved Fatherland his obedience and his devotion, even his blood. And the Fatherland had kicked him through the gates of hell.

"Number Two Six Three Three Six!" an urgent voice blared into the loudspeakers. "Number Two Six Three Three Six to the hospital. Schnell!"

The hospital. He hesitated a second, then broke into a clumsy run across the deserted Appelpatz, hounded by the cold voice thundering his number all over Dachau. Why the hospital? It couldn't be because of the ulcer on his neck. One of the SS might have noticed and reported it, but for a wound such as that one they don't summon you to the hospital at Dachau. They have other ways of dealing with you. If they judge your wound or disease incurable, they simply dispatch you out of the camp to an unknown destination, and you never come back. And the SS clerks enter in the logs, next to your name: "Invalid, sent away to be exterminated."

Out of breath, he stopped before the entrance to the hospital and, following regulations, removed his clogs. An SS guard, wearing a large red band on his left arm, admitted him into a small office. Inside, another SS was sitting behind a tidy desk, leafing through the pages of a fat brown file. 26336, still breathing heavily, took off his hat and stood still. The SS looked at him, his eyes clouded, indifferent. "Yes?"

The prisoner recited aloud. "Jew in protective custody Number Two Six Three Three Six reports as ordered, Herr Blockführer."

The Nazi was looking at him attentively. For a split second, 26336 discerned a glimpse of sympathy in his eyes.

"Are you in good health?"

"Yes, Herr Blockführer."

"Turn around. Like that. What do you have there on your neck?"

He tried to control his voice. "An ulcer, Herr Blockführer." Now they knew.

"Wait here."

The SS got up and walked out, closing the door behind him. 26336 was left alone in the office. Frantic thoughts were rushing through his mind. What if they wanted him for the medical experiments? It was supposed to be a secret in Dachau, but through the prisoners' grapevine the blood-chilling news was spreading all over camp. In some of the huts, the SS were carrying out atrocious experiments on living humans. In Block 5, a certain Dr. Blaha was said to conduct experiments on tuberculosis. Five hundred prisoners had been isolated in the block and infected with the disease. Rumor had it that once the experiment was over, they would all be exterminated.

Worse even were the activities of Professor Schilling, the malaria expert. Number 26336 had seen him once, getting out of a car: a spare, narrow-chested old man with sparse blond-white hair, a thin mouth, a pointed goatee, and small, birdlike eyes behind rimless spectacles. One of the prisoners employed at the hospital as a sanitation worker had been in Schilling's laboratory. He had seen there cages full of mosquitoes, the labels saying they had been brought over from the Pontine marshes in Italy and from the Crimea. Professor Schilling supposedly would use his mosquitoes to sting healthy prisoners and infect them with malaria virus; then he would observe the progress of the disease until his patients died. He used mostly Jews and Polish priests.

And finally there was Dr. Rascher, the fanatical Nazi who was reported to carry out experiments on blood crystallization. He wouldn't hesitate to wound you, by knife or by bullet, and watch your blood flow slowly out of your body. He was experimenting with a new drug, Polygal, supposed to coagulate your blood, and would meticulously measure the time it took you to die.

The door opened. The Nazi was back, followed by an SS doctor wearing the rank insignia of Sturmführer. The physician approached 26336 and reached for the dressing of his wound. "Donnerwetter!" he exclaimed, an expression of utter disgust painted over his face. "What a mess!" He turned to the SS. "Take him to the sick bay immediately. Tell the nurses to clean this filth with alcohol. Lots of alcohol. And I want it cleaned real well. I shall be there in a moment."

At the sick bay, 26336 was asked to sit down on a leather-covered seat. He had a strange sensation, as though he were dreaming. Three male nurses hovered around him, their hands full of cotton pads soaked with alcohol. They thoroughly cleaned the ulcer of their Jewish patient. The stinging and the pain were unbearable and brought tears to his eyes, but he didn't make a sound. In the corner, an SS guard was standing, watching them. Once in a while he would holler "Lots of alcohol. Clean it properly!"

He should be as dumbfounded as me, 26336 thought. *Alcohol is very expensive in Germany nowadays. And to waste such quantities on a dirty Jewish prisoner, whose days are numbered. . . . Why are they doing this?*

"Attention!"

A dry clicking of heels heralded the appearance of the

doctor, who walked in purposefully, bent over 26336, and examined the ulcer. "Tweezers," he ordered, stretching his hand. "Cotton pads. Bandages." He meticulously dressed the prisoner's wound, then walked around and faced him. He had a narrow, clean-shaven face and a prominent Adam's apple.

"You stay here, at the hospital," he said. "Understand?"

"Jawohl, Herr Doktor."

"As of now you're under my personal responsibility. You'll take your meals here. You'll not go to work. Understand?"

"Jawohl, Herr Doktor."

As the physician left the room, 26336 couldn't help sliding his hand to his thigh and pinching himself. Was this luck real?

A week followed of delightful idleness, of rest, good care, succulent meals. 26336 felt as if he had gone to a distant world. From his window he could see a patch of low sky, unmarred by the gruesome black smoke from the crematorium chimneys. Still, a few hundred yards away, in the huts, on the Bock, in the torture chambers, in the fields, people were dying. Once in a while, the dry discharge of a pistol would break the silence of the hospital and remind 26336 that only a couple of brick walls stood between him and the living hell of this most sinister Nazi camp. But calm reigned in his hospital room. The orderlies and the nurses fed and pampered 26336 with utmost care and devotion.

And yet one question would keep coming back, torturing him, shattering his hopes, filling his sleep with nightmares. Why? Why were they treating him like this? Now that he knew he wasn't going to be exterminated, or turned into a human guinea pig, a new suspicion had slipped into his brain and had quickly become a haunting obsession. *Gleiwitz*, a voice kept whispering inside him, *remember what they said about Gleiwitz? About the prisoners? Remember what happened to them?*

The appalling story of Gleiwitz had been told to him by the kapo of his block, a former SA trooper who had excellent connections. In August 1939, when Hitler had decided to start a war, he had ordered his aides to find a pretext for an attack on Poland. The Fuehrer's cronies, Himmler and Heydrich, had hastily conceived the ideal provocation. Two detachments of SS special troops, posing as Poles dressed in Polish uniforms, would stage an attack on German units at the Polish-German frontier posts of Pitschen and Hochlinden. A third detachment would take over the Gleiwitz radio station, which was near the Polish border. They would broadcast a short speech insulting Hitler and the Reich, and claiming that Breslau and Danzig were Polish. Then they would "retreat." To add credibility to the simulated attacks, the SS chiefs decided to leave about fifteen corpses dressed in German and Polish uniforms. The photographers and journalists who would be rushed to the radio station and the frontier posts would thus find evidence that the Poles had indeed crossed the German border during the night and cowardly attacked German troops.

The SS therefore needed freshly killed bodies to justify Germany's subsequent retaliation and its full-scale attack on Poland. It was rumored that General Heinrich Müller himself, the dreaded chief of the Gestapo, had supplied the future corpses: fifteen inmates of concentration camps. They had been kept somewhere for two weeks, given abundant food and promised immediate release if they agreed to participate in a harmless masquerade on the night of August 31. As night fell, the prisoners had donned the German and Polish uniforms that had been supplied by the secret service; a few minutes later, they were writhing in agony, poisoned by lethal injections. They were then riddled with bullets, and their bloodied corpses were transported in unmarked cars and strewn at the scenes of the three border incidents. The most talked-about incident, largely reported in the German newspapers the next morning, was the Polish attack on the Gleiwitz radio station. The body of a dead "Pole," a tall blond man of about thirty, lay near the station entrance. On the following day, September 1, 1939, Hitler had launched his war against Poland.

Remember what they told you about Gleiwitz? the inner voice would repeat over and over again. *Remember what they said about those corpses? They had also been prisoners like you. They had also been Jews and political dissidents. They had also been separated from the others and had received extra rations, good care, and were allowed to sleep. And now they are dead, silent partners in the devious deception concocted by Hitler.*

"Somebody is very interested in you," the chief nurse said. "If you weren't Jewish, I'd say they were preparing to release you. But a Jew . . ."

He is right, the inner voice said. *No Jew has ever left Dachau alive. Not one.*

Thus, lying awake in his hospital bed, gnawed by uncertainty and dark foreboding, 26336 saw the dawn of the seventh day, April 16, 1941.

"Number Two Six Three Three Six!" the loudspeakers roared. "Number Two Six Three Three Six to the political department. Schnell!"

He sprinted toward the low, oblong building that housed the "Politische Abteilung," the political department—better known under another name, Gestapo.

The room was Spartan. Two desks. Two chairs. An old armchair. A large photograph of the Fuehrer, in military uniform, hung on the wall.

Two men in civilian clothes were seated behind the desks. One of them wore thick round glasses. He was waspish, sallow-skinned, with sparse, light blond hair. His conservative black suit loosely hung from his rawboned frame. He was about fifty years old. His nose was pointed, his lips thin, bloodless, curved in a permanent leer. The liquid eyes, strikingly huge beneath the powerful glasses, fixed 26336 with a cold, unblinking stare.

The other man was tall, well built, in his early forties, with wavy brown hair and an open face. He wore a blue double-breasted suit. His shirt and tie were of fine quality and his hands, resting on the desk, were well manicured. But the man was by no means a city dandy. His deep tan and upright posture marked him as a career officer.

26336 stopped by the door and quickly knelt to remove his clogs. The regulations in Dachau were very strict: A subhuman should always be barefoot in the presence of a master.

"Don't take off your shoes." The officer had spoken. His voice was mild but firm.

The prisoner awkwardly stepped forward, conscious of the insistent stare of the two men. He put his feet together, pressed his fists to his hips and recited, "Schutzhaft Jude, Number Two Six Three . . ."

The officer raised his hand. "Please." Then he gestured toward the armchair, smiling.

"Would you please sit down, Herr Fackenheim?"

Flabbergasted, he slowly settled into the cushioned armchair. He couldn't remember when he had last sat in an armchair. Nor when somebody had called him by his name, or addressed him as "Herr"—sir. A sudden sense of fury gripped him. These people couldn't be serious. Nobody would call a Jew "Sir" in Dachau. What was this, a farce? Were they trying to ridicule him? To apply a new, refined method of mental torture?

"Herr Fackenheim." The officer again. "My colleague and I, we have come here to ask you a question. Would you like to get out of here? I mean, would you like to be set free?"

He froze, staring at the two men before him. For a moment he didn't budge, unable to grasp the meaning of the officer's words.

The German seemed prepared for such a reaction. As Fackenheim gazed at him, speechless, he went on in a calm, low voice. "We can have you released today and take you with us. Right away. You see, you're not a stranger to us, Herr

Fackenheim. We know quite a few things about you. During the First World War you have distinguished yourself in battle. You've fought bravely for your country. You have been awarded the Iron Cross, First Class. You have been a loyal German all your life. You have talents and qualifications that can be useful to us. Useful to you too, actually. You have stressed and repeated on many occasions since your imprisonment that, despite all that's happened to you, you remain a German. That's good. We can provide you with the opportunity to prove what you say. If you indeed feel yourself a German, would you be ready to do something for your country? And be free?"

In dismay, Fackenheim continued to stare, unable to digest the deal that was so casually offered to him in the Gestapo headquarters at Dachau. An offer that a Dachau subhuman couldn't imagine in his wildest dreams. Immediate freedom. As if Dachau had never existed. He took a deep breath. His hands, clutching the armrests, trembled. *Do something for your country,* the man had said, *and you will be free. Do something for Germany. But why me? Why did they pick me out of all the Dachau prisoners? Perhaps Colonel Metger, my commanding officer during the First World War,* has intervened *on my behalf. We were on close terms until I was arrested.*

"What do you mean by asking me to do something for my country?"

They ignored his question. "What do you say, Herr Fackcnhcim?" the officer finally asked. "Would you like to get out of here?"

"Of course I'd like to get out of here. Have you ever seen anybody enjoy burning in hell?"

For the first time, the other man spoke. "Very well." He had a cold, high-pitched voice. "It's settled then."

"Wait!" 26336 cried out, half rising from his chair. The two men looked at him inquisitively. "I have an old mother. She lives in Frankfurt. She is sick. She is a widow, and I am her only son. She doesn't have anybody else in the world." He paused. "Neither do I."

The officer nodded. "We know that," he said matter-of-factly.

"That woman lives in fear and need," 26336 went on. "I . . . I must have your word that she won't be molested in any way, and she will be taken care of."

The two Germans exchanged impassive glances. "I think we can guarantee that," the officer said. The older man beside him nodded absently. "It's settled then," he repeated, and his hand slid under the desk, reaching for a concealed button.

The door on their right opened and the chief of the Gestapo in Dachau stepped in. He didn't even glance at 26336. He clicked his heels and bowed respectfully toward the thin blond man. "Jawohl, Herr Regierungsrat."

"Regierungsrat." Government adviser. Another piece of the puzzle fell into place. That stranger must be a high-ranking government official.

The adviser stood on his feet. His sharp voice was authoritative, habituated to command. "This gentleman is going to be released. Take all the necessary steps so he can receive his clothes and his personal effects."

Not a muscle twitched in the Gestapo chief's face." Jawohl, Herr Regierungsrat." And turning to Fackenheim, with a polite, civil voice he said, "This way, please." They walked out of the office, leaving the two strangers behind.

Starting then, each moment proceeded as if in a dream. The trip to the "Effektenkammer," the prisoners' belongings store, amid a crowd of hastily retreating prisoners who were astonished at the sight of one of them walking beside the dreaded Gestapo chief. The restitution of his clothes—overcoat, suit, shirt, tie, underwear, socks, and shoes. The handkerchief, the keys, the watch, the wallet, and the loose change he had in his pockets, all thoroughly recorded. Even the half-consumed packet of cigarettes was intact. The small valise with some clothes and toilet articles. The medal, Iron

Cross, First Class, still pinned in his lapel. Since the anti-Jewish measures had been put into effect by the German authorities, he had been wearing the medal in sign of protest. "Who gave you that?" The man in charge of the store, SS Oberscharführer Mursch, asked him in surprise.

"It was awarded to me," 26336 answered. The SS shrugged. "Sign here," he said.

The return to the hospital for a routine medical examination. Then to the camp administration building to the office of the camp recorder. The recorder, a prisoner himself, stared in disbelief as he handed 26336 a single sheet of paper. "Will you fill this out and sign?"

The release declaration. "I, Paul Ernst Fackenheim, born in Frankfurt, Land of Hesse, on February 8, 1892, hereby declare that I was released today, April 16, 1941, from Internment Camp Number Three at Dachau. I undertake under oath not to reveal any information to anybody about the Dachau camp and/or about my imprisonment here."

A signature. The first Jew to be officially released from a Nazi concentration camp since the beginning of the war. How could he know that in the bloody history of the "final solution" he would remain the only Jew to be willingly released by the Nazis? The only one of six million.

In front of his block, he ran into his kapo, the former SA trooper, imprisoned there since the Röhm putsch. "I am free!" 26336 shouted at him, for the first time letting his ecstasy show. The kapo ceremoniously shook his hand. He was not a bad man after all, not like the kapos of the other blocks who were worse than the SS. When Fackenheim had arrived in Dachau that night nine months ago, shivering with cold and fear, the kapo had thrust a bowl of pea soup into his hands. "Eat, Jew," he had grunted.

The kapo was the one who had told him about Gleiwitz. The man had good sources, Fackenheim thought, and on a sudden impulse he caught him by the arm. "What's happening on the front?" he asked. The war situation might have something to do with the Reich's sudden generosity toward him. They could be planning another provocation like Gleiwitz.

"It seems that we've occupied Greece," the kapo said. "And in North Africa, Rommel has just liberated Benghazi and taken over most of Cyrenaica. The Italians are furious." He chuckled. "The English beat the hell out of their army, and here comes Rommel with a handful of tanks and single-handedly takes everything back. They should stick to singing and macaroni, those Italianos." He grew serious. "Why do you ask?" he inquired, frowning at Fackenheim.

The released prisoner shrugged, and climbed the wooden steps to the hut door. Inside the empty block, he changed his clothes and stuffed his meager belongings into the small valise. The change of clothes, oddly enough, brought with it a change of mood. His exuberance died, giving way to a muted anxiety. Out of the block again, he realized that he was trying to avoid the other prisoners. A vague sensation of guilt crept into his heart, as if he were deserting his friends, abandoning them to their fate. He knew he couldn't do anything for the others, of course; he had to seize the unique chance that was offered to him. Each and every one of the other inmates would have grabbed with both hands such an opportunity to get out of Dachau. Still, he felt deep compassion for the wretched skull-shaven figures moving about the camp, and a disquieting malaise for being different now, dressed like a free man, on his way to the world of the living. Instinctively he hastened his pace and kept close to the walls.

An SS soldier was waiting for him in front of the block to escort him out of Camp Three. They didn't speak and walked in silence along the row of huts. By the camp gate they ran into "the Hound," Oberscharführer Beck. The SS sergeant major was casually leaning against a lamppost, whistling a romantic tune. At the sight of 26336 in civilian clothes he stopped abruptly, slowly straightened up, and stepped forward. He tilted his head aside, staring at him. "What are you doing with that Jew?" he finally asked the SS escort.

"He is being released."

The Hound hesitated a moment, then approached his former prisoner and patted his shoulder. "Well, aren't you lucky!"

Back in the Gestapo building, Fackenheim was shown into the same office where he had met the two men earlier. The room was empty now. He put down his valise and, slowly, still hesitating, settled in the armchair. The two gentlemen, his SS escort had said, would be back soon. He had to wait for them. All the formalities were over.

The door suddenly burst open. "You filthy Jewish pig!"

He turned to his right. In the doorway stood the most feared man in Dachau, Haupsturmführer Egon Zill, the camp commander. He was a small, wiry man, his face pale with a yellow hue. His beady eyes were brown and piercing. Fackenheim had first seen him on that rainy night when he had arrived at Dachau in a trainload of Jews, Catholic priests, and Jehovah's Witnesses. As the dejected, badly scared prisoners disembarked in the white glare of the floodlights, a multitude of SS guards had emerged from the dark. They wore steel helmets branded with the death's-head insignia; heavy revolvers were stuck in their belts and they carried whips in their hands. Some were struggling with the leashes of huge German shepherds that barked furiously. Egon Zill, in full SS uniform, stood in the middle of his men, and his smile hadn't left his lips as the SS had hurled themselves on the prisoners, shouting obscenities, kicking and whipping them.

Zill had been there all the time, when they had been herded to the political department, recorded in the logs, fingerprinted, and photographed, full face and side view—all done under an unending hail of blows and lashes. Even the chair in which they sat for the photograph had a built-in cruel device, said to be Zill's invention: a concealed long needle that shot into the prisoner's flesh as soon as his picture had been taken. Zill also supervised the questioning of the prisoners by the SS. The new arrivals were asked to describe their crimes against the Reich. Those who said they had no idea as to why they were imprisoned were savagely beaten. Fackenheim was among them.

Later, Zill had watched prisoner "barbers" hurriedly shave the heads and bodies of the new inmates, lacerating and scratching their skin. He had followed the bleeding nude men into the showers, where other SS guards had doused them alternately with ice cold and boiling hot water till they were screaming with pain. Then Zill had stepped forward, grabbed a bullwhip from one of the guards, and whipped the naked, defenseless bodies that writhed in agony under the showers. Fackenheim took the beating in silence, biting his lips. Some who tried to resist were chosen by Zill for the Baum torture, which was his favorite pastime. He had personally supervised the manacling of the prisoners' wrists behind their backs, had checked if they had been properly attached to the pole hooks, and had himself kicked the stools from under their feet. As they dropped in the air, screaming, he went on whipping them with sadistic pleasure. Fackenheim had escaped that torture, and had never found himself face to face with Zill. Never, until the present moment in the Gestapo office.

Instinctively, he jumped to his feet and froze in attention. But after a second he realized that he didn't have to, not anymore. *I have nothing to fear,* he said to himself, conscious of his new status. *I am a free man now. He has no power over me.* He forced himself to step backward. Nodding politely at Zill, he sat down in the armchair.

"You bloody bastard, Jewish son of a bitch! I'll have your hide. I'll have you hanged. I'll make you mourn the day you were born!" Zill was yelling, beside himself with fury.

"You'll beg me to kill you! I'll make you taste the worst tortures ever, and I . . ."

He was interrupted by the sudden opening of the door. The blond man with glasses, the enigmatic government adviser who had interviewed Fackenheim earlier, stood on the threshold. His cold fish eyes focused on Egon Zill. He seemed as cool and imperturbable as before. He almost didn't raise his voice. "This man is no longer under your orders, Herr Zill. I beg you, Herr Zill."

The flood of obscenities stopped. For a moment, Zill stood in place, breathing heavily and glaring at the Regierungsrat. Then, fists clenched and face purple with rage, he pivoted on his heels and slammed the door behind him.

The government adviser calmly turned toward Fackenheim, as if the incident with Zill had never happened. "This way, please."

Outside, a gray automobile was waiting, its engine running. It was a Mercedes-Benz, of the kind used as staff cars by the German army. But this car wasn't a military vehicle. Its registration plates were civilian. The driver was also dressed in civilian clothes: a pair of woolen, neatly creased trousers, a visor cap, and a leather jacket. He respectfully opened the rear door for Fackenheim, who settled in the far corner, his small valise on his knees. The officer who had interviewed him slid into the seat beside him. The Regierungsrat took the seat beside the driver.

The car moved forward slowly. Even now, as the sinister buildings of the death plant named Dachau disappeared behind him, Fackenheim refused to believe he was being released. The change was too abrupt, too unreal. He clung to the car window, staring with a mixture of anxiety and elation at the prisoners and the SS guards.

The sentries must have been forewarned, he reflected, when he saw them hurriedly open the gates and raise the barriers before the approaching Mercedes. The car passed the first electrified fence, then the second and the third. They reached the main gate, with its notorious inscription: Arbeit macht frei. Behind them, the last watchtowers turned into indistinct shapes.

The Mercedes took a left turn, and soon they were gliding on a well-paved road. They were on the Munich highway now. A couple of civilian cars and some trucks drove past them. A light breeze danced in the blooming trees planted on both sides of the motorway. Spring was in the air. The sun was shining in a spotless blue sky. He felt as if he were on another planet.

Fackenheim turned to the officer beside him. "Only now I start to believe that I am really safe."

"Keep quiet."

The officer touched his lips with his finger, nodding his head toward the driver's large back. He shouldn't know, the gesture meant.

Fackenheim leaned against the seat, silent but happy. "I am free," he kept repeating to himself. "I am free."

Still, as he watched the grim profile of the Regierungsrat and the sealed expression of the officer beside him, he again felt a pang of anxiety. "Do something for your country," the officer had said. What did he mean? A secret mission? A spying assignment?

In total silence, the Mercedes sailed toward Munich.

II

The Fackenheim File

THE SPYMASTERS of the Abwehr, the German army intelligence, had done a thorough job. They had found the right man, the right Jew.

Paul Ernst Fackenheim was Jewish by blood; he was Prussian by spirit. His grandfather was the Chief Rabbi of Mühlhausen, in Thuringen. But his classmates at the Goethe Gymnasium in Frankfurt were the young princes of Hesse and the Emperor's nephews. On his thirteenth birthday Paul had chanted biblical psalms as he celebrated his bar mitzvah in the Frankfurt Synagogue, his shoulders shrouded in an immaculate tallith, his head covered with an embroidered skullcap, and his left arm bound by black phylacteries. But at the age of ten he already knew by heart the German hymns, war songs, and military marches. With his pious parents he would eat matzo on Passover, pray in the synagogue on Rosh Hashanah, and fast on Yom Kippur. But the holiday that would really thrill him was September 2nd, Sedan Day, the anniversary of the decisive German victory over France in 1870. In that battle Emperor Napoleon III had been defeated; five months later the German Empire was proclaimed in the Hall of Mirrors at Versailles and the new Germany emerged for the first time as a major European power. Paul would celebrate Sedan Day with his classmates and teachers in the ancient forests surrounding Frankfurt. Those were unforgettable days of songs, games, sporting events, trophies, martial parades, and patriotic speeches that stirred deep emotions in young Paul.

He was the only son of a severe and tyrannical businessman who dealt in metal tools, bicycles, and sewing machines. His mother was the youngest daughter of a rich leather-goods manufacturer from Offenbach. Hedda Fackenheim was a beautiful, statuesque woman suffering from fragile health. She bestowed all her love and affection upon her little boy, who grew up with an unusual attachment to her. But his childhood was also marked by the imperialist winds that rose over the Reich at the turn of the century.

Still, arrogant, warlike Germany maintained a liberal attitude toward its Jewish citizens. Paul never experienced any discrimination. He was accepted as equal by his Gentile friends and treated as such. His adolescent world was similar to that of most German youngsters: a boundless admiration for the flamboyant Kaiser Wilhelm; dreams of wars, victories, and heroics; horse riding in the foggy German forests; Wagnerian mythology; dance lessons; formal parties in tuxedo, bow tie, and patent leather shoes. And the final product was a "German of Jewish faith," more German than the Gentiles, more nationalistic than the Kaiser.

On August 1, 1914, the First World War started. The next morning, young Fackenheim reported at the headquarters of the 81st Infantry Regiment in Frankfurt and volunteered for the service. He was turned down. As a former student he was to be drafted only in a couple of years, for a short service as officer. The Reichswehr had enough soldiers and didn't need any college boys. Paul didn't give up. Using family connections, he obtained an audience with the commanding general of the Frankfurt military region. Once inside the office of the old officer, he plunged into a patriotic speech about his yearning to be on the front with his comrades in those crucial battles for Germany's future. But the old general didn't even hear his discourse. The man was deaf, actually, and when his adjutant introduced the young visitor, he thought he heard "Falkenhayn"—the name of the impetuous war minister in the imperial Cabinet. Convinced that his young visitor was the nephew of the minister, the general nervously reached for the telephone. The next morning, Fackenheim was sworn into the 63rd Artillery Regiment.

After his initial training, Private Fackenheim was dispatched to Belgium to join his unit. He spent some months in the flatlands of Flanders and in the region of Liège. Then he crossed with his unit into France and took part in the fighting at Saint-Quentin. During the murderous battle of the Somme, a French artillery shell destroyed the telephone line connecting the regiment headquarters with the command post of a battery of field cannon. Paul volunteered on the spot, crawled under the dense French fire, and laid a new telephone line. The division commander awarded him with the Iron Cross, Second Class. Paul went on fighting and was rapidly promoted: corporal, sergeant, cadet officer. In 1917, at Montdidier, he was placed in command of a battery of 75-millimeter field guns mounted on special trailers. Those cannon were Germany's response to the new British wonder weapon, the first tanks. At the outskirts of Montdidier, Paul's battery fought with courage and inflicted heavy losses on the British armor. Paul was awarded the Iron Cross, First Class.

In an officer's mess at Eupen, in Belgium, the newly decorated cadet struck a warm friendship with a fat, jovial pilot who commanded the flying squadron of the "Red Devils." The name of Fackenheim's new friend was Hermann Goering.

Goering wasn't the least bothered by the Jewish origins of his comrade in arms. Fackenheim was just another young German, brave, strong, handsome, a loyal friend and a fine drinking companion. He had a way with women and had made quite a few conquests among the Belgian country girls. But most of all, he was a sworn daredevil, ready to volunteer for any unusual mission. Paul's commanding officer, First Lieutenant Metger, treated him with an esteem that soon turned into friendship. The two men were to remain close friends long after the war ended.

Paul Fackenheim was deeply distressed by the final defeat

of Germany in 1918. He regarded it as a national shame, the result of an ignoble act of treason. The Germans themselves had stabbed their Kaiser in the back. He firmly believed that the popular revolution that shook Germany after the war was nothing but eyewash intended to justify the vile deeds of a bunch of robbers and criminals. The leaders of the Spartacus League, Rosa Luxemburg and Karl Liebknecht, were the real traitors trying to destroy Germany from within. He rejoiced at their death when they were murdered in Berlin. Instead he sympathized with the numerous free corps of right-wing soldiers and officers that emerged all over Germany. He regarded them as the bearers of the genuine German spirit.

Back in Frankfurt, Paul spent his days in the streets, wearing his uniform and carrying his service revolver, like so many nationalistic soldiers. The rebel sailors who had occupied the Frankfurter Hof Hotel aroused his fury. In his eyes, they were nothing but hoodlums who spent their life partying. A few times he saw some of those "phony revolutionaries" rolling drunk in the gutters—a sight that influenced his attitude toward socialism in general. He didn't miss an opportunity to pick a fight with the "traitors" and take part in the bloody brawls and street clashes that were so common in postwar Germany. Even when the turmoil settled down, Paul Fackenheim kept hoping that the army would carry out a counter-revolution, bring the Kaiser back from exile, and establish a new defense line along the Rhine. Then the war would start again, until the final victory of the Fatherland.

His awakening from those glorious dreams was painful. Germany was beaten, the economy was destroyed, inflation was soaring. The day came when he had to take off his uniform and try to adapt to civilian life. But a second deception was in store for him. Paul wanted to go back to college and study journalism. Since his early childhood, he had been writing short stories. At the age of fifteen he had even had a couple of them published in the renowned *Frankfurter Allgemeine Zeitung*. He truly believed that journalism and writing was his true vocation. But his father wouldn't even listen. Business was bad, bankruptcy was around the corner, and he wouldn't assume another burden, especially one that seemed so dubious. "Brot lose Kunst," he would repeat stubbornly—in art you can't earn your bread. He refused to pay for Paul's studies and forced him to join the staff of a leather-goods factory whose manager was distantly related to Paul's mother. The young man, deceived in his dreams, embittered against his despotic father, could think only of running away.

Finally he revolted. One summer evening, strolling by the Rhine, he met a svelte blond girl, Gretchen. She wasn't Jewish, but he didn't mind. Her beauty and wit captivated him, and he soon was madly in love. He married her on a whim, without even telling his father. Hedda Fackenheim, his mother, was the only one to assist at the secret wedding. After the ceremony Paul didn't return home. A few weeks later he got a job that fulfilled his wildest dreams. In Hamburg, young Mr. and Mrs. Paul Fackenheim boarded a luxury liner that was to take them to the other end of the world, the Far East.

At the beginning, it was indeed like a dream. Paul had been appointed roving representative of several German hardware companies, and was constantly on the move. He drifted through the exotic, mysterious lands of the Orient, whose very names carried an aura of adventure and excitement. Java. Sumatra. Bali. Hong Kong. Singapore. Shanghai. The romantic young man was enticed by the tropical jungles, the tigers, the snakes, the herds of wild elephants, the ritual dancers, the dark superstitions. He witnessed the strange customs of the native tribes, the practices of the secret sects; he experienced the eerie sensations induced by the exotic drinks and drugs of Asia.

In a battered car with his Malayan driver he crisscrossed the jungles, reaching the farthest villages. Aboard a native boat he set sail for the Indonesian islands and the neighboring countries. He saw the dragons of Komodo, the flying serpents of Borneo, the sensuous dancers of Bali. He discovered dead native villages exterminated by the plague. He described his fascinating journeys in articles he sold to several German newspapers.

Paul did well in his business, and his financial situation was excellent. The main base for his operations was Batavia, the capital of Dutch Indonesia. He lived in a spacious, sprawling house at the outskirts of the city. He was a respected member of the German Club, very active in its social life. His easy manner and natural sense of humor earned him many friends. Intrigued by the unusual flavors of Asian cuisine, he became an amateur cook. He had a skill for languages and quickly mastered some of the local dialects. In Batavia, Paul Fackenheim became a happy man.

But soon his private life turned sour. Gretchen, his wife, lacked the curiosity and imagination that could turn life in the Far East into an everlasting adventure. She longed for home. From the day she had set foot in Indonesia she had been complaining about the humid climate, the dirty natives, the barbaric customs, the tropical diseases. She wasn't interested in traveling to the neighboring countries; the social life of Batavia irritated her. She angrily rejected Paul's timid hints that he would like to have a child. After a year in Indonesia she returned to Germany for a cure. Paul became very lonely without her, but he received no answer to his letters. Soon, however, letters of a different nature started piling on his desk: His old friends were writing to him from Frankfurt, warning him in veiled terms about Gretchen's infidelities. "It's not a secret anymore," one of them finally wrote to him, "and Gretchen doesn't seem to mind. You have no other choice but to draw your own conclusions."

He wrote to his lawyer in Frankfurt and divorced Gretchen without even meeting her. He was never to see her again. He remained all alone. The casual affairs he had with a few bored wives of Dutch officials and European businessmen left him bitter and disappointed. A romantic man, in need of warmth and affection, he hardly tolerated the solitude. His material success couldn't make up for the loneliness that haunted him. In late July 1931, a letter from his mother arrived, bringing an avalanche of bad news. The crash of the New York Stock Exchange had caused the collapse of his father's enterprise, and his father had died from a heart attack. Hedda Fackenheim was alone, sick and suddenly impoverished. She appealed for his help. Without thinking twice, Paul abandoned everything and was on the first boat to Europe.

Frankfurt was grim and hostile. Hedda Fackenheim was desperate. Her husband had died, leaving behind a heavy debt. Paul had brought back all his savings. He paid his father's debts to the last penny, and showered his mother with presents. In the Orient he spent without counting, and for a while life in Germany was pleasant and easy, but one morning he awakened to find out that he was totally broke. After the years of dolce vita in Batavia, Paul suddenly had to face a new, harsh reality.

Unemployment was reaching unprecedented figures. He failed to find a job in the city and boarded a train to Berlin, hoping for better luck in the capital. He couldn't be choosy anymore; he had to feed his mother. He was soon to become a man of all trades. He worked in offices, shops, hotels, restaurants; he became a sales representative, a repairman, a clerk, a lab technician. He was ready to do any work, as long as he could send a money order to Hedda Fackenheim at the end of the month.

Even in that bleak new life, Paul remained an incurable romantic. In a sidewalk café on the bustling Kurfürstendamm he met a slender blonde with huge, sad blue eyes. Her name was Luzi Schiller. She reminded Paul of Gretchen. She was just recovering from a disastrous love affair; she was pregnant and didn't want the other man's child. Her plight, coupled with her unusual beauty, made her irresistible to the sentimental young man. Paul courted her. Within a few weeks he convinced her to marry him, promising to give his name to her baby. After a modest wedding, they rented a small apartment in the eastern outskirts of Berlin. Six months later, Luzi gave birth to a little boy. They named him Willy.

Paul redoubled his efforts to get a permanent job. He now had a family to take care of. Finally he was hired by a textile factory, his first steady employment since he came back from Asia. Still, deeply disillusioned with the weakness of the German government, he hoped that new leadership would emerge and that new men would impose law and order in the country. Less than a year after his return, general elections were held in Germany. Naïvely, he cast his vote for Hitler. Paul thought Hitler's Nazi propaganda was empty and ridiculous and would soon be forgotten. On the other hand, he believed that the man would restore the German economy and get the nation on its feet again. Soon he was to discover that he had committed a monstrous error.

On January 30, 1933, Hitler became Chancellor of the Reich and formed the first Nazi government. To Paul's amazement, the new Fuehrer of Germany started immediately to apply in reality the same ludicrous and absurd slogans he had spoken in the past. In 1934, as the anti-Semitic measures intensified, Fackenheim was fired from his job. That was too much for him. Little Willy had been sick all winter, and there were more and more bills to be paid. Paul had never been a coward; unafraid of any possible consequences, he dispatched an angry letter to his former army buddy, Hermann Goering, saying, "I demand to get my job back immediately." A week later, he got a formal letter from Colonel Bodenschatz, Goering's assistant: "Herr Goering regrets that he cannot do anything for you."

Furious, Fackenheim wrote a second letter, this time to Rudolf Hess, the close and trusted friend of Hitler. "I served Germany with loyalty and devotion during the war," Fackenheim wrote. "I have always been a good and patriotic

German. I warn you that I shall not accept being treated like this by my country."

He had barely posted the letter when he realized he had made a grave mistake, a mistake that might cost him his freedom. The Nazis wouldn't tolerate such language, certainly not from a Jew. He could expect any day now a visit from the dreaded secret police, the Gestapo. But the man who knocked on his door a week later was not a Gestapo agent; he was a representative of the Deutsche Arbeit Front, the German Labor Organization. He brought Fackenheim a letter from the Front, informing him that "following Mr. Hess's intervention," he would be reinstated in his job.

But not for long. Four weeks later, he was summoned to the Arbeit Front offices in Berlin. The official who received him was cold and harsh. "We regret to inform you, Herr Fackenheim, that we cannot guarantee your personal security. We would like to continue to employ you, but as you know, anti-Jewish feelings are spreading widely in Germany as of late. If you don't resign from your job of your own will, you are in danger of being assaulted and brutalized by the population. That might also have grave consequences for your comrades at work, who would suffer because of you. Therefore all that I can do is ask you to quit your job willingly."

Unemployed again, Fackenheim started wearing his Iron Cross on his lapel as a protest against the anti-Jewish discrimination. He couldn't believe that his beloved Germany was treating him now as a pariah. Friends helped him to get through the winter; a kindhearted official of the "Winterhilfe"—the organization for help to members of the Nazi party—personally provided the Fackenheims with flour, sugar, and meat. But the sporadic charity of an individual couldn't obliterate the humiliations, the insults, and the rejections that had become Fackenheim's daily lot. And at the height of those days of despair, disaster hit him again. Luzi had been violently quarreling with him, and their relations had turned bitter. But he was still very much in love with her when she died in a supposedly minor operation. He had barely returned home from the hospital, still stunned, when a group of thugs in Nazi uniforms stormed the door of his apartment. At their head was Luzi's father. The old man had long suppressed his hatred for his Jewish son-in-law. But now that his daughter was dead, there was nothing to hold him back. He snatched Luzi's little boy and took off, while his Nazi cronies ransacked the apartment and chased Fackenheim across Berlin.

Paul didn't give in, though. He decided to stay and fight back. Those Nazis were nothing but scum, of course, and Germany was still a civilized nation. Or so he thought. He lodged a complaint with the police, demanding to get little Willy back. He assailed the courts and the government offices with petitions, appeals, and angry accusations. "I shall not tolerate such a hooliganism," he wrote. "I am a German citizen and I demand the assistance of the law." At first, the ministry clerks and the police officers were amused by the stubbornness and cheek of this shabby, medal-toting Jew. But finally they got tired of the game. One morning, shortly before dawn, a police officer and two Gestapo agents woke him up. "You have fifteen minutes to dress and get out of here," one of them said. "And we want you out of Berlin by tonight." Alone again, jobless and homeless, Paul boarded a train to Frankfurt. He had nobody left but his mother.

Ages ago, when he was a small boy in Frankfurt, he adored his exquisite mother, who was in his eyes the most beautiful, kindhearted, and intelligent woman in the whole world. She was his only ally and with her he was safe from his father's wrath. He felt so secure when he would bury his face in that silky hair scented with delicate lavender perfume, and so proud when he would watch her discuss music and literature with her friends at the weekly women's parties she held in their elegant living room.

But the woman who waited for him that night at the

Frankfurt railway station was no longer the proud, attractive Hedda Fackenheim. Gone was the vivacious brunette whose melodious laughter and gay flowery dresses would light up their home. Facing Paul, shivering in a shabby gray coat and cracked shoes, stood an old woman, her shoulders sagging, her sparse white hair hastily drawn in a loose bun, lines of bitterness etching her face. She had had to give up art, reading, and music, she said to Paul. She had sold most of the furniture, the paintings, the piano, and the Persian carpets. Now she barely survived by subletting rooms and cooking for some Jewish friends who took their meals at her apartment. But that too was bound to end soon. Her neighbors openly persecuted her and some had already lodged a complaint with the Gestapo against "the illicit business of the Jewess Fackenheim."

Paul was distressed by his mother's suffering. Even his own misery seemed to pale against her physical and mental collapse. He spent a sleepless night trying to figure out a way to save his mother. And at dawn he was already out in the cold, trying to elbow his way through a tumultuous crowd of Jews and German dissidents who besieged the gates of the British consulate. England seemed to be the only hope left now, the last haven for those trying to flee Hitler's mutating Germany.

After long hours of waiting, he was finally admitted to the office of the vice-consul, Arthur Dowden. Through a large window Paul could see a group of Jewish refugees, camping in the consulate garden. He inquired about a visa to England for himself and his mother.

"Do you have any relatives in England who could lodge you and provide for your needs?" Dowden asked. He was a slim man, quite young, with wavy brown hair and a soft voice.

"I don't think so," Paul said. There was a distant uncle who had emigrated to England years ago, but they had lost contact.

"Perhaps you could get a job in England," Dowden suggested. "A letter from your future employer would be quite adequate."

Fackenheim shook his head. "I don't know anybody over there."

"In that case," Dowden said, lowering his eyes, "I am afraid we can't be of any help. The immigration regulations are quite explicit, you know, and you must understand that there are thousands in your position."

"Yes," Fackenheim murmured. "Yes, of course." He shook Dowden's hand and left the consulate. In the future he would often recall that episode. He would repeatedly accuse himself for having given up so easily. He should have spared no effort to obtain that visa. He should have located his uncle in England and appealed to him for an affidavit, or tried to find a job, any kind of job, with a British company. Instead, he had meekly resigned himself to the idea that the gates of Germany were closed. Like many other German Jews, he would later bitterly admit, he had been blind. He had refused to see the reality. He stubbornly clung to the conviction that things would get better, that Nazism was only a fleeting phenomenon. *Hitler isn't Germany,* he kept repeating to himself; *the German people are not Nazis. Germany is my homeland.*

Fackenheim would always recall two Jewish gatherings that he had happened to witness in Berlin on the same day, in September 1933. In the morning, his job hunting had brought him to a leather factory in the southern part of Berlin, quite close to the railway station. Outside the station he had run into a huge crowd—two, maybe three thousand Jews, waving blue and white flags stamped with the star of David, singing songs in which he recognized a few Hebrew words. The crowd was effusively parting from a group of about a hundred young men and women laden with bags and suitcases. Some were hugging them, patting their shoulders; others were crying. "What's going on?" Fackenheim had asked a tall, unkempt youth who carried a cardboard sign bearing the word "Shalom."

"They are leaving for Palestine," the young Jew had answered, his face flushed with excitement. "For the land of Israel. Are you Jewish?" Before he could answer, some girls had started singing "Hatikva," the Zionist anthem, and the huge crowd had joined, chanting with quasi-religious devoutness the strange words of the slow, sad hymn.

Fackenheim had watched the crowd for a few moments, then had crossed the street and walked away. He had never been a Zionist, and Palestine had no attraction for him. He was German, his wives had been Gentile, and his faith had never interfered with his profound attachment to his country. The flags, the chants, and the songs of the people gathered by the station left him indifferent.

But that same evening, walking aimlessly down the Kurfürstendamm, he had come across another group of Jews, massed in front of a big concert hall. They were not carrying flags or signs, but the posters displayed on the glass doors of the building announced a meeting of "the Jewish community of Greater Berlin." Out of curiosity he had walked into the packed concert hall and listened to speaker after speaker proclaim their total devotion and loyalty to their German homeland. He had joined in the enthusiastic applause. The purpose of the meeting, the old gentleman sitting next to him had explained, was to make it clear that the Jews of Germany totally identify with their nation. Fackenheim agreed wholeheartedly.

As time went by he would recall his visit to the British consulate in Frankfurt, and deep in his heart he would admit that perhaps he hadn't wanted to leave Germany at all. That was why he didn't hear the warning bells. He did not want to know. Meanwhile, Jewish families mysteriously disappeared from Frankfurt, and rumors had it that they'd been sent to concentration camps, beaten, tortured, even massacred.

On November 9, 1938, Fackenheim read in the papers that a Polish Jew, Herschel Grynszpan, had murdered the German diplomat Ernst von Rath in Paris, hoping to arouse public opinion against the persecution of Jews in Germany. Paul condemned the assassination. The same night, the Nazis launched their collective revenge against the Jewish communities in Germany and Austria. In a carefully planned pogrom, which they named Kristallnacht—the Crystal Night, Nazis burned hundreds of synagogues, shops, warehouses, and offices belonging to Jews, murdered thirty-six of them and arrested 30,000 others. Half were deported to the Buchenwald concentration camp. Paul Fackenheim was arrested too, but was released after a couple of days. Some of his friends disappeared that night, never to come back. But he carried on with the obstinacy of the blind. All that counted for him was to provide for his mother's old age.

Under the new anti-Jewish restrictions, he encountered growing obstacles finding a job. Fortunately, his old hobby, cooking, turned out to be quite handy. For a few months he worked as a cook in the Jewish hospital of Frankfurt. Later, he opened a private cooking school for Jewish women who were trying to obtain jobs abroad as maids or cooks. One of his pupils was a young, very attractive girl by the name of Marion Kobliner. She was the daughter of Irma Kobliner, a widow who had been a subtenant in his mother's apartment. Paul timidly started courting the pretty Marion. But the Kobliner family managed to obtain a visa to England and left the country a few weeks before the outbreak of the war. Paul helped them get out of Germany. Nevertheless, Marion's image wouldn't leave Paul's mind. She kept returning in his dreams as a faraway, inaccessible woman whom he could have loved in a different world. But he couldn't imagine that her name would surface again in his life years later, under the most fateful circumstances.

On September 1, 1939, the Second World War erupted. New restrictions were placed on the Jews. By chance, Paul learned that his old friend, Lieutenant Metger, was a colonel now and had recently assumed command over the Frankfurt Artillery Regiment. He hurried to see him, and asked him for help. Oberst Metger listened to him in silence. "I will do my best, Paul," he said sadly, "but I'm afraid my powers are very limited. I'll talk about you to the Gauleiter of Frankfurt, although . . ." He stopped in midsentence. "Listen, I have an idea. Try to enlist in the Wehrmacht. Volunteer for the service. They won't take you, of course, but they'll have proof that you are a good German and a patriot. Maybe they'll spare you, you and your mother."

That same afternoon, Fackenheim reported to the Frankfurt recruitment center. He spread his military papers before the officer in charge and asked to be sent to the Eastern front. The young lieutenant looked at him strangely, and called two other officers from the inner office. They asked him to repeat his request, and watched with amusement this curious Jew who wanted to fight for the Reich. "Well, mein Herr, I am afraid we don't need your services right now," the chief recruiting officer chuckled. "If things turn worse, I assure you that we shall not fail to call upon you, of course."

Fackenheim walked back home in the rain that swept Frankfurt. He had run out of resources, and there was nothing more he could do.

The following months passed in misery and ever-present fear. And finally the night came when two men wearing brown hats and raincoats knocked on his door. Gestapo.

The train to Dachau. The fear. The cold. The hunger. The fat Bavarian policeman whom he met by chance in the crowded aisle and who murmured in his ear, "You'll be lucky if you get out of there alive."

And Dachau. The living hell.

The German secret services had studied the Fackenheim file thoroughly. The Abwehr experts knew all about 26336: his life story, his military record, his family status. They were aware of his courage, his easygoing nature, his candor and honesty. They possessed detailed reports about the Asian chapter in his life, his misery in Berlin and in Frankfurt, his fluency in foreign languages. They had established that, like many Jews, he had relatives all over the world, including England, the United States, and even Palestine. They knew that he had voted for the Fuehrer in 1932, but regarded Fackenheim's political naïveté as a unique asset that could make their handling of his case much easier. By systematically analyzing police reports from Berlin, SS reports from Dachau, and copies of letters he had written to his mother, they had reached the conclusion that their man firmly believed the official propaganda about the war. On numerous occasions he had told his fellow inmates in Dachau that he believed Hitler would soon be deposed or assassinated by the army and that the old liberal Germany would emerge from its ashes. There couldn't be any doubt about his fervent patriotism either. In his letters to his mother, copies of which they kept on file, he would doggedly reiterate his attachment to Germany. "I am doing my best to fulfill my duty as I should. Mother, you know I have always been a good German, and in spite of whatever has happened to me, I remain a loyal German. I do hope that Germany will win and will not be destroyed in this war."

A loyal German. Of all the files of German Jews, the Abwehr picked Fackenheim's. The spymasters of the Reich had decided to bet on his political ignorance, his attachment to traditional values, to the military code of honor, to his German Fatherland. They had decided to make the best of the trump cards they held up their sleeve. A magnificent bait to lure him: his release from Dachau. A formidable threat to pressure him into total submission: the life of his mother, who was at the mercy of the Gestapo.

The Abwehr chiefs knew well that 26336 had no choice. In their hands he was nothing but a puppet, a pawn in their devious game.

III

The Red Card

THE MERCEDES slowed down as it approached the lively center of Munich. Fackenheim watched in wonder as the magnificent skyline of the city emerged before them: the eleventh-century tower of St. Peter's, the green cupola of the Theatiner Church, the sleek spire of the Salvatorkirche, the famous twin towers of the Frauenkirche. A noisy, cheerful crowd strolled on the sunswept sidewalks. Many men were wearing the traditional Tyrolean outfit: green felt hats adorned with feathers, lederhosen held by large, colorful suspenders, heavy mountain shoes and woolen socks. Soldiers on leave clustered around photo shops or stared hungrily at the young women in the street. The pretty Bavarian girls, oblivious to the crisp weather, had already discarded their winter clothes and minced daintily on the sidewalks, their thin skirts dancing sensuously around their legs. Fackenheim stiffened and took a deep breath, trying to remember the last time he had made love to a woman.

"Hauptbahnhof—München," the driver said. The car stopped in front of the huge sprawling structure that housed the main railroad station. The man who had been sitting in silence beside Fackenheim got out quickly and held the door for him. "This way please." The Regierungsrat didn't even turn back. He sat stiff and immobile in the front seat, dispassionately watching the crowd streaming through the station gates. Fackenheim suddenly felt with absolute certainty that the "government adviser" was in deep disagreement with what was happening; he had been reluctant, reserved, even hostile all along and didn't seem to approve of the liberation of a Jew from Dachau. While the officer who had interviewed Paul had treated him with genuine compassion, the Regierungsrat seemed to be a potential enemy who right now was acting against his will. Paul was to recall this feeling months later when he would become the cause of a bitter feud between the secret services of the Reich.

Fackenheim got out of the car. A man had stepped out of the crowd and stood beside the officer. He was very tall, blond, dressed in a smart gray suit. The officer turned to Fackenheim. "This gentleman will take care of you now. Good-bye." He slid into the Mercedes, which departed at once. Fackenheim followed the car with his eyes, puzzled by the abrupt disappearance of the people who had taken him out of Dachau. He had read in a spy novel about the techniques of contact and compartmentalization, but had never taken the cloak-and-dagger stuff seriously. And after all, they were in Munich, not on enemy territory.

"Follow me, please," the man in gray said. Fackenheim obeyed. As they made their way across the big hall for departures, he stopped by a newsstand. Several newspapers announced in banner headlines the glorious German victories in North Africa. One of them displayed a photograph of a short, dusty general standing in the middle of the desert, with tanks and armored troop carriers in the background. A pair of desert goggles were fastened to his cap. The picture was crowned with the caption: ROMMEL, THE HERO OF TOBRUK. Another paper carried an exclusive photograph of the triumphant entrance of the Wehrmacht in Belgrade. The Yugoslavian capital looked like a heap of rubble.

"Will you hurry please?" the man in gray said to him in a low voice. "We'll be late for our train." On the platform, people were clustered around a fast-food stand. Paul winced at the tantalizing smell of the "Munchen Weisswurste," the veal sausages, that were grilled in the open. A fat Bavarian was devouring his sausages and Brezeln with gusto, washing them down with a huge stein of beer. As he watched him, Fackenheim found it hard to believe that barely ten miles to the north, in Dachau, people were dying.

The man in gray led the way into a first-class car of the express train *Munich-Cologne*. A subservient steward ushered them into a reserved compartment and placed Fackenheim's small valise on the upper luggage rack. The compartment had a touch of old Europe about it. The heavy window drapes and the upholstery of the seats were made of brown velvet. The tan, soft carpet was spotless, and starched lace doilies gleamed immaculately on the head supports. Framed photographs of the Rhine valley and the snowcapped Alps hung on the walls. The German locked the door from inside and pulled down the shades.

"Who are you?" Fackenheim asked.

The young man hesitated a moment, then said, "I am employed at the consulate general of Germany in Belgium."

"Belgium?" Fackenheim stared at him in surprise. "May I know your name?"

The blond man returned his stare, but didn't speak. He broke his silence only after the train began moving on its northbound journey. "Did you have breakfast?"

Breakfast. He hadn't realized that it was still morning, and all the dramatic things that had happened to him—the interview, the formal procedure of his release, the journey to Munich—had barely taken a couple of hours. He smiled bitterly. "They don't serve you breakfast at Dachau."

His companion bent toward him. "Now listen to me." He seemed highly strung and blinked nervously several times before resuming. "I don't know who you are. I don't have to know and I don't want to. I've got my orders. I have to deliver you in good shape at your destination. That's all."

He took a bag from the luggage rack and emptied its contents on the folding table, in front of Fackenheim. Paul could hardly believe his eyes. A whole roast chicken, a stack of sandwiches, boiled eggs, sliced ham, a thermos flask full of coffee, a big bottle of red wine.

Without waiting to be asked, he hurled himself at the food. A man who had subsisted for months on a half loaf of bread, a bowl of soup, and twenty grams of margarine a day could hardly be expected to stick to etiquette.

When he finally raised his head and let himself relax on the padded seat, the small table looked as if it had been devastated by a hurricane. For the first time, the shadow of a smile touched the lips of his companion.

"Where are we going?" Fackenheim asked.

"My orders are to escort you to Brussels."

"Brussels? Why should I go to Brussels?"

The blond man didn't answer. He meticulously repacked the meager leftovers of Fackenheim's meal and put them in the bag. He cleaned and folded the table, then took a key from his pocket and opened his briefcase. He handed Fackenheim a folded red card. "These are your papers," he said. "From now on your name is Koch. Herr Paul Koch."

Fackenheim stared at him in bewilderment. Koch! They seemed to know all about him, those mysterious people who were now in control of his life. Even when selecting his nom de guerre they had displayed an intimate knowledge of his past. And a peculiar sense of humor.

"Koch" meant cook in German. And cooking had always been the favorite hobby of Paul Fackenheim. He had suffered his most memorable thrashing by his father's hand at the age of twelve, when he had broken fourteen eggs in a vain attempt to concoct a huge cream cake. He hadn't given up, though, and had continued buying cookbooks, experimenting with unusual recipes and cooking gourmet dishes. In the Far East, he had learned from the native Indonesians and Chinese the rules of their exotic cuisine. And back in Germany, his hobby had saved him in his worst hour of need, when he had opened the Fackenheim Cooking School in Frankfurt. He had taught cooking to many high-class Jewish women who had never before bothered to step into their kitchens and were now so keen to get a job as maids or cooks abroad. The fees he collected had allowed him and his mother to survive in the darkest months before his deportation to Dachau.

And now the German Abwehr had decided to give him a pseudonym fitting his talents. The former *cordon bleu* had become Herr Koch.

Fackenheim examined his new identity card. It was a rectangular piece of red cardboard, as big as a postcard. There was no photograph. The letterhead, in big, bold print, read HIGH COMMAND OF THE GERMAN FORCES IN BELGIUM. Under it, a typewritten text:

> The bearer of this document, Herr Paul Koch, travels on official business in Germany and in the occupied territories.
>
> He has been entrusted with a mission by the High Command.
>
> All the services of the army and the party are hereby required to give him all assistance and protection he may need.

The illegible signature was stamped with the seal of the German military governor of Belgium.

"I was instructed to inform you that Paul Fackenheim doesn't exist anymore," the man in gray said stiffly, as if reciting a text he had learned by heart, "and that you're not allowed to reveal your real name, your creed, and your past to anyone."

"Koch" didn't answer. His eyes were glued to the official seal which showed the German eagle clutching the swastika in its claws. For the first time in his life the Nazi cross, symbol of persecution and death for his people, was to guarantee his protection and well-being.

"What do you want of me?" he asked, swept by a wave of sudden fear.

His companion kept silent.

"You must tell me," Fackenheim insisted. "I must talk to you about a subject which is of the utmost importance for me."

"If you have any questions, I can promise to transfer them to the proper authorities." The man seemed like a robot trained to deliver impersonal and prefabricated answers.

"So tell this to the proper authorities: I have a mother, an old and sick woman who lives in fear and need, in Frankfurt."

The man in gray nodded. Even though he pretended to be uninvolved, he seemed to know much more than he wanted to admit.

Fackenheim went on. "I spoke about my mother with your . . . friends who brought me over to Munich. I told them, and I am telling you: I shall cooperate with you only if you guarantee the well-being of my mother. I must be assured that she will not be persecuted in any way, and she will be taken care of."

The German smiled. "I believe I can promise you that your mother will be protected. You have nothing to fear."

They continued their journey in silence. While the glorious German spring rolled before the train windows in a breathtaking display, Fackenheim tried to put some order to his thoughts. The uncertainty about his future overshadowed his initial elation. What would become of him? Why were they taking him to Brussels of all places? Was it because of his fluency in French? But they didn't need a Jew from Dachau for that. Or perhaps they wanted him to question Jewish prisoners? He went on imagining and discarding the wildest ideas, but failed to come up with a logical explanation.

For a while he absently leafed through some old copies of the soldiers' weekly, *Signal*, which his companion had brought with him. Every photo displayed a new, martial Germany, sure of the final victory: giggling French girls and cocky German officers by the Eiffel Tower in Paris; King

Boris of Bulgaria signing the Axis agreement; Hitler greeting Mussolini at the Berghof during a visit of the Duce to Germany; victorious German troops sweeping through Greece and Yugoslavia. He cast the magazines aside as a wave of remorse overcame him. How could he cooperate with the Nazis, with the assassins of his people, with those who invented Dachau? And then the answer, bitter and cruel, took shape in his mind. What else could he do? Die in Dachau? Abandon his mother? He wanted to live!

During their short stop at Nürnberg, he saw a boy running along the platform, selling newspapers. Rommel had taken the port of Bardia, in Cyrenaica, the headlines screamed. The hero of the Reich was about to cross the Egyptian border, on his way to Cairo.

In the late afternoon, the phone rang in a shabby apartment on Kernerstrasse Street in Frankfurt. A white-haired woman, dressed in black, picked up the receiver.

"Hedda Fackenheim," she said.

"Mother?"

She flinched at the sound of the familiar voice, a voice she thought she would never hear again.

"Mother, it's me, Paul."

She clutched the phone, unable to utter a single word.

"Mother, do you hear me? Mother?"

"Paul?" she managed to whisper into the mouthpiece.

"Mother, I am free."

"Where are you, Paul? Where are you calling from?"

There was a short silence. "I can't tell you. I can only tell you that I am free, that I feel fine, and you'll hear from me again."

"Aren't you coming home?" she asked anxiously.

"No. Not now. But I am all right. And you, Mother? How are you?"

"Paul . . ." The quivering old voice tried to compose a

message. "Paul, I saw your friend, Colonel Metger. He asked about you. He sent you his best wishes." The old colonel had come to visit her a few weeks ago.

"Metger? I see."

Paul paused. Was it Metger, he wondered, who had helped him to get out of Dachau?

"Mother, how are you?"

"I am fine, Paul, everything is fine. God, I am so excited. I am so happy that you're free, Paul. When shall I see you?"

"Listen, Mother. You will not suffer anymore. I promise you. Everything will be fine from now on."

He hung up. For a moment, Hedda Fackenheim didn't move, still pressing the receiver against her ear. Where was he? "You will not suffer anymore," he had said. What did he mean by that?

That same night, somebody knocked on the door. A man she had never seen before stood on the landing. "Frau Fackenheim?" he inquired politely.

She nodded.

He handed her a sealed envelope and disappeared in the dark staircase. She hastily locked the door and tore the envelope open. Inside she found 300 deutsche mark. There was no letter for her.

From that day on, the anonymous envelopes were delivered to her every month. No explanation ever came about their origin, and after a few fruitless inquiries, she didn't ask the messenger anymore.

In Brussels, an automobile stopped on a small street not far from the Porte de Namur. Once again it was a civilian car with a civilian driver. Fackenheim got off. His companion rolled down the window and leaned toward him.

"That's the end of your trip. You're going to live here, on the first floor, in the private pension of Madame Leclerc. She is expecting you. Your room has been reserved and prepaid. You don't have to fill out any forms or answer any questions.

Madame Leclerc is very discreet, anyway, and I don't think she'll try to get any information from you. She is from Luxemburg. If your French is inadequate, you can talk to her in German."

Fackenheim listened, gripping his small valise. Still, he failed to understand. Were they going to let him free? Why did they leave him like this in the middle of a Brussels street, a man who only this morning was a prisoner in Dachau? But on the other hand, where could he go? How could he escape? Those people knew they had absolute power over him.

"When shall I hear from you?" he asked.

"You'll never hear from me again. My mission is over. But somebody else will get in touch with you. And don't forget: Your name is Paul Koch. Good luck."

He shook the hand of 26336. "Oh, I almost forgot. You'll need some money for your expenses." The German pressed a thick wad of bills into Fackenheim's hand.

"Auf Wiedersehen."

The car jolted forward and disappeared at the first intersection. Fackenheim looked around. A quiet, bourgeois street. The massive nineteenth-century houses, the clean sidewalks, the well-tended tiny gardens and sturdy trees—all bestowing an atmosphere of peace and calm on the neighborhood. There was still light in some windows, and somebody was playing a Chopin sonata on the piano. He heard steps on the far side of the street and the throaty laughter of a young woman. He found it hard to believe, here in the opulence of fat, carefree Europe, that a war was going on, that Hitler and Dachau could even exist.

He shivered slightly. The night was chilly and he had no overcoat.

He turned back. Nobody was following him and nobody watched him. He was all alone. Free.

IV

Nightmares of
an Abwehr Spy

T HAT NIGHT, Paul Fackenheim
had a strange dream.
He had fallen asleep only
at the first light of dawn. Yet when he had walked into the
cozy little room in Madame Leclerc's pension, he could think
of nothing else but sleep. Madame Leclerc was a plump,
dark-eyed woman in her early fifties, with black hair, a heavily painted mouth, and a clipped accent. She had greeted him
politely and led the way up the stairs to his room, blurting out
questions like an automaton. Was he tired? Did he want her
to draw him a bath? Would he like some supper? Some tea
perhaps? He had courteously refused, had locked the door
behind her, and collapsed on the bed. The dramatic events of
that day and the long journey to Brussels had left him utterly
exhausted. The featherbed had a softness he had forgotten,
the clean sheets were scented with lavender.

But he hadn't fallen asleep and had restlessly shifted and
tossed in the dark. It took him hours to realize that something
was missing, and that it was Dachau—the night in Dachau.
The mixture of moans, sighs, and tears of those hundreds of
living dead; the icy wind that blew through the open windows, piercing the thin blankets and cruelly assailing the
frail, shivering men; the smell and the feel of the unwashed
bodies huddled against each other on the wooden cots in a
vain search for warmth and security.

Dachau was haunting him now, forbidding him from enjoying the soothing calm of the Brussels night. In the blackness that surrounded him he could vividly see the scores of

48

eyes, full of envy and despair, that had focused on him when he had walked away in his shabby suit, clutching his small valise.

And only when the first gray haze had started creeping over the still city had he sunk into a heavy, agitated slumber.

He dreamt he was standing in the middle of a vast prairie amid a huge crowd of men, women, and children. Some were wearing civilian clothes, others feldgrau uniforms; many were dressed in the striped pajamas of the Dachau inmates. All around, the horizon was strewn with watchtowers and fortified positions; machine guns were pointed at the crowd. And the crowd stood still, immobile, as an eerie silence hovered over the field.

All of a sudden, from thousands of loudspeakers, the voice thundered over the assembly. The familiar voice every German knew so well, a demented, hysterical, and yet enrapturing voice, threatening, inflaming, overwhelming. There were no words in the voice, there was no message, only the strident sound, rising and falling, hissing in hatred, cajoling in promise, thundering in demonic harangue. Yet the crowd, suddenly electrified, responded to the voice with a roaring ovation, an explosion of joy and enthusiasm.

Paul was the only one in the exultant crowd who knew that the voice was lying. He broke into a run across the field, grabbing the men by their shoulders, shouting the truth in their faces, striving to tear them away from the false prophecy. But his warnings were drowned out by the thunder of the voice, and the men ignored him, their burning eyes looking through him as if he didn't exist.

The voice suddenly faded out. Heavy black clouds crept across the sky. A cold wind rose in the north and swept the prairie, turning into a roaring tempest. The watchtowers collapsed like matchsticks, and the terrified crowd dispersed in all directions. A ghastly yellow glow lit the far horizon, and four solitary riders emerged under the frenzied clouds.

Paul knew who they were even before discerning their

death's-heads etched against the blackness of their hoods. The crowd also recognized the Four Horsemen of the Apocalypse and rushed madly away. But they were all doomed. The dark horses, growing to monstrous sizes in the eerie sulfurous light, hurled themselves onto the men, trampling row after row of screaming human beings.

Paul was trapped in the middle of the field, unable to move, knowing there was no escape. The horsemen approached like lightning. Paul glimpsed a gleaming skull in the folds of a black mantle and the hollow eyes of a huge horse as it stood on its hind legs, froth streaming from its mouth. The horse then struck him, sudden blackness enveloped him, and he fell into a bottomless abyss.

He woke up bathed in sweat. Daylight streamed through the lace curtains. All his body was aching, and he shivered with fever. The ulcer on his neck shot a sharp pain throughout his body. His lips were cracked and dry, his mouth foul.

Swaying like a drunk, Fackenheim managed to dress, his fingers numbly struggling with his shirt buttons. The nightmare obsessed him, its smallest details vividly present in his mind. He burst out of his room and down the stairs, as if he were running for his life. The front door wasn't locked. He yanked it open, and the next moment he was standing outdoors in sunny, cheerful Brussels, whose fresh spring air he gulped with abandon.

Off the Namur Gate, he found a pleasant restaurant called Aux Deux Clés. He picked a corner table by the large window, and he ordered a beer from a young waiter in a white vest with golden epaulets who was proudly smoothing his oily forelock. The waiter nodded coldly, pursed his lips, and strutted away. Only when the waiter had returned and carelessly set the mug down, spilling some of the beer on the tablecloth, did Fackenheim notice the hostile, disgusted expression on his face. He cast a quick glance about him. The other patrons were also looking at him strangely. There was aversion in their eyes and an instinctive fear, as if they were watching a leper. He got up without touching his beer and hurried to the men's toilet.

In the mirror he saw the face of a stranger. Haggard, red-rimmed eyes stared at him from a hirsute, hollow-cheeked visage. He saw dark, sunken eye sockets, sagging pouches beneath the eyes, waxen skin, bloodless lips. His skull was shaven, his neck scrawny; his jacket was threadbare and baggy, and the stained bow tie on his loose collar only emphasized the image of debauchery and misery that he presented. *You look like a tramp*, he said to himself, *a bum who has just been released from prison.*

Back at the table, he left some money beside his untouched beer and escaped to the street. But here too he had the feeling of being watched; the passersby seemed to gape at him with disdain. He suddenly wanted to be away from all those people and their spiteful stares. He bought a few toilet articles in a small shop and hastily made his way back to Madame Leclerc's pension. His room seemed to him the last sanctuary on earth.

He was wrong. A man was sitting by the window, his back turned to the door. He was tall, corpulent, and was dressed in an inexpensive tan suit. As the man turned to face him, Fackenheim noticed his shock of brown hair and his black eyes. He had an oval face, a double chin, and big, thick hands. He seemed to be in his early thirties.

"Good morning, Herr Koch," he said in German. His voice was deep and calm.

"Who are you?"

"My name is Schmidt. I'll be taking care of you."

"May I see your papers? I don't want to take unnecessary risks."

Schmidt threw back his head, studying him thoughtfully. Out of his breast pocket he took a cigarette that looked tiny between his sturdy fingers, lit it, and blew a spiral of smoke. Finally he nodded. "All right," he said. He took a black wallet from his inner pocket and unhurriedly scanned the documents inside. "My real name is Müller," he said impassively. "I always use an alias. Regulations, you know." He handed Fackenheim a folded document. It was a military pass delivered by the German high command in Belgium. The name was printed in Gothic letters, without any mention of rank. HANS MÜLLER.

"Fine," Fackenheim said. "I'll call you Müller, if you don't mind."

The big man shrugged.

"And what exactly do you want?" Fackenheim asked.

Müller wasn't offended by his belligerent tone. "The chief directed me to work with you. To start, I must instruct you in Morse and radio signals."

"What for?"

"You'll know that in good time." Müller's voice was calm but firm.

"Who is your chief?"

"It would be better for you not to know too much. You'll see him tomorrow, I'll take you to his office."

"My mother . . ."

"Your mother is well. We are taking care of her. You can write to her. I'll forward your letters. Of course, you shouldn't mention Brussels. You shouldn't mention your employment either. I'll make sure that your mother gets your letters regularly and can write back to you. Here is some money for your expenses. If you need more, just let me know." He left an envelope on the table and shook Fackenheim's hand.

"One more question," Fackenheim said when Müller was at the door. "Where is your office? I might have to get in touch with you in case of an emergency."

"Sorry. I am the one who is in charge of the contacts. I'll come to pick you up tomorrow at ten."

"You are with the Abwehr, aren't you?"

Müller shrugged again. "I guess you've figured that out already. Tomorrow morning, then."

The big man was punctual. Fackenheim had barely finished his breakfast the next morning when Müller knocked on his door. "You can't see the chief today," he said. "He had to leave."

"When shall we go to your office, then?"

Müller slowly lit a cigarette. He seemed to find refuge in smoking whenever he needed time to formulate a delicate answer. "We'd better meet here," he finally said. "It will be safer for you."

"What do you mean?"

Müller exhaled some smoke, walked to the window, and pulled the curtains. He turned on the ceiling light, returned to his chair, opened his briefcase, and took out a small dummy of a radio transmitter. "Let's start working. Do you have any experience in Morse?"

"I spent some time with Signals in the Great War."

"Fine. Let's refresh your memory, then."

For two hours, Fackenheim practiced transmitting code words and messages in Morse on the tiny device.

"That will be enough for today," Müller said. "That's not bad at all. You'll be ready quite soon."

"Ready for what? What kind of mission do you have in mind? I have the right to know."

Müller shrugged and hastily changed subjects. "I'll come to see you again this afternoon. I must buy you some clothes. Yours are in bad shape."

"I fell very awkward when I go out," Fackenheim admitted. "I am a civilian, I speak German, and I carry that strange red card your friend gave to me. People keep away from me."

Müller leaned back on his chair, watching him attentively. "I'd like to make you an offer," he said. "You're free to accept it or refuse it. It might make life easier for you." He paused and lit another cigarette. "We are asking you to accept a uniform of the German army."

"What?" Fackenheim couldn't believe his ears.

Müller kept his calm. "A uniform of the Wehrmacht. With the rank of captain. I have the official authorization of the chief for that proposal."

Fackenheim was deeply perturbed. *How dare they offer me a German uniform after all the ignominies I've seen committed in the name of the Reich?* But on the other hand, wasn't that a token of their trust? Dress him in a uniform of a German officer and let him be free in the center of Brussels?

The Prussian in him took over. "If you had offered me that uniform and asked me to enlist and go fight the enemy on the Eastern front, I would have agreed. But not on your conditions. I am Jewish. I was a prisoner in Dachau. I can't do that."

Müller nodded without speaking and went out.

After the door had closed behind him, Fackenheim burst into nervous laughter. A German uniform. The former 26336 from Dachau promoted to captain in the Wehrmacht. He did well to refuse; that would have been too much. Make him the Jewish officer of Hitler!

How could he know that his friends from the Abwehr wanted to make of him something worse, much worse than a Jewish officer in the Reich's army?

A month passed. The newspapers reported new German victories. Yugoslavia was defeated. The occupation of Greece was completed, after airborne German troops parachuted over Crete and overpowered the British garrison there. Winds of panic blew in Cairo and Alexandria as Rommel swiftly advanced, determined to reach the Suez Canal. In Poland, the Jewish population was herded into ghettos. In utmost secrecy, the mass executions of Jews had started. But the Nazis, dedicated perfectionists of horror, were still busy searching for quicker and more efficient methods to exterminate the Jews.

No news of the atrocities in Poland reached Brussels, however. And in Brussels, the life of the Abwehr's private Jew had settled into a cozy and pleasant routine. Every morning at ten o'clock, Müller would knock on his door. The big, cheerful man would meticulously arrange his books and equipment on the table, light a cigarette, and start the daily training: two hours of Morse, radio transmissions, ciphering, and coding; how to use a portable transceiver, how to encipher and decipher a message, how to establish a coding grille, how to use a codebook. Müller led him easily through a quick course in elementary cryptography, in which the code was based on the one-time pad system. They then advanced to the next stage, the mastering of more sophisticated cryptographic methods. At noon, Müller would pack his equipment, shake Fackenheim's hand, and go away. The rest of the day was free.

The two men did not discuss Fackenheim's mission. He knew he was going to be dispatched to enemy territory as a spy—the nature of his training left no doubt about that. But there was no use in asking any questions. Müller wouldn't say a word and Fackenheim suspected at times that the Abwehr agent himself didn't know what kind of mission was being planned.

On the other hand, Fackenheim had made his own private inquiries. A few times he had discreetly followed Müller across the city; he had struck conversations with German officers and civilians he had met in the cafés and restaurants of Brussels, subtly slipping a question here and there. He now knew that the Abwehr had established one of its important centers in town soon after Belgium had been conquered by the German army in 1940. He had heard that the Métropole and Les Ambassadeurs hotels were used by the Abwehr to put up some of their special guests, who, given a crash course in espionage, disappeared after a week or so, never to be seen again.

He also knew there was a big training center for Abwehr spies at Number 5, Rue de la Loi. Müller's office was there too. But why didn't they admit him there, with the others? Because he was Jewish? For his protection? Or for theirs? Could his missions be so secret? Or perhaps they intended to sacrifice him and didn't want anybody to know?

Still, life went on, and the Brussels spring was magnificent. Fackenheim enjoyed his new existence. His health improved and he became his old self again. He spent a few days in the First Military Hospital of the German army on Avenue de la Couronne. A good surgeon operated on his neck and his ulcer was removed. He bought new clothes and became smartly dressed. His head was full of hair again; his eyes no longer had that haunted look.

Paul devised a means to correspond with his mother without submitting his letters to Müller's censorship. In the military hospital, where he came once a week for routine checkups, there was a soldiers' mailbox. He used it to send letters to his mother; he hadn't written her in so many words where he was, lest something might happen to her. But walking in the center of Brussels once, he asked a street photographer to take a picture of him under a sign reading Rue Neuve. His mother had traveled a great deal in Europe, and he was sure that she could guess where he was when she got the picture.

Fackenheim took long strolls around town every day, and took his afternoon cocoa on Boulevard Trevuren at the Café Marquand, which was supposed to have the best pastries in Belgium. He often sat next to a fighter pilot of the Luftwaffe, who was clad in a brown leather flight jacket. They chatted like old friends. The pilot never told him his name, but Fackenheim had seen his picture in the papers. The man was

Adolf Galland, one of the famous aces of the German air force.

For dinner, Fackenheim went often to the Novada restaurant on Rue Neuve. Because he spoke flawless French and had a pleasant way with people, he was able to befriend the entire staff. The maître d'hôtel, Louis, reserved the best tables for "Monsieur Paul" and served him his most exquisite dishes.

His life was agreeable. Except for those frightful nights, when an iron hand would seize him and nail him to his bed. His old nightmares were always there, together with his cruel memories, his fear, his ever-present remorse—he knew that in spite of all outward appearances he was still a prisoner in the enormous Nazi machine. And he was all by himself. Night after night the questions would assail him, filling his mind with torment: What to do? How to escape? What would become of him? And the answer was always the same. *You can do nothing. Your brothers are dying. Your world is falling apart. And you are nothing but a toy in the hands of your former jailers. But if you want to survive, if you want to save your mother, keep quiet. Obey. Do what you're told. As long as they don't order you to betray your people and your faith. There is no other way.*

He tried to escape those nights of mental torture, but the nightmares were beyond his control. One morning, when he was in the hospital, he had woken in a strange room where he was all by himself. His pretty nurse, the blonde, blue-eyed Elli, was sitting on a chair beside the bed, her face distraught, her eyes red from lack of sleep. He remembered well that he had gone to sleep in a room shared by three other patients. "Why am I here?" he had asked. "What happened?"

"You had high fever tonight, and you spoke in your sleep."

"What did I say?"

"Nonsense," she said, lowering her eyes. "Absolute nonsense. You shouted and screamed and said things that nobody should hear. I got scared. When one is under the influence of drugs and develops high fever, he might imagine things, you see? He might imagine that those things have happened to him, while the truth is that he has only heard about them. One should let sleeping dogs lie. Anyway, I didn't want the others to hear you. It could be dangerous for you. So I had you moved here."

"What did I say?"

Her eyes were blank. "I forgot," she said.

Nurse Elli could forget. But Paul Fackenheim could not. That's why he walked the streets, devoured life with abandon, yearned for human warmth, for company. At night he was the last to leave the Novada restaurant. He haunted the bars but avoided the cheap cabarets frequented by German soldiers. He spent long evenings at the Café de la Paix Mondiale with a carefree crowd of young Belgians.

That's where he met, one evening in May, Jacqueline-les-Lunettes.

V

The Dead Houses

JACQUELINE-LES-LUNETTES: Jacqueline-the-glasses. He was to discover the origin of her nickname when he slowly undressed her one night by the open window of his room. When she stood naked before him, the milky whiteness of her body offering itself to his touch, he reached for her glasses.

"I'll keep them," she said briskly.

He almost burst out in laughter, but restrained himself. "Why?" he asked. "What do you need your glasses for?"

"I want to see your face when you make love to me," she said softly. "People's faces change totally when they make love. Some look as if they are in pain, others smile like children. Will you tell me how I look when we are together?"

She was sweet, fresh, young, and disarmingly frank. There was something childish in the way she gave herself to him totally, in her uninhibited delight in sex, in her candid way of exploring his body. She was a country girl, rosy-cheeked, small-breasted, and always cheerful. She had come from a small Walloon village to Brussels eager to taste the good life depicted in the popular novels. She had been spared the inevitable disappointments only because of her capacity to enjoy the smallest pleasures of life. Jacqueline lived in a tiny room with two other young women and worked in a porcelain factory in the northern outskirts. But Brussels enchanted her, a new pair of stockings made her happy, an invitation to a meal in a second-rate restaurant made her feel like a duchess. She was delighted by Paul's manners, and found his interest in her exhilarating. He was much older than her, a

59

foreigner, a gentleman and a man of the world, she explained to him gravely, and she was flattered by his attention.

The times he spent with her were to be the most blissful memories Paul would keep of Brussels. She made him feel how wonderful life could be, how easy it was to enjoy it. She didn't read papers, didn't listen to the radio, and didn't care about the war. With Jacqueline he felt safe from the nightmares that haunted him; he felt protected from the memories of the past and the uncertainties of the future. With her firm body under him, his large bed would metamorphose into a safe world, and he would sink into a joyful state of calm, that would brutally dissolve with the first light of day.

There had also been some other women in Brussels. There was Simone, who refused to come to his room because she was afraid of being involved with a German. And there was Flo, Florence, the clever, pretty divorcée, a former research assistant at the University of Liège who worked now for a publisher of textbooks. She was in her late thirties, a striking, slim woman who had the elegance and sophisticated allure that Jacqueline would never acquire. She too would not speak of the war, but he suspected that her reasons were the opposite of Jacqueline's. She was an intelligent, passionate woman with strong views about everything, and he wouldn't have been surprised if she turned out to be a member of the underground. She never gave herself to him fully; even in bed she never stopped asking him questions and watching him closely, doubtfully, through her half-closed eyelids. Flo was the only person he had met in Brussels who apparently didn't accept his cover story. He was certain that she saw through him and didn't believe one word about his job as a civilian employee of the German occupying forces in Belgium. Flo was too clever for that, but she liked him and she enjoyed sleeping with him, and that was what counted, finally.

His love life till then had been nothing but a failure. His first adventure, at the age of sixteen, had been rather typical of its times. His parents had left for a short weekend at the fashionable resort of Bad Godesberg, and the maid, the plump, blond Marie, had gaily plunged in the bed of the young virgin and initiated him in the joys of sex. The youngster had been thrilled by that first experience and became a frequent visitor to Marie's tiny room. But he didn't dare make use of his newly acquired skills in his budding love affair with the daughter of a rich Protestant businessman. Fearing the mother of his teenage Dulcinea, he had valiantly protected her virginity, despite the girl's assiduous efforts to get rid of it. Then the war had come, and he had experienced the soldier's quick, casual sex with easy girls. In Germany, France, and Belgium he had had a few sexual encounters that had no emotional meaning for him. And the more he tasted that kind of sex, the more he idealized the image of the woman he would meet, love, and marry one day.

It was only natural, therefore, that he would be spellbound by the first beautiful woman who encouraged his courtship after the war. Certain that he had found the love of his life, he had hastily married Gretchen. That had been a mistake which cost him dearly.

He had awakened to reality only in Batavia, in the Dutch Indies. Quite often, when he came back from his long trips in the countryside, he wouldn't find Gretchen home. Several times she returned only in the morning, mumbling something about a night spent with a woman friend. He guessed the truth, of course, but pretended to ignore it. And how could he blame her? He was fascinated by the exotic Orient and spent most of his time on the road, while his young wife hated Asia and was terrified by the prospect of wasting her youth far away from the glittering cities of Europe. He hadn't objected to her decision to return to Germany for a long rest. And he had been only mildly surprised by his friends' letters that informed him about her love affairs. His lawyer had had no difficulties in obtaining the necessary evidence, and the divorce had been quick and smooth. He had heard later that she had remarried, her new husband a dashing young businessman.

He had made his second mistake when he returned to Berlin. He was lonely, miserable, yearning for love, and was still used to life in Indonesia, where a white woman was regarded almost as a goddess. When he had met Luzi, he had been dazzled by her beauty. When she had burst into tears and told him about her pregnancy, he had not hesitated. "I'll give my name to your child," he had offered. And just for a few months, he believed that this time he had married the right girl.

But when he had lost his job, and poverty had struck, she had grown restless. She had started disappearing in the evenings and didn't bother telling him where and why. One night he had seen her wearing a new necklace, then other pieces of new jewelry, silk scarves, expensive blouses. On her dressing table he had seen unopened bottles of perfume. "These are from my savings," she had said. "I am saving on the money you give me." He had wanted to believe it, smothering his suspicions—until the night he had come home and had found her lying on the bed, unconscious, in a puddle of blood. She had become pregnant again, from somebody else, and had tried to abort with a knitting needle. At the hospital, the doctors had assured him that she suffered only from a hemorrhage and would recover quickly. An hour later, she had died in surgery.

And he was alone again. Alone in Frankfurt, with no friends, and no woman. Alone in Dachau. Alone in the Abwehr net. Crushed under the weight of his terrible secret, unable to share it with a living soul, to ask advice from a true friend. And so he clung with desperation to his ephemeral love affairs, to those stolen moments in the arms of foreign women.

And then came the stroll in the old city that almost made him break down.

That night he had slept badly. A hot and humid summer had settled on the city, and the muggy air was almost suffocating. Fackenheim got up early, donned a short-sleeved shirt and lightweight trousers, and went out, delighting in the freshness of the early morning.

The city of Brussels was waking up. Working people were already hurrying along the streets, children's laughter echoed in the open windows, food stores raised their blinds. Peasants' carts, drawn by sturdy Belgian horses, were carrying fresh produce, milk, and fowl from the country.

Taken by the cheerful sights and sounds, he didn't even realize that he had deviated from his usual path and wandered into terra incognita. He was pacing down the avenue that led to the North Brussels railway station, and without any reason took a left turn. It was a long and narrow street, most of it still in shadow. He walked slowly on the deserted sidewalk, in pleasant relaxation, when a vague feeling of malaise made him stop and look around. Something was wrong. He turned and looked back. There was nobody in the street. All was quiet and peaceful.

The realization came slowly. It was the silence that was wrong. The street was too quiet. There was no sign of life, no sound, no movement. He studied the houses on both sides of the street. The doors were locked and bolted, some of them barred with planks nailed to the framework. The windows were shuttered, the shops closed. Garbage was piled on the corners. In one open garbage pail, he saw torn books and broken china. In one house a bolt had broken on the upper floors and a shutter was swaying in the morning wind, repeatedly rapping on the wall. There was something sinister in that regular beat that dryly echoed in the deserted street.

He heard the sound of footsteps on the pavement and turned around. A frail old woman, dressed in black, trudged along past the dead houses. She was carrying a milk can. He waited for her to come near him. A black gutter cat ran in front of her and found refuge in an alleyway across the street.

The old woman crossed herself hastily and squinted at him.

"What's going on here?" he asked in French. "Why does nobody live in that street?"

She looked at him suspiciously, inched closer to the wall, and plodded on, trying to bypass him.

He caught her scrawny arm. "Not so quick, grandma. Answer me!"

The old woman faced him. "Why do you ask?" Her toothless mouth produced a hoarse, croaking sound. "Everybody knows that."

"I don't. I'm not from here, grandma."

"You're not?" She bent her head sideways and studied him doubtfully. "Come on, now, you're German, aren't you?"

"No."

She left her milk can on the sidewalk and stepped toward him. "The Jews used to live here." Her crackling voice was low, conspiratorial. "They owned all those houses, and the shops as well. The Germans said that they could be dangerous for the security of their army. They took them all away. Nobody knows where." She stared at him for a moment, then picked up her can with a sigh and walked away.

He watched her saunter along the walls until her stooping black shape disappeared like a shadow. That was the Jewish quarter, then. The familiar feeling of remorse and helplessness stirred inside him. *Nobody knows where they are.* But he thought he knew. He could visualize them all, men, women, and children, dressed in the striped uniforms, the stars and numbers stamped over their hearts, amid the watchtowers and the electrified fences. The memory of Dachau struck him, vivid and real, as if he had never left it.

He turned to the house to his right and crashed his fist on the door, several times. But there was no response. He started running from one house to another, knocking on the locked doors, shaking the closed shutters. It couldn't be, they couldn't have taken them all. Somebody must have stayed behind! A rotten board broke under his blows, and drops of blood appeared on his knuckles. He went on pounding, desperately hoping to find a living soul behind the windows.

The blows echoed in the empty hallways, the closed shops, the abandoned apartments. But there was nobody there.

Later, he failed to remember what he had done for the rest of the day. He must have walked for hours like a robot, the sight of the phantom street engraved in his mind. Nobody knew where the people had gone.

He surfaced from his daze only late that night, in Florence's room. Lying beside her, his eyes closed, he tried to regain control over himself. All that he wanted was to run away and disappear. But as always, the inner voice objected, whispering its maddening questions: *Run away, but where? Disappear, but how? And your mother?*

Nevertheless, just for a moment, he thought he had made a decision. He turned to look at Florence. She was the only person in the world who could help him now.

"Flo, I must ask you a question. I need your help."

She was looking at him, puzzled, intensely studying his face with her green eyes. She had never seen him in such a state.

"Flo, I must get in touch with the Resistance. I think you know some of them. It's terribly important. You must help me find them. Please."

She kept looking at him for a while, propped on her elbow. *She knows them,* he said to himself, *she can contact them. They'll help me run away, they'll find a hiding place for me.* And then he saw doubt and mistrust creep into Flo's eyes, and he knew that he would never make it.

"I don't know what you're talking about," Flo said, and turned her back to him.

Two days later, on June 15, at 10 A.M., Müller knocked on his door. At first Paul didn't recognize him. Müller was wearing the uniform of a sergeant major in the Wehrmacht.

Müller noticed the surprise in Paul's eyes, but didn't let him ask any questions.

"I came to ask you to pack your things," he said calmly. "We are leaving tomorrow."

"Tomorrow?" That was totally unexpected. "Where are we going?"

Müller hesitated a second, but quickly made up his mind. "My orders are not to disclose anything to you, but I don't see what difference it could make. We are going to Berlin."

VI

The Fox Lair

THE TWO SS SERGEANTS had almost completed their evening beat. Their routine circuit included a portion of the Kurfürstendamm, Berlin's most famous avenue, and several of the adjacent streets. Tonight's patrol had been quite uneventful—some harmless crowds at the entrance of the cinemas, a soldiers' brawl over a couple of girls, a few drunks whom they left to the regular police. Their functions were purely political. They knew the Berliners well. As time went by, they had developed a sixth sense that would detect any unusual phenomenon. Occasionally they would stop a passerby as a matter of routine, check his papers, ask a few questions. In most of the bars and restaurants, one quick look would be enough to reassure the SS that all the patrons were loyal and devoted subjects of the Fuehrer.

The big beer cellar on Tauentzienstrasse was packed. Harried waitresses in white blouses and green skirts were elbowing their way through the crowd, carrying huge steins of beer and plates filled with sausages, sauerkraut, and potato salad. Heavy cigar smoke hung in the air and the audience, mostly men—blue-collar workers, clerks, and soldiers—shouted, joked, and bellowed with laughter. In a corner, a group of drunk soldiers, their faces flushed and their tunic collars unbuttoned, were unsuccessfully trying to start a beer song.

The younger SS was the first to notice the stranger. He was leaning on the counter, taking long gulps of beer from the glass mug he held in his hand. Beside him lay a packet of foreign cigarettes. He was of medium height, well dressed, but the cut of his gray suit seemed foreign too. His wavy brown hair, his profile, and, most of all, the furtive looks he cast once in a while immediately triggered the alarm in the preconditioned SS mind. That fellow wasn't a Berliner. He looked Jewish. He seemed to fear the SS. Three good reasons to get to know him better.

The two sergeants made their way through the crowd, and stood behind the stranger. The younger one cockily slipped his thumbs in his leather belt. "Your papers, please!"

The stranger turned quickly. He attempted a smile, but they noticed a flash of anxiety in his brown melancholy eyes. He left his drink on the counter, produced a wallet from his inner pocket, and fingered its contents.

"Just a moment! What have you got there?" The SS noticed some foreign banknotes among the man's papers. He stretched out his hand. "Let me see that."

"That's nothing," the man said in perfect German. "Those are Belgian bills."

"Where did you get them? You're Belgian?"

The man shook his head. "No." He took a folded rectangle of red cardboard from his wallet. "Here are my papers."

The SS eyed the red card with surprise. He had never seen anything like it.

"Those are your papers?" he asked, incredulous. He studied the document and bent to read it in the dim light. "The German high command in Belgium." He turned to his partner. "What's that supposed to be?"

The older SS shrugged, confused. "I'd rather run a check on that fellow."

A deep silence had settled in the vast "Bier Keller." The waves of laughter and the saucy jokes had faded away. Even the drunk soldiers had stopped bellowing their songs and were staring about them with glassy eyes. All attention converged on the confrontation between the SS and the stranger. The SS might be arresting a foreign spy or a dissident. In such cases, the best tactic was to keep away.

Tiny beads of sweat formed on the stranger's forehead

and he blinked nervously.

"Come with us," the older SS finally said, keeping his voice down. "Herr Koch, is it?" he added after glancing again at the red card. He sounded skeptical.

The crowd parted silently to give them way. The three men got out in the street. The SS sergeants shoved the stranger, none too gently, into a dark doorway and flanked him on both sides. Their hands came to rest on their revolvers. They knew from experience that when pinned to a wall, alone with two armed SS, the suspect would feel cornered and would break down quicker. "All right," the older sergeant said harshly. "We're not playing games anymore. Where did you get those papers? Who gave them to you?"

The stranger's reaction was unexpected. He stuck out his chin and folded his arms on his chest. His voice was laced with arrogance. "I have been instructed not to give any explanations to anybody. You can see yourself who delivered that document and that should satisfy you. If you want more detailed explanations, you'd better ask for them at Tirpitz Ufer."

The shot scored. The SS knew well that at Number 74–76 of the Tirpitz Quay was located "the fox's lair," the headquarters of the chief of the Abwehr, Admiral Wilhelm Canaris. They exchanged looks, and the older man asked, in a milder voice, "And what are you doing here?"

"I've come to attend some business. I am staying at the Brunhilde pension, on the corner of the Kurfürstendamm and Fasanenstrasse."

They nodded. He could see by their reaction that they knew the Brunhilde well and were acquainted with the kind of clientele it serviced. The name seemed to dissipate their last doubts.

"That's all right." The tone had become conciliatory, and the SS smiled. "I am sorry, but we mistook you for a Jew. You know, comrade, if you have the opportunity, you ought to get yourself a new nose."

Laughing, the two sergeants amiably slapped Herr Koch on the back and walked away.

He remained alone in the dark street. His hands were still trembling, but he was quite proud of his little performance. He had concealed his fear, and luck had been on his side tonight.

He walked back into the Bier Keller. When he appeared at the door, the laughter stopped abruptly. He felt as if he had created a vacuum about him. He stepped back to the counter. Nobody had touched his beer and his dish of sausages. Keeping his cool, he swallowed his drink in a long gulp. "Another one," he said to the barmaid. As if on cue, the place came back to life, the conversations and the singing resumed, and the crowd's interest in the stranger quickly waned.

This outing had been a mistake, he admitted to himself. Müller had warned: "Stay in your room and don't go out. We are not responsible for you and can't guarantee your safety if anything happens. Officially, we don't even know you."

Müller might have been right, but Paul refused to shut himself in a pension room in the middle of summer. Müller didn't need him. Since their arrival in Berlin on the sixteenth of June, Müller had changed into civilian clothes again and disappeared. He was spending most of his days in high-level meetings at the Tirpitz Ufer. He hinted vaguely to Paul that one of the subjects on the agenda was his own mission. But Paul had grown used to treating Müller's disclosures with skepticism. The man was very secretive, and never let him know more than he wanted him to know. Paul also refused to believe that Müller was nothing but a sergeant major in the Wehrmacht. A sergeant major doesn't participate in planning sessions at Abwehr headquarters. He guessed that his grade was much higher. Perhaps Müller thought that in railway stations and airfields, where security was tight, he would be able to protect him better if he was wearing an army uniform.

Paul didn't doubt either that Müller had ordered him to

stay in his room out of concern for his safety. But Paul hadn't been able to resist the temptation for more than forty-eight hours. He had to go out, and trusted his lucky star. He had taken to the streets and had almost run to the Kurfürstendamm, to stroll once again on the elegant avenue and mix again with the carefree crowds that would invade the lively cafés, restaurants, and nightclubs.

He went out, night after night. He saw two new movies, one German and one French. He took his lunches at the sunny terrace of a sidewalk café and watched the crowd flow by. Berlin seemed to him more festive and cheerful than ever. He felt almost as if he were dreaming as he sipped his drink, the sun caressing his skin, and throngs of soldiers, officers, and cheerful Berliners paraded by. But he couldn't suppress a twinge of anguish each time he saw an SS uniform in the crowd. He didn't dare speak to anyone. And he resisted the temptation to phone his mother in Frankfurt. Quite a few times he noticed Jews in the crowd strolling down the Kurfürstendamm. Most Berlin Jews were still free. But he knew he had no way to tell them what destiny Hitler was forging for the Jewish people.

He kept going out every day, determined to enjoy as much as he could of that Berlin life he loved so much—and which he'd missed out on in the dark periods of his life. Still, some strange urge made him walk one night to the Tirpitz Quay and get a glimpse of the Abwehr headquarters, where his future was being decided. The house was dark, a graceless gray stone edifice five stories high, looming over the black waters of the narrow canal.

As Paul watched the building, he thought about the enigmatic chief of the Abwehr, Admiral Canaris, who certainly lurked in one of the dark offices even at this time of night. Nobody knew much about Canaris, and his name, which he had heard whispered furtively by German officers in Brussels, evoked strange stories and legends. He was small, gray-haired, and sallow-skinned. His Greek blood and uncommon name came from an obscure ancestor, whom Canaris's admirers described as a freedom fighter, and his enemies described as a bloodthirsty maverick.

It was said that Wilhelm Canaris had killed a man once, in an adventure worthy of a cloak-and-dagger film. During the First World War he had been arrested by the Italians as a spy not far from the Swiss border and thrown in prison in Genoa. He had asked to confess, and when the prison priest had entered his cell, he had strangled him, put on his cowled habit, and sneaked out of jail.

At the end of the war Canaris had been one of the leaders of the conservative officers' group that had occupied the Eden Hotel in Berlin, and as such had been involved in the murder of the Spartacist leaders, Karl Liebknecht and Rosa Luxemburg. He had tried to protect some of the assassins. Later he had joined in an attempt to restore the Kaiser. He had also participated in the secret rearmament project of the German navy. Rumor had it that in this capacity, as well as on special missions for German intelligence, he had traveled throughout Europe under elaborate disguises and false names and taken part in endless conspiracies. He was a staunch anti-Communist, although he was not a Nazi.

Nevertheless, Canaris had been among those who had greeted Hitler's ascension to power. And two years later Hitler had given him full control over the shadowy world of the Abwehr. This man, Paul thought, had saved his life. But he wouldn't hesitate a moment to sacrifice him, if doing so could serve his secret plans.

Paul Ernst Fackenheim didn't know that at the very moment he was being questioned by the two SS, a top-level meeting was being held at the Tirpitz Ufer. A small conclave of generals, political experts, and spymasters were reaching a secret decision that was to be of crucial importance for his future.

Late that night, Müller knocked on his door. He looked

exhausted. His face was drawn, unshaven, but his eyes were glowing with excitement.

"Come on, my dear Koch, let's celebrate."

At the restaurant, Müller ordered a bottle of French Burgundy. Fackenheim watched him with wonder. French wine was quite expensive in those days, and he doubted if Müller could put it on his expense account.

Müller raised his glass. "Well, my dear Koch, we may indulge tonight. I must congratulate you and wish you luck. We just reached a decision concerning you. Tomorrow morning you're leaving for Athens."

"Athens?" He cast a puzzled glance at Müller. "Why in heaven should I go to Athens?"

Müller's smile seemed strained. "You'll see." He took a sip from his glass. "You'll be told in good time."

Paul put his glass on the table. "What about you?" he asked. "Are you coming with me?"

"I'll join you in a few weeks." Müller lit a cigarette and turned to watch a party of high-ranking officers being seated by a round table at the far end of the restaurant. A flurry of waiters held out chairs and rearranged the cutlery, while the manager himself hovered around the table, repeatedly nodding his bald head.

"I'll come as soon as possible," Müller went on. "I must attend to some urgent matters before I leave."

"Anything to do with my mission?"

Müller disregarded the question. "I'll take you to the airport tomorrow. He smiled faintly. "You'll need me there to spare you all those stupid questions about passports and travel permits."

Paul sat stiffly in his chair as the restaurant manager rushed past them. He felt utterly helpless once again. They were moving him like a pawn on a chessboard and he had to obey. First Brussels, then Berlin, and now Athens.

In different circumstances he would have been thrilled by the forthcoming trip. He had always dreamed of visiting

Greece, whose ancient civilization he admired. He could still recite long passages in ancient Greek that he had learned by heart in his youth. But he strongly doubted if he would be able to enjoy the splendors of the Parthenon or the magic of the Aegean. Greece had recently been occupied by the Wehrmacht and was already being transformed into a staging area against British strongholds in the Mediterranean.

His own training seemed to be over. Otherwise Müller wouldn't have taken him to Berlin. Müller seemed elated. He must have convinced his superiors that Fackenheim was ready for his mission. And Athens was probably only a stopover on the way to . . . But where were they sending him? He had wrongly assumed that they were interested in his experience in the Far East, in his fluency in the local dialects and customs. And secretly, in his heart, he had been hoping to return to Indonesia and leave far behind the nightmare that Germany had become. After so many years and vicissitudes his memories of the Far East had acquired a romantic halo. The years he had spent traveling in those exotic, mysterious lands seemed to him now as the happiest in his life. He would have gladly gone back there, even if he was asked to risk his life in perilous missions. But Athens?

"What are you thinking?" Müller was watching him closely, his head tilted to one side.

He shrugged. "Nothing special. Greece, I guess. I'd love to go there. But I'm worried about what would come later."

Müller shook his head. "Even if I wanted, I couldn't give you any details. But don't be upset. You'll be briefed very shortly, believe me."

Behind them, the officers burst into laughter as somebody popped the cork in a champagne bottle.

On June 21, at dawn, Müller shook Paul's hand on the foggy runway of Berlin Airport. Paul suddenly realized that he was going to travel alone.

"There's nobody to escort me?" he asked Müller, incredulous.

Müller chuckled. "You're a big boy now. You can manage on your own." He patted his shoulder and quickly walked away, vanishing in the brume. Paul couldn't help feeling flattered by this token of trust. The Abwehr people were men of honor, real soldiers, unlike those Nazi brutes. But on second thought he realized the Abwehr wasn't risking anything with him. Where could he go? And how? He was their prisoner. No matter how much slack they gave him, they still held the rope in their hands.

The plane was a military "Aunt Ju," an old, slow Junkers that had known better years. It was full of Wehrmacht and SS officers. Paul was the only civilian aboard. During the flight he kept to himself, answering in monosyllables the infantry captain seated next to him. After a short stopover at Vienna, they landed in the Bulgarian capital, Sofia, in the early afternoon.

They got off the plane amid one of the most fascinating spectacles Paul had ever seen. The airfield was jammed with hundreds of German planes, as if the entire Luftwaffe had been flown there overnight. Fighter aircraft and bombers stood in endless lines along the runways. There was feverish activity everywhere. Ground crews were pumping fuel into the aircraft tanks, loading heavy bombs into the bays, arming the cannon. Pilots and air crews were inspecting their machines under the watchful eye of heavily armed sentries deployed all over the field. It was obvious that a military operation of unprecedented scope was in the making.

The young officers who had got off the Junkers with Paul gazed at the unusual sight with shining eyes. The older officers, especially those wearing decorations from the First World War, looked more preoccupied. Nobody seemed to know the reason for the military buildup, but Paul kept recalling the champagne party of the Wehrmacht officers in Berlin the previous night.

Only the next day was Paul to learn why Hitler had concentrated such a huge air fleet in scores of airfields throughout Eastern Europe. The next day was June 22, 1941, D Day of Operation Barbarossa, the surprise onslaught of Nazi Germany on Soviet Russia. It was to be Hitler's most risky gamble, and the beginning of his end.

In Sofia, Fackenheim changed planes. Aboard a booty Douglas, taken from the British, he resumed his southbound flight. They refueled at the sleepy Salonika air base—a single landing strip swept by moving sands—and landed in Athens in the early evening. Paul caught a glimpse of the Acropolis bathed by the setting sun. But the hectic activity around him quickly diverted his mind from the majestic sight. The airport swarmed with people. The German soldiers and "Feldgendarmen"—military police—seemed overwhelmed by the throngs of Greeks laden with bags, suitcases, and parcels. Some military policemen directed Paul and the other passengers toward a hangar, where harried German officials were checking papers and luggage. Fackenheim had barely reached the end of the line when a Wehrmacht officer appeared beside him.

"Herr Koch, I presume?"

It was a young captain, wearing the Iron Cross. His uniform was hanging on his skeletal frame. Nothing seemed to be in place. The officer owlishly stared at Fackenheim with his nearsighted eyes, hugely magnified by thick glasses, then made a swift comparison with a photograph he held in his long bony fingers. He nodded to himself. "Will you follow me, please?"

"May I?" Fackenheim picked the print from the captain's hand. It was an excellent photograph, taken recently in a Brussels street. That was strange. He had never seen the snapshot before and couldn't recall posing for it. So here was proof that his freedom in Brussels had been an illusion after all.

His good friends from the Abwehr had kept a very close watch on him.

The captain beckoned to an elderly soldier, who picked up Fackenheim's suitcase and carried it to a military Mercedes parked by the runway. The soldier opened the car door for Fackenheim and bowed stiffly, then slipped into the driver's seat and started the engine. The Mercedes smoothly crossed several roadblocks, the Feldgendarmen saluting deferentially, then got on the main highway to Athens.

"You are well organized," Fackenheim said to the captain. "I'd like to meet your chief as soon as possible."

The young officer shrugged in embarrassment. "I'm sorry, mein Herr. I don't belong to this operation. I was ordered to pick you up at the airfield and take you to your hotel, that's all. All the rest doesn't interest me, not really." He smiled timidly. "You see, I'm not exactly a glorious career officer. The army has never been of any interest to me. My profession, in civil life, is philology. I speak Greek quite well, and I've lived in Athens for a few years, working at the university. That was enough for them to make me a captain and pin this on me." He touched his Iron Cross.

Fackenheim frowned. The story could be true, but he doubted that the Wehrmacht would decorate anybody just for being a good linguist. However, he kept his thoughts to himself. The captain wasn't going to tell him the truth anyway.

The car came to a stop at Odon Universidad, one of the main avenues of the Greek capital. A doorman, whose cruel, sharp features reminded Paul of a pirate, emerged toward them from the entrance of a decrepit building. On the worn-out, dirty yellow facade, a sign in big bold letters presumptuously proclaimed HOTEL MAJESTIC.

"We part here," the officer said as he politely shook Fackenheim's hand. "Enjoy your stay in Greece." He clumsily got back in the Mercedes, which slowly moved forward.

Fackenheim crossed the hotel lobby. A noisy crowd of Germans, officers and civilians, clustered on the frayed sofas and around the tables. The swarthy Greek behind the reception desk bowed obsequiously. "Welcome to the Majestic, Herr Koch." He sported a well-trimmed mustache and his coal-black hair was shining with brilliantine. "We have been expecting you."

His room was spacious but shabby. The furniture was quite old and the carpet of poor quality. But Paul didn't mind. He barely looked at the bustling street below. He knew exactly what he wanted to do, and he couldn't wait. He freshened up and hurried out, stopping at the reception desk to change some money.

A half hour later, he was at the Acropolis. Night had fallen, and the towering hill was deserted. The sky was clear, full of stars, and a gentle breeze blew from the Mediterranean. The silence on the top of the hill, the sparkling lights of Athens below, and the silvery infinity of the Aegean beyond the port of Piraeus bestowed upon the place a magic-filled air of peace and serenity. Paul, spellbound, slowly walked among the splendid columns and statues of the Parthenon. All his troubles seemed so far away now, suspended in time, irrelevant and utterly unreal. He sat down on the marble steps leading to the temple, enjoying the moment to the hilt.

A light rustle made him raise his eyes. On top of the Parthenon, a huge banner swayed in the wind. It was bright red, with a big black swastika on white background in the center. He shuddered. The very sight of the Nazi symbol hovering over the Acropolis shattered his illusion of tranquillity. He couldn't think of anything more obscene, more revolting, than the swastika floating over the site of the most ancient democracy in history.

He rushed down the hill, almost running. He knew he wasn't going to visit the Parthenon again, not with that banner on its top. At the foot of the hill, he saw a small souvenir shop, still open. He walked in.

"Oui, Monsieur?" A smiling Greek came to meet him. Fackenheim absently picked an evzone doll. He cast a look at the shopkeeper. The man was tanned and black-haired, a typical Greek. Still, his eyes betrayed him. The soft, somber eyes of a Jew.

"Are you Jewish?" Paul blurted abruptly, in French.

The merchant stared back, surprised. "Yes," he admitted after a short hesitation. "Why do you ask?"

"I am Jewish too." For the first time since his release from Dachau, Paul had revealed his real identity. It could cost him his life, but right now he didn't mind. He was still haunted by the giant banner on the Acropolis.

"Listen to me," he said quickly. "Go away. Leave the country. You certainly do have a family. There must be a way out." He took a deep breath. "I just arrived from Germany. I know the Nazis. You couldn't imagine what they are doing to the Jews. Your turn will come, too, now that they are here. Leave Greece, before it's too late."

The shopkeeper was watching him fixedly. The surprise and fear in his eyes slowly melted into an opaque, expressionless look. He busied himself with the doll, smoothing the short puffed skirt of the evzone soldier, pointlessly touching the drooping hat and the red tassels. "You must be very tired, Monsieur," he said gently, wrapping the doll and counting the change. He came from behind the counter, softly placed his hand on Fackenheim's shoulder, and steered him to the exit. "Why don't you go now and have a good rest? The journey must have been exhausting."

"But I told you, I just flew over from Germany! I saw them. I was at . . ."

"Good night, Monsieur. Enjoy your stay in Athens."

VII

The Chief

"MAY I SIT DOWN?"

Fackenheim shrugged. "Suit yourself."

The lobby of the Majestic was packed, as it was every night. A merry crowd of German servicemen—pilots, navy officers, paratroopers—carried on the noisy drinking party that would regularly transform the shabby hall into an effervescent night spot. Imported bottles and willing women smoothly made their way from hand to hand. Only a few taciturn civilians seated at the far corners failed to take part in the feast, condescendingly watching the crowd get wilder and happier as the hours passed.

The man who had stopped by Fackenheim's table was a navy captain, reasonably intoxicated. He collapsed in a chair and banged his fists on the table. "Waiter!" He looked around, merrily windmilling his arms, until he caught the eye of one of the Greek waiters. "Ouzo! A whole bottle!"

He leaned toward Fackenheim. "You'll share the bottle with me, comrade, all right? That's an order." He burst into thunderous laughter. He was a huge, barrel-chested man, with bulging arms, a heavy-jowled red face, a bulbous nose, and bloodshot blue eyes. "What's your name? Koch? Well, my old Koch, how's business in Greece? Made any good deals lately? No? Well, I have no reason to complain." He took the bottle of ouzo from the waiter, splashed a generous measure of the colorless liquid in two glasses, and, ignoring the carafe of water, gulped down the fiery liquor. "I like it straight," he said, wiping his lips with the back of his hand. "Come on, take your drink. We must celebrate tonight. I just made a little fortune in drachmas, whatever they are worth. Like to hear about it?"

He didn't wait for Paul to answer. "Now listen. A few weeks ago, I was having breakfast at the Café des Artistes. You know it?" He poured himself another drink. "By the way, the Café des Artistes is the best place around here. Take my word." He patted Paul's shoulder. "The food is first class, the wine is perfect, and the girls . . . you'll see, the prettiest girls in Athens.

"As I was saying, I am sitting there, eating my meal, when I see a Greek, a fat guy with a mustache, coming toward me. He starts speaking to me in bad German. 'Do you know Athens?' he asks. 'Yes,' I say. 'And Piraeus too?' I say yes again. The Greek sits down beside me. 'You know where the big sugar warehouse is, the one that burned down during the bombardment?' 'Yes, I've been there once,' I say. 'All that's left is a heap of burnt and melted sugar. Wherever you look, that black mass is all over the place, at least three feet high. The fire over there must have been something, believe me!' Then I say, 'What a pity for that good sugar.' 'It depends,' the Greek says to me with a curious smile. 'I can still use that sugar. You can't do nothing with it, for you it's just a pile of garbage. But not for me. I want to bring over a few trucks, load them, and clean the whole place. For each truckload you let me take, I'm ready to pay 5,000 drachmas.'

'Buy it then,' I say to him." The captain's glass was empty again, and he reached for the bottle. 'Impossible,' the Greek says to me. 'The place has been requisitioned by the army, it's guarded by German sentries. One corporal and two privates. I need a German officer.' He looks at me. 'All that this officer must do is tell the sentries that every day, at a certain time, a few trucks will come to the warehouse and load the burnt sugar. And I'll pay 5,000 drachmas, cash, for each truck. You see, Mister Officer, it will start raining soon and the sugar will be lost for good, as the warehouse has no roof anymore. But I can still make use of it.'

'Use it for what?' I ask. The Greek bastard smiles. 'Brandy,' he whispers. 'Did nobody tell you, Mister Officer, that you can distill brandy from burnt sugar? I have a liquor distillery. Do you get it now?' "

The captain regretfully turned the ouzo bottle upside down and signaled the waiter for another one. "So I said to him 'All right' and I took care of the matter. And in a few weeks I made a small fortune for myself. That calls for a celebration, doesn't it? Have another drink. How they say in Greek? Yassou!"

Fackenheim swallowed the anise-flavored liquor and got up to leave. He had grown used to that kind of story. His great talent was knowing how to listen. And every evening, wherever he was, he would meet German servicemen and civilians only too eager to narrate their adventures to a sympathetic audience. In Athens he had heard the most extraordinary narratives of daring commando raids, murky espionage affairs, astute black market operations. Some of those nights, when a casual companion cast an inquiring look at him, he would also feel the urge to tell his story, to share his terrible burden with somebody, anybody. And over and over again he would remember the cruelty of his fate, forbidding him to communicate with his fellow men, compelling him to hide behind a barrier of lies or silence. The loneliness that had been his lot for most of his life now haunted him again, although in a different way.

Three months had already passed since his arrival in Athens. He had made quite a few acquaintances among the officers stationed in Greece and the employees of the Hermann Goering Works. He had encountered black market wizards, Berlin businessmen, American journalists, and the usual assortment of informers, collaborators, and prostitutes that would always cluster around a conqueror's headquarters. In the sunny streets of Athens he had met many veterans of the Albanian campaign, poor devils mutilated by shrapnel or amputated for frostbite, who were now in invalid chairs being pushed by young German nurses. He had discovered that the Majestic was an Abwehr hotel where secret agents would spend several lonely nights before discreetly vanishing in old fishermen boats bound for the Middle East. Oddly enough, the Gestapo and the SD—the Nazi security service—also lodged their teams of torturers and interrogators in the tacky, untidy Majestic. It was apparently considered safer than the opulent Hotel Grande Bretagne, which was the official headquarters of the German high command in Greece.

Athens held no more secrets for Paul Fackenheim. He had systematically explored the city and its suburbs, the port of Piraeus, the picturesque streets of Fallerum, the serene villages in the countryside. Night after night he would return to the old quarter, the "Plaka," and spend long hours in the small taverns, which the locals had deserted with the appearance of the Wehrmacht soldiers. As time went by, his anguish grew deeper, more depressing. He would seek refuge in the Plaka taverns, drinking till the early hours, listening to the plaintive Greek songs, and trying to forget a terrible past. He wrote regularly to his mother, but got no letters in return. Since he had left Brussels he had heard no news from her.

The news that electrified Athens that summer of 1941 came from the fronts. In Russia, the Wehrmacht had launched a murderous blitzkrieg, and a stunned world heard daily of new, unprecedented German victories. By the middle of July, barely three weeks after Operation Barbarossa started, forty-five Wehrmacht divisions under the command of Field Marshal von Bock had advanced 450 miles into Russian territory and had only 200 miles to go before entering Moscow. To the south, Field Marshal von Rundstedt led his thirty-eight divisions toward Kiev, the capital of the Ukraine. And far to the north, twenty-seven divisions commanded by Field Marshal von Leeb thrust across the Baltic states on their way to Leningrad.

In North Africa, General Rommel had achieved a decisive victory against the British in mid-June, thwarting their

Battleaxe offensive intended to break his siege on the strategic port of Tobruk. The prospects of a lightning thrust into Egypt and the Suez Canal looked brighter than ever.

The glorious victories of the Reich's army on the battle-field stirred contradictory feelings in Paul Fackenheim's heart. In spite of his misfortunes, he had remained a German patriot with conservative views, staunchly anti-Communist, wishing that his country would defeat its enemies and win the war. Yet the symbol of the swastika and the presence of Hitler hovering over each German victory profoundly disturbed him. He wanted the victory of Germany. He hoped for the defeat of Hitler. And again, forbidden to air his own views, he had to play the game, to take part in the general merri-ment in the Majestic lobby after the announcement of each new feat of arms. He had to drink to the victory of the Reich, join his voice to those of his companions as they toasted their beloved Vaterland, their beloved army and leader, while deep in his heart he felt like crying.

These had been three long, nerve-racking months. On ar-riving, he had assumed that Athens was to be merely a short stopover before he was sent on his mission. But the local Abwehr people seemed in no particular hurry. The morning after he came to Greece, a young man had knocked on his door. He was no more than twenty-five, blond, stiff, and ar-rogant. He had introduced himself as Braun and had taken Fackenheim to several shops to buy him new clothes. He had meticulously packed the old clothes of "Koch" and taken them away. When Paul had asked to meet his superiors, Braun had feigned not to understand. "I don't know what you're talking about. I have been sent by the Telefunken com-pany in Berlin to teach you Morse and radio transmitting. I have no superiors here."

"You haven't, of course. How stupid of me."

"Don't try to be too smart," Braun had said. "I wouldn't if I were you."

Fackenheim had swallowed his pride. He had no choice

but to comply. And the old Brussels routine had started all over again: the usual knock on his door every morning at ten, the two hours of training, the long walks in the hot, humid city. He had felt genuinely relieved when three weeks later Müller had arrived and taken over. The two men had become good friends. Müller had listened sympathetically to Paul's complaints about Braun. "Leave him to me," he had said. Paul never saw Braun afterward.

Müller intensified Paul's training. He initiated Paul in the formulas of the three main brands of "G-Tinten," the secret inks used by the Abwehr. They were called "Apis," "Betty," and "Pyramidon." The Apis was an excellent ink, but it required too many chemicals to develop—ferrous chloride or calcium ferrocyanide, both mixed with cooking salt. Müller preferred the Pyramidon, concocted with the base of real pyramidon pills, an analgesic drug that could be easily purchased in any pharmacy. Several of those pills diluted in water could be transformed into invisible ink. No developers were needed. The writing was done on regular paper—generally between the lines of an innocuous letter—with small wooden sticks. It vanished immediately and reappeared when the paper was held over a flame.

Paul's training in wireless transmissions now entered the operational stage. In Brussels and during his first weeks in Athens, Paul had been trained with some obsolete Morse radio sets. Now Müller brought to his hotel the best piece of equipment the Abwehr was using. It was a special "spy radio" developed by the Telefunken company and called the "Afu" (for "Agenten Funkgerät"). The radio was quite compact, fitting into a small suitcase. It had been built by Telefunken on the special request of Admiral Canaris. Although small, it was very powerful and could be used for long-distance transmissions. It weighed less than thirty pounds and had a maximum power of twenty watts. Müller told Fackenheim that in the Abwehr slang, the cute little Afu was nicknamed "Klamotten," which meant "junk."

As his training advanced, Paul grew more tense in antici-
pation of his forthcoming departure. And for the first time,
his confidence in Müller was somewhat shaken. He gradually
developed serious doubts about the competence of the
Abwehr—and for good reason. Müller and his assistant, a
closemouthed balding giant named Kurt, would often drive
Paul to a charming little restaurant on the beach, at
Fallerum; they would have some Greek specialties for dinner,
wash it down with coarse red wine, then push their plates
aside and place the Afu radio on the table. Paul would put
the earphones on his head and start his daily practice of sending and receiving. "You must be out of your mind," he told
Müller over and over again. "Everybody is looking at us."

"Never mind those Greeks," Müller would answer, with
the impassive Kurt rocking back and forth on his chair. "They
don't understand a thing. Carry on."

Fackenheim had no right to argue. Still, he remained
convinced that Müller was disregarding the most elementary
security precautions. To make things worse, at the end of
August he had been initiated into a new, sophisticated
Abwehr code that Müller called the "most recent and most
secret code of the German army." The Abwehr didn't seem to
mind training an agent who knew that priceless code in full
sight of the entire population of Fallerum.

The only time during that period when he saw Müller lose
his cool was the day after Paul had had a strange encounter in
the old quarter of Athens. While Paul was strolling in the
street, two Germans in civilian clothes came up to him and
asked for directions to Hommonia Square. Since he had nothing to do, he agreed to accompany them, and accepted their
offer of a drink in the Military Club. The first glass soon became a bottle, and another bottle, and Paul's new friends
grew more convivial and talkative. They told him they
worked for a German company importing olive oil from
Greece. Then they started questioning him with an insistence
that at first he attributed to mere curiosity or too much drink-

ing, but that finally aroused his suspicions. Who was he? What was his name? Where in Germany did he come from? Did he know the Kochs from Munich? What was his profession, and what was he doing in Athens? Where did he stay, and whom did he know among the local German dignitaries? Trying to duck the hail of questions, he said he worked for a radio company.

"Oh, radio! Ta ta ta—ta ta," one of his interlocutors exclaimed, imitating the sounds of a Morse transmission. The other burst out laughing and winked at Fackenheim, his face expressing complicity and secret knowledge. "Sure, pal, if you want, you can call it that. And you're here on a mission?"

He had finally managed, rather clumsily, to evade the question, and had left, puzzled and disturbed. As he got up from his chair, he noticed that one of his new friends was wearing a tiny swastika, the emblem of the Nazi party, pinned under his lapel. Why was he concealing it? Wasn't the swastika, after all, the official symbol of German power in Greece?

The next morning Müller burst into his room, furious. "Tell me, Koch, have you lost your mind? Do you want to break your neck?"

"Why? What happened?"

"As if you don't know!" Müller was fuming. "You met two men yesterday, didn't you? You might be interested to hear that they already submitted their report on you."

"What report? To whom?"

Müller ignored the question, pacing back and forth across the room, his big fists clenched. "They believe that you're a suspicious character, maybe even a British agent. They say that your behavior is exuberant and conceited. They say that after a couple of drinks you started boasting about your mastery of radio transmission techniques."

"I never . . ."

"I must tell you," Müller went on, "that after reading their report we discussed your case the whole night. The report has aroused serious doubts about your ability to achieve your mission."

"What kind of doubts?"

Müller turned to face him. "Doubts so that, at a certain moment, we considered the possibility of sending you back to where you came from."

Fackenheim stared at him, speechless. Send him back to Dachau! And for what? Trying to keep his cool, he told Müller the full story of his meeting with the two strangers.

It took Müller a long time to calm down. "Why the hell did you have to talk to them at all?" he grunted.

"And why not?" Fackenheim countered. "Am I forbidden to talk to people? To Germans?"

"And why did you go drinking with them?" Müller asked stubbornly. But his voice seemed less belligerent. As Paul didn't answer, he finally shrugged. "Well, maybe your version is the right one." He slumped in a chair. "You might be pleased to hear that the chief believes the incident happened the way you describe it."

"Your chief is here? In Athens?"

Müller nodded guardedly, then resumed. "Perhaps that whole affair wasn't your fault after all. But I have to warn you, Koch. Keep your mouth shut. Don't give any information to anybody. Don't trust anybody, do you hear me?"

"It was a trap, wasn't it?" Paul said slowly, and as Müller didn't answer, he went on. "But who would want to trap me? Except the Abwehr people, who should be reliable, who could even know of my being here?"

"You ask me too much. How could I know that?" Müller looked away, and Fackenheim suddenly knew with certitude that he was lying.

"I believe," Paul said, his eyes glued to Müller's face, "that somebody wants my hide. And that he sent those two spies with the express purpose of making me trip. Who were they? Gestapo? SD?"

Müller didn't answer. But for the rest of that day he remained tense and preoccupied. And it dawned on Paul that behind the scenes there was something much bigger concerning him—that somebody indeed was lying in wait to ensnare him, and Müller was genuinely worried. If not, why should he be so disturbed by a harmless encounter Paul had had with two other Germans? And why would they report him, twisting the facts? And to whom did they report?

The following morning Müller came to his room shortly after dawn. Paul was still in bed. Müller looked concerned, but there was no anger in his voice. "Come on, Koch, we are leaving this place. We've booked a room for you in another hotel. You'll be better off there."

An hour later, Fackenheim checked into the Minerva Hotel, situated opposite the Hotel Grande Bretagne, headquarters of the German high command. Except for Paul, the Minerva was populated exclusively by military personnel. Mysterious civilians didn't swarm in the lobby as in the Majestic.

After he unpacked, Paul went down to the bar, where Müller was waiting for him.

"My chief wants to meet you," Müller said without preamble. "Tonight, at eight sharp, at the Alex tavern."

"But I don't know him. How shall I . . ."

"He knows you. Alex, at eight. Be on time."

Alex was a typical Greek restaurant of great renown. The ceiling was low, uneven, spotlessly whitewashed. The floor was covered with glazed red tiles. Colorful tablecloths, ornate with embroidery, were spread upon the massive wooden tables. On the walls hung strings of red peppers and dried garlic. In the middle of the vast dining room, on large stone counters, was spread an impressive variety of raw foods: all kinds of fish, crabs, lobsters, calamari, and shrimp; fowl, chunks of red meat, choice cuts of lamb and pork. After making their choice of a main dish, the patrons would give their instructions to one of the cooks, who were clad in immaculate

aprons and hats. Then the patrons would return to their tables and taste Greek appetizers to the sound of a small bouzouki band playing in the far corner.

Paul made his way across the crowded restaurant, anxiously looking around him. A tanned man, sitting alone by a
table under the window, rose and smiled at him. They shook
hands. The man's face was oddly familiar, but Paul failed to
place it.

"Sit down, please," the man said. He was dressed in an
elegant gray suit, a white shirt, and a discreet dark-blue tie.
"You look surprised. Müller told you that I'd be expecting you
here, didn't he?"

Fackenheim pulled up a chair and sat down. So this was
the mysterious chief.

The stranger smiled again. "Remember me? April the sixteenth?"

April the sixteenth. The day of his release from Dachau.
"It was you who . . ."

"Yes. It was me who got you out of . . . that place."

The man was the officer who had questioned him at
Dachau, together with the "government adviser."

Fackenheim felt more relaxed, as if he were meeting an
old acquaintance. This man, after all, had saved his life.
"How should I address you?" he asked.

"As you wish. Most of my men simply call me 'Chief.' "

"Very well."

They ordered a bottle of ouzo, which was brought to their
table together with the traditional tray of hors d'oeuvres—
huge black olives, stuffed vine leaves, baby shrimp and calamari, coarse feta cheese, all bathed in thick green oil.

Paul watched the chief pour drinks. He had rehearsed his
little speech meticulously. He had many questions to ask, he
had complaints about the uncertainty in which he lived, the
lack of news from his mother, the sloppy security in Fallerum.
But his encounter with the man who had arranged his release

from Dachau stirred cruel memories in his heart. And it suddenly seemed to him so unreal, so unfair, to be sitting there, amid that merry crowd, listening to the clinking of glasses, the silvery laughter of women, the playful music of the bouzouki. He didn't speak, and just stared at the glass he clutched in his hand.

And then the strangest thing happened. The chief pushed aside his untouched plate, propped his chin on his two hands, and said, "Tell me the truth about Dachau."

The question was so unexpected that Paul froze, unable to utter a word. He had anticipated everything, except that direct question. The old fears and suspicions surfaced in his mind. Could this be another trap? The chief seemed to be a man of honor and integrity. Yet Paul didn't know if he could trust him. He knew that one mistake would be enough to send him back to Dachau.

"I am sorry, Chief. I can't. I have sworn not to reveal anything on this subject. I was told to erase Dachau from my memory."

The chief's face turned purple. "Don't be a fool," he said with suppressed anger. "Who do you think I am? Gestapo? SS? A Nazi official? I am a professional soldier, and so are most of my colleagues. It's time for you to understand, if you don't already, that in our service the Nazis are not welcome." The man was speaking the truth, Fackenheim admitted to himself. Over the last three months he had overheard enough conversations in the lobby of the Majestic to know that the Abwehr was considered the worst enemy of the Nazi organizations inside the Wehrmacht. Rumor had it that were it not for the special esteem and sympathy the Fuehrer felt for Canaris, the Abwehr would have been dismantled a long time ago.

"I give you my word of honor as a German officer," the chief went on, "that I shall not repeat anything you choose to tell me without your permission."

Fackenheim still hesitated. He knew what had happened to people who had dared to speak about their experience in the Nazi concentration camps.

"I can either tell you all," he finally said, "or nothing. I prefer to remain silent, just because I doubt if you would believe me."

He discerned a spark of compassion in the chief's eyes, and the officer's voice was soft, friendly. "Was it that horrible?"

"Worse than you could ever imagine," Paul said impulsively. He no longer tried to restrain himself. And once he started, he plunged headlong into his story. All that he had suppressed during those long, lonely months—the emotions, the pain, the urge to share his terrible secret—erupted now in his narrative. He spoke for three quarters of an hour, describing everything he remembered, omitting no details. For some reason, though, he couldn't look at his companion while he spoke. His clenched fists lay on the armrests, slightly trembling; his eyes were out of focus, staring vaguely at the rough pattern of the tablecloth.

A tense silence settled upon them when he was through. The chief didn't speak. Paul raised his eyes. The officer sat stiffly on his chair, his face livid, his lips pressed tight. After a moment, he seized his glass and downed his drink with one gulp.

"Good God." His voice was low, weary. "I would have never imagined such a thing. If I hadn't heard it from you, I wouldn't have believed it. And if I had known all that before . . ."

"Then?"

"Then"—he said slowly, his eyes riveted to Fackenheim's, "then probably I would have never had you released from Dachau. Don't repeat what you told me to anybody. Not even to Müller."

He reached for Paul's hand and pressed it strongly. "Now listen to me. I can promise you that the day will come when we, the army, will clean up all that filth. We'll make all those who have such monstrosities on their conscience pay for their crimes.

"But first we must win the war. At the present time, any internal crisis or a civil war could bring Germany's end.

"We'll take care of Hitler and his gang. They'll have to account for the atrocities they have committed in the name of Germany. But you must understand, as I do, that we can't take risks before we win the war. I know quite a few things about you, and I know that you are, first of all, a German. Do you want Germany to be destroyed? Do you want Stalin to bring us to our knees? I know that you want to fulfill your duty. You have expressed your wish to contribute to the cause of Germany, in spite of all the evil that has been done to you. My esteem for you is deeper now after all that you've told me. I trust you as before. But I must ask you to trust me as well."

Fackenheim was too moved to answer.

They ordered their dinner and ate it in silence. They drank another bottle of ouzo. Before they parted, the chief told Fackenheim, "If you have any particular wish, don't hesitate to turn to me. Müller will serve as our go-between."

After he left the restaurant, Fackenheim walked for hours in the deserted streets of Athens. He felt deeply relieved by the sincere words of the chief. He had also been provided with a means to absolve himself, to ease his own conscience. *It is not for Hitler and his butchers that I am risking my life*, he said to himself, *but for my homeland, for my comrades, for the German nation that is the victim of a fit of folly. The chief didn't know anything about the concentration camps. That is a fact. And if such an important man didn't know, how could all those millions of simple Germans know?*

The chief is right. We should win the war. That's all that counts now. Afterward, the army will take care of Hitler.

Fackenheim felt a surge of confidence and gratitude toward the chief. Still, when the pale light of dawn spread through the sleeping streets of the city, he felt he was trying to evade the truth. And the truth was that he trusted the chief because he wanted to. The chief's compassion and his promises were for him a solid anchor, a glimmer of hope, a source of strength. If he didn't trust him, Paul realized, he would crack. And he had no one else to turn to.

Müller was waiting in his room. He didn't ask him where he had spent the night.

"I have been authorized to inform you that you'll soon be leaving on your mission."

"Where?"

Müller paused before answering.

"Palestine."

Palestine. The land of Israel. All of a sudden, everything became clear. That was why they had rescued him from Dachau. That was why he was in Athens, at the threshold of the Middle East. That was why they needed him: a Jew to spy on Jews, to betray his own people. It was a stroke of genius, shrewd and utterly cynical.

"No," he said. "Anything but that."

VIII

Our Jew in Palestine

ANARIS'S PLAN was simple, yet glowed with genius. The old man wasn't interested in Palestine, not yet. He was fascinated by a long, narrow strip of muddy water cutting straight across the Egyptian desert: the Suez Canal. From the barren wastes of Libya, Rommel coveted that vital link between England and its distant empire. And Canaris was determined to provide "the desert fox" with the one weapon he so badly needed: intelligence.

Rommel had landed in North Africa in February 1941, following a desperate appeal from Mussolini to Hitler. The much publicized Italian offensive into Egypt, launched from Libya a few months before, had turned into a humiliating debacle. The soldiers of pompous Marshal Rodolfo Graziani had fled in panic from the British, and by the end of January 1941, the strategic port of Tobruk had fallen to the troops of Lieutenant General Sir Richard O'Connor.

Hitler, who had been infuriated by Mussolini's ill-advised and ill-fated initiatives in Albania and North Africa, had finally given way and dispatched the brilliant Erwin Rommel to the rescue. Rommel had already earned tremendous prestige for his decisive role in the French campaign in June 1940. Leading his panzer division in a murderous blitzkrieg, he had swept across Belgium, breached the "impregnable" Maginot line, taken Cambrai, Arras, Lille, and finally reached the coast of the English Channel near Dieppe, blocking the escape route of thousands of British soldiers. He had ended his lightning raid through France by occupying the port of Cherbourg on June 18. He had captured 97,000 prisoners and destroyed hundreds of French and British tanks. Hitler had bestowed on him the Knight's Cross, and the German press had showered him and his "Spook Division" with praise and glory. An overwhelmed writer had compared him to "one of the horsemen of the Apocalypse" and his armored division to "a ghost fleet."

It was that horseman of France's tragic apocalypse that Hitler now sent to save Mussolini's tarnished honor in North Africa. Rommel indeed succeeded in reversing the situation quickly. On March 2, his Afrika Korps launched a lightning offensive against the British army. On March 24 the British front collapsed. Ten days later Rommel took Benghazi, and after six more days he entered Sollum. He besieged Tobruk, and in June blocked the British counteroffensive, "Battleaxe."

In Germany, Rommel's fame soared again. He became the hero of newsreels, magazines, enthusiastic teenagers, and Nazi women's organizations. The British, too, were aware that they were facing a most formidable foe. In the House of Commons, Churchill claimed Rommel alone was responsible for British setbacks in North Africa. In a few months the British would send a commando to Rommel's headquarters in Libya with orders to kill or capture the legendary general. The operation would turn into a bloody fiasco.

Still, at the beginning of the summer the front had apparently stabilized. The besieged British garrison in Tobruk valiantly resisted Rommel's repeated assaults. The continuous warfare in the scorching heat, the deficient supply lines, and the sandstorms decimated the German panzer force. There could be no doubt that the British would soon throw fresh reinforcements into the battle in a desperate effort to save the Suez Canal. But what kind of reinforcements? Of what magnitude? How armed and equipped? To obtain that vital knowledge Canaris had to infiltrate his agents in enemy territory and penetrate the main British bases. The bulk of the British army was concentrated in the big military camps along the canal and farther north in the coastal plain of

Palestine. Those camps had to be the major objectives of the Abwehr in the Middle East. Actually, the decision to undertake a special intelligence effort in that region had been reached at Tirpitz Quay as early as February 1941, when Rommel set foot in Africa for the first time. Paul Fackenheim was then nothing but an anonymous number in a Nazi concentration camp.

This wasn't the first initiative of Canaris in the Middle East. As early as 1937, the agents of the Reich had started infiltrating Palestine, Egypt, Iraq, and other Arab countries. They had repeatedly attempted to exploit the growing hostility of Arab nations toward British domination. When the world war had broken out, Germany was nurturing ambitious designs for the Middle East: to raise in arms the Arab nations and instigate rebellions in the Arab armies against the crown. The plans of the Reich were partly inspired by the legendary adventures of Lawrence of Arabia in the First World War, when the strange, charismatic Welshman had launched the tribes of the Arab peninsula against the Ottoman Empire.

Following this new Arab revolt and a sweeping German offensive, Berlin expected that the Britain era in the Middle East would be terminated and a German epoch would commence. Egypt would be conquered, the Suez Canal would be closed, and Britain would be cut off from her Eastern empire. Palestine, Transjordan, and Iraq would then collapse and the fabulous oil reserves of the Persian Gulf would fall into German hands. The Reich would then launch its drive toward Iran, India, and the vulnerable soft belly of Soviet Russia.

Erwin Rommel was the perfect choice to carry out that grand design. He was a brave general and an unequaled master of deception. But neither his cunning nor his formidable panzers could win the battle of Egypt without a steady flow of first-rate military intelligence. In March Rommel had been led to believe that the British were unloading troops and armor in the port of Tobruk, while the truth was that they were withdrawing their best units from Libya for their forthcoming—and doomed—expedition in Greece. He had lost precious time, and maybe a decisive victory, by guessing too late the reason for the puzzling British retreat. The information he obtained by aerial reconnaissance and interception of enemy radio messages was too fragmentary. What the German high command needed were detailed reports about the enemy forces, their emplacements, their defense lines, the characteristics of their armor and artillery. "Any trustworthy item of intelligence is worth a dozen panzers," Canaris had said in February 1941, when the Libyan campaign had started.

Surprisingly, Canaris's determination to put in place a first-class espionage network for Rommel was not shared wholeheartedly by Hitler and the German high command. Hitler and his generals were putting the final touches to their plans for the conquest of Soviet Russia. For them the Barbarossa invasion was all that mattered. Rommel's victories in the desert pleased them immensely, of course, and filled them with pride. But they didn't attach to them too much strategic importance. When Rommel flew to meet Hitler in Berlin in March 1941, the Fuehrer refrained from revealing to him the secret of Barbarossa. The high command bombarded Canaris with requests for detailed intelligence about the Russians. Egypt and the Suez Canal could wait.

Canaris, however, thought otherwise. He held Rommel in high esteem and was personally committed to his success. It also seems that with his legendary sixth sense Canaris had already detected the deeply buried anti-Nazi streak in Rommel, and saw in him a potential ally in any future move against Hitler. And so the old fox, lurking in his Tirpitz Ufer lair, went out of his way to help the younger fox of the Libyan desert.

Canaris started his new intelligence campaign in the Middle East with one of the most ambitious operations in the history of the Abwehr: the attempt to abduct the commander in chief of the Egyptian army, Masri Pasha. The abduction was to be carried out with the full consent of the victim, as Masri Pasha was a leader of a secret officers' organization dedicated to the liberation of Egypt from British rule. The anti-British feelings of many high-ranking officers had grown when Winston Churchill decided to exclude the Egyptian army from any participation in the defense of their land. The Egyptian units who had been stationed in the western parts of Egypt had been disarmed and evacuated, replaced by British and colonial troops. These decisions, added to the sincere admiration many Egyptian officers had for Germany, reinforced the determination of the secret military organization to take action against Britain. The humiliated officers, as well as some powerful political leaders in Egypt, hoped for a German victory. Some of them were ready to actively assist the German army in its campaign to take over Egypt. Two lesser-known members of the group were the young officers Gamal Abdel Nasser and Anwar el Sadat.

Canaris and Rommel attached tremendous importance to the projected abduction. As commander in chief of the Egyptian army, Masri Pasha could supply the Abwehr with invaluable information about the enemy's strength. Because the Egyptian army had been working in close cooperation with the British, Masri seemed to be the ultimate prize every master spy in history had ever dreamt about. Canaris, therefore, intended to whisk him straight to Germany for a long and detailed debriefing.

The execution of the project was entrusted to one of the Abwehr's most able agents, Major Nikolaus Ritter of the Luftwaffe. Ritter was the James Bond of the German secret service. He was the man who had established the Abwehr espionage network in the United States and smuggled the secret plans of the Norden bombsight to Germany. He had run double agents in England and Portugal, flown to an emergency rendezvous in the open sea, briefed special envoys to

America, pried into the secrets of the United States consulate in Antwerp, and supplied to Canaris's agents genuine American passports with the help of a ravishing spy, Jennie Lemaire. Assigned to the Masri Pasha case, he considered abducting the Egyptian in a submarine along the Egyptian coast, close to the delta of the Nile. Later he changed his plans and decided to dispatch a plane to a rendezvous site in the desert, south of Cairo. On June 7, 1941, shortly before sundown, Ritter took off from Libya aboard a Heinkel-111, another Heinkel following close behind to protect him from the Royal Air Force. The airplanes crossed, undetected, into Egyptian airspace, dived to low altitude over the desert, and overflew the rendezvous spot. No living soul was visible in a range of many miles around. The Heinkels returned to Libya. A few days later Ritter was to learn that Masri Pasha had panicked at the last moment, fearing capture by the British.

Canaris and Ritter didn't give in. In utmost secrecy a special unit trained in Germany, in an isolated compound of the Brandenburg Regiment. The unit was code-named Z.-b.-V.800, and numbered several scores of volunteers who were ready to undertake the most perilous missions. They were being schooled in various kinds of undercover activities—spying, sabotage, parachuting, commando raids, agitation of native populations. They were going to be infiltrated in Egypt, Palestine, Iraq, and Iran. The first agents to be picked by Ritter were a tall, burly man named Mullenbruch and a small, agile, quick-witted fellow of about fifty, appropriately named Klein. Their goal was to penetrate into Egypt and Palestine equipped with Afu radio transmitters and initiate a continuous flow of intelligence reports to the Abwehr listening installations. They were also to recruit agents among the Arabs in Egypt and Palestine. Klein was to establish contact with the anti-British officers' underground.

The two men seemed to be the ideal choice for the mission, as both had been born in the Middle East and spoke Arabic fluently. Mullenbruch grew up in the German

Templar community in Palestine. He had been instructed to reach the city of Haifa, where he had lived before the war. Klein, a native of Alexandria, was going to return to his hometown.

A few weeks after the attempt to snatch Masri Pasha, two other Heinkel-111s took off from Darnah airfield in Libya. Aboard were Mullenbruch, Klein, and the unrelenting Ritter. The plan for their infiltration into Egypt was quite ingenious. After the idea to cross the Sahara by car had been abandoned, Ritter had decided to fly the two agents into Egypt and land in the desert about sixty-five miles west of the Nile. An old camel trail would serve as a landing strip. From that point, Mullenbruch and Klein were to continue their journey on powerful motorcycles until they reached Cairo and went their separate ways. The agents had been trained to ride motorcycles in Darnah, and were now packed, briefed, and ready for their mission.

But once again, luck wasn't on the Germans' side. When the aircraft reached the landing site, the pilot of the leading Heinkel panicked and refused to land. Major Ritter pulled rank and threatened him, but the pilot stubbornly refused, pretending that the trail was unfit for landing or takeoff. The two Heinkels had to turn back to Darnah. However, when they reached Darnah they were to find that the airfield there was undergoing an RAF bombing raid. In the meantime the leading plane had run out of fuel and developed engine trouble, forcing the pilot to attempt a night landing at sea. The results were disastrous: Ritter was severely injured, Klein had a dislodged shoulder, Mullenbruch was killed. The equipment, the radios, the forged documents, and the motorcycles were lost. Another operation of crucial importance to Rommel's offensive had ended in catastrophe.

To make matters worse, units of the British army and the Free French under General Catroux occupied Syria and Lebanon at the end of July, routing the pro-German Vichy forces. Thus an important German stronghold in the Middle East was lost, one that could have served to infiltrate agents and monitor British army activities in nearby Palestine and Iraq. Special units of British counterintelligence roamed the countryside hunting for remaining Abwehr agents in Syria and Lebanon. At the very eve of the new Rommel offensive, the need for highly qualified agents inside Egypt and Palestine became more acute.

That was the moment when Herr Koch emerged on the scene.

Canaris had kept him up his sleeve till the last moment. While Mullenbruch and Klein were still being trained at the Brandenburg facilities, he was already working on the idea of dispatching a Jewish spy into the Jewish land of Palestine. He had reached the conclusion that only a real Jew could melt into the scenery and mix with the Jewish population; only a real Jew, posing as an illegal immigrant, would be assisted and sheltered by the local population. A Jewish illegal immigrant would not be suspected either by the Jewish community or by the Arabs and the British for failing to know the language or being unfamiliar with the country.

That's why he had started to look for a Jewish spy. And he had found Paul Ernst Fackenheim.

The operation hadn't been easy. In order to retrieve "Koch" from his Dachau torturers, the Abwehr had to overcome the furious objections of the Gestapo, the SS, and other Nazi party organizations. The fanatic Nazis were violently opposed to the liberation of a single Jew from their camps. They feared that one day, far from their reach, he might reveal the gruesome truth about their kingdom of terror, and they were revolted by the idea that a Jew, this traitor, enemy, and subhuman, could be incorporated into the Reich's war machine and contribute to its victory.

Even after Fackenheim's liberation from Dachau the SS didn't give up, and the implacable struggle between the party and the Abwehr went on. The Abwehr spymasters were well aware they were being watched and spied upon by the party fanatics. They knew that the smallest error could send Fackenheim back to Dachau. Therefore, until Fackenheim was trained and ready to set out on his mission, the Abwehr had to protect him not only from foreign spies, but from the various Nazi polices as well. Once liberated from Dachau, he simply had to vanish from the earth. That was the reason for his hurried journey to Brussels, and for his isolation from any contact with Abwehr officials in the Belgian capital. He had to be trained in utmost secrecy. In Brussels, at 5, Rue de la Loi, the Abwehr had indeed established an important training center for selected agents. But Fackenheim was never admitted into the building. He was trained individually, and very few Abwehr officers on Rue de la Loi even suspected his presence in Belgium.

Fackenheim had been kept incommunicado in Brussels as long as Canaris was expecting to get hold of Masri Pasha. After the failure of the project he had been moved a square forward, but still in waiting position. He had been flown to Berlin, where a decision had been taken to intensify his training and prepare him for his mission. He was then dispatched to Athens. But in Athens he was also isolated, while a few hundred miles away hectic preparations were being made to infiltrate Mullenbruch and Klein into Egypt. Only when that effort, too, had failed did Canaris decide to use Paul Fackenheim.

Till now, "Koch" had been deliberately kept in the dark regarding the character of his mission. Except for the vague hints about "doing something for his country," he had had no inkling whatsoever about the purpose of his training. The main motive for that Abwehr policy was security, of course— never let an agent know more than he needs to, never brief him on a future project, which might always be canceled or modified. But there was another reason for the silence that surrounded Fackenheim: Had he known from the start that he was about to be sent to Palestine, he might have refused to cooperate. The Abwehr chiefs figured that only at the very eve of the operation, when the plans were ready, when he had established a bond with his case officer, when he had developed some feeling of belonging to the Abwehr community— only then could he be told and persuaded to set out on his mission.

When Müller came to see Fackenheim that morning, the time had finally come. The Abwehr had decided to play its trump card—a Jewish spy—in the decisive battle for control of the Middle East.

And at that very moment, Fackenheim said no.

"I shall not go to Palestine. I shall do nothing against my people. I shall do nothing that could harm any other Jew."

Müller stiffened and for a moment was speechless, apparently at a loss. But he regained control and sat down, facing Paul. He knew his pupil well. He knew that this time he couldn't break Paul's resistance by threats implying a return to Dachau or warnings about his mother's fate. There was only one way to make Paul cooperate: Paul's deep attachment to the values of military honor.

"I can promise you and assure you," Müller said, groping for the right words, "that we shall refrain from any action which could harm your people. I can solemnly guarantee that this will never happen."

Watching Paul's haggard face, he went on. "We ask you to collect intelligence about the British, and only the British. Not about the Jews. Furthermore, you know well how the British are treating the Jewish refugees. You know they prevent them from entering Palestine. The enemy is England. Not the Jews.

"You also are aware of the situation at the desert front. The British are busy preparing a new offensive." Indeed, by the end of September a few reports had reached Berlin and Rome warning of a forthcoming major British offensive. Still, Müller didn't know that the British offensive would be launched in November 1941. "The lives of thousands of

Tracts distributed to the Arab population, warning against German paratroopers. "This is the fifth column . Hit them in their hearts!"

Geschäfts-Nr. der BfA

Erklärung

de**s** _Journalisten Heinrich Berzeviczy_ , geb. am _10.3.1911_
(Beruf, Vor- und Zuname, bei Frauen auch Mädchenname)

wohnhaft in _2 Hamburg 64, Hoheneichen 4_
(postalische Anschrift)

über die Beschäftigungs- und Versicherungsverhältnisse de**s** _Schriftstellers Paul Fackenheim_
_____, jetzt wohnhaft in _2359 Ulzburg_

aus der Zeit vom _März 1941_ bis _März 1946_

Mir ist bekannt, dass Herr Paul Fackenheim im März 1941 auf Betrei-
ben der Abwehr auf dem Konzentrationslager Dachau entlassen wurde,
um für militärische Zwecke in Ägypten eingesetzt zu werden. Mir ist
ferner bekannt, dass der Obengenannte von Oktober 1941 bis Anfang
März 1946 in Ägypten und Palästina war und von der britischen Armee
interniert wurde. Als Angehöriger derselben Abwehrgruppe wie Herr
Fackenheim kenne ich diese Vorgänge aus Erzählungen meiner Vorgesetzter

An die

Bundesversicherungsanstalt für Angestellte
Berlin-Wilmersdorf
Ruhrstraße 2

Der Zeuge soll mit eigenen Worten ausführlich schildern, was ihm über die Art und Dauer der Beschäftigung des Versicherten, den von ihm erzielten Verdienst und über Anzahl und Höhe der von ihm entrichteten Beiträge zur Invaliden- und Angestelltenversicherung bekannt ist. Die Anschriften der Arbeitgeber sind, soweit möglich, anzugeben. Die Darstellung darf nicht allgemein gehalten sein, sondern muß vom Zeugen mit Angaben über bestimmte Daten und Tatsachen belegt werden. Dabei muß er auch angeben, woher er seine Kenntnis hat, ob eigene Kenntnis oder Beobachtung, oder Mitteilungen des Versicherten oder anderer Personen.

(19/3321)

I. 1045 a - Anlage -
8/61 - 100 000

Bitte wenden!

Meine Angaben beruhen auf eigener Kenntnis, weil ich (genau angeben, woher die Kenntnis erlangt ist)

die mit dem Einsatz von Herrn Fackenheim in Ägypten direkt
zu tun hatten.

Ich kenne den/di**e** _Paul Fackenheim_ seit _1941_ und bin mit
ihm - i~~hr~~ - weder verwandt noch verschwägert.

Ich versichere wahrheitsgemäß, daß ich obige Angaben nach bestem Wissen und Gewissen gemacht habe.
Ich bin bereit, erforderlichenfalls meine Angaben vor Gericht zu beeiden.

Die eigenhändige Unterschrift wird hiermit beglaubigt:

Hamburg , den **13. 10 67** 19___   _Hamburg_ , den **13. 10 67** 19___
(Ort)   (Ort)

Freie und Hansestadt Hamburg
Bezirksamt Wandsbek
Ortsamt Alstertal
Einwohnerabteilung

(Vor- und Zuname des Zeugen)   (Unterschrift und Amtsbezeichnung)
                                      (Polizeibehörde) Regierungsoberinspektorin

---

Affidavit by Mr. Heinrich Berzeviczy, a former Abwehr officer,
confirming the main points of Paul Fackenheim's story.

Ludwig Dischler
Oberst a. D.

19. 1. 69.

Herr Fackenheim ist 1941 oder 1942
der Abwehrstelle Athen zweck Einsatzes
in Palestina überstellt worden.
Mit der Ausbildung und Einzel-
heiten des Einsatzes hatte ich als
Leiter der Abwehrstelle nichts zu
tun. Diese Aufgabe oblag ausschließ-
lich den hierfür bestimmten
Personen. Daher lernte ich Herrn
Fackenheim erst im Lager
Neuengamme, wo wir beide ein-
sassen, kennen. Deckname: Koch.

Dischler.

Statement by Colonel D (Dischler),
former chief of the Abwehr in
Athens, about "Koch's" departure
on a mission in Palestine.

Paul Fackenheim's reproduction of
his drawing containing the message
he had tried to convey to the
Abwehr. The Morse signs are
clumsily concealed in the curtain.

BUDAPEST

B	U	D	A	P	E	S	T
B	R	U	D	E	R	H	Ö
R	T	O	I	E	S	I	B
N	A	L	E	A	U	F	Z
U	M	L	E	T	Z	T	E
N	O	E	F	E	C	H	T

BRNUN × RTAMO × ÜDLLE ×
DIEEF × EEATE × RSUZO ×
HIFTH × ÖOZET ×

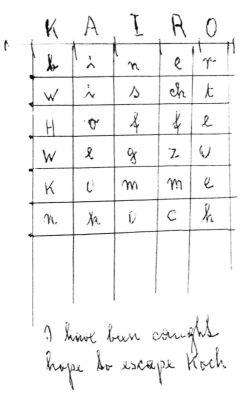

I have been caught hope to escape Koch.

Paul Fackenheim's reproduction of his grille and the message to the Abwehr.

PETER F. STUDER-MAYR   2 HAMBURG 39 · SIERICHSTR. 69 · TEL. 27 25 24

5. Februar 1969

Herrn
Paul Ernst Fackenheim
2359 U l z b u r g
      Beckersbergring 171

Sehr geehrter Herr Fackenheim!

Ich danke Ihnen für Ihren Brief vom 21.1.1969.

Gerne bestätige ich Ihnen, daß Sie in der Zeit, in der ich
in dem Internierungslager Monastry bei Latroon in Palästina
war und zwar von Ende 1944 bis Ende 1945, ebenfalls dort interniert waren.

Meiner Erinnerung nach waren Sie schon vor mir, also vor Ende
1944, in dem vorgenannten Internierungslager. Da ich das aber
nicht genau weiß, kann ich es Ihnen somit auch nicht ver-
bindlich bestätigen.

Ich hoffe, daß diese Bestätigung, daß wir gemeinsam bis Ende
1945 in Monastry waren, genügt.

                          Mit freundlichen Grüßen!

                          P.F.Studer-Mayr

Letter of P. F. Studer-Mayr to Paul Fackenheim, confirming they had been
interned together in the Latrun convent.

Paul Fackenheim soon after his liberation in 1941.

Paul Fackenheim around 1970.

Mrs. Irma Kobliner at the time of Paul Fackenheim's court-martial.

The reports and summaries of British Intelligence in the Middle East, which describe the activities of Paula Koch and Colonel Falkenheim. (British Archives, Public Record Office, London)

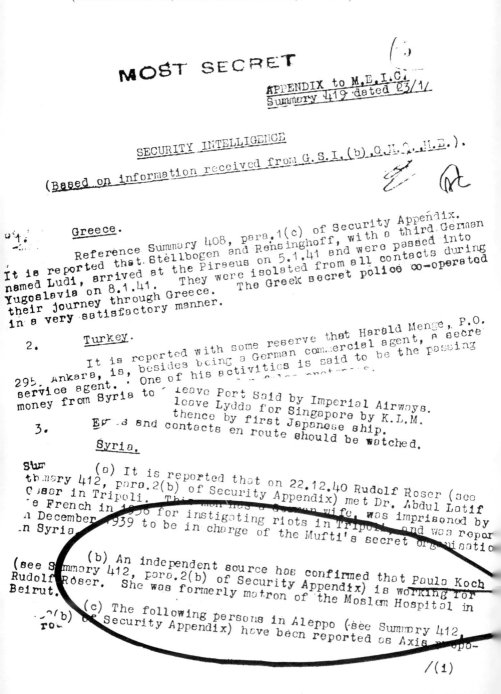

MOST SECRET

APPENDIX to M.E.I.C.
Summary 419 dated 23/1/

SECURITY INTELLIGENCE

(Based on information received from G.S.I.(b),G.H.Q.,M.E.).

1. Greece.

Reference Summary 408, para.1(c) of Security Appendix.
It is reported that Stellbogen and Rensinghoff, with a third German named Ludi, arrived at the Piraeus on 5.1.41 and were passed into Yugoslavia on 8.1.41. They were isolated from all contacts during their journey through Greece. The Greek secret police co-operated in a very satisfactory manner.

2. Turkey.

It is reported with some reserve that Harald Menge, P.O.
295, Ankara, is, besides being a German commercial agent, a secret service agent. One of his activities is said to be the passing money from Syria to

3. leave Port Said by Imperial Airways.
   leave Lydda for Singapore by K.L.M.
   thence by first Japanese ship.
Eg__s and contacts en route should be watched.

Syria.

(a) It is reported that on 22.12.40 Rudolf Roser (see Summary 412, para.2(b) of Security Appendix) met Dr. Abdul Latif Caesar in Tripoli. This man has a German wife, was imprisoned by the French in 1936 for instigating riots in Tripoli, and was reported in December 1939 to be in charge of the Mufti's secret organisation in Syria.

(b) An independent source has confirmed that Paula Koch (see Summary 412, para.2(b) of Security Appendix) is working for Rudolf Roser. She was formerly matron of the Moslem Hospital in Beirut.

(c) The following persons in Aleppo (see Summary 412, (b) of Security Appendix) have been reported as Axis

/(1)

MOST SECRET

APPENDIX to M.E.I.C.
Summary 428 dated 3/2/41.

SECURITY INTELLIGENCE.

(Based on information from G.S.I.(b), G.H.Q., M.E.).

1.   Egypt.

(a) It is reported from Istanbul on authority described as reliable that Ferenc de Marossy, the new Hungarian Chargé d'Affaires in Egypt (see Summary 410, para.1(b) of Security Appendix) is of German origin and took a Hungarian name only two years ago. He is said to be pro-Nazi and a close collaborator of General Goemboes, the former totalitarian Prime Minister.

(b) Reference Summary 419, para.3(b) of Security Appendix. Shiniti Tanabe left by air for Palestine on 27.1.41. Present information states that he will travel to Japan via Istanbul, Moscow and Siberia.

(c) Gustavo Testa, the Apostolic Delegate to Egypt and Palestine, with his secretaries Josepho Micossi and Carlo Perico arrived in Egypt from Palestine on 24.1.41. Micossi had left Syria on 21.1.41. All three are Italians with Vatican diplomatic passports.

2.   Syria.

(a) It is reported that Commandant Teze, formerly of the Deuxieme Bureau, has arrived in Syria from Vichy with final instructions for the ?? French policy of Syria.

... been in touch w...

(c) Reference Summary ... that the influence of Baron von Hentig reports have recently been received ... is said to be ... officer, Colonel Woldfries, who is expected to visit the Syrian-Transjordan ... ezireh and is expected to visit the Syrian-Transjordan, where news of the ??ch on the other hand, a statement from Iraq, declares that no Germans have been ?? of should be fairly reliable, therefore, that this and similar repo?? ... It is suggested ... may be part of the "war of nerves".

(d) Paula Koch (see Summary 419, para.4(b) of Security Appendix) is now employed at the Swiss Consulate at Beirut. The Consul, Werner Raths, has already been reported as a suspect (see Summary 363, para.4(f) of Security Appendix). Mrs. Alma Marcopoli of Aleppo is in contact with Koch. Paul Marcopoli, of Aleppo, is known as an Italian agent.

(e) Cesar or Qaisar Agu??, a prosperous Baghdad merchant with branches in Hamburg, Aleppo, Beirut and Teheran, who recently ??ited Turkey and Germany, has been making propaganda since his ??rn. He is in touch with the following firms in Athens:-

(i) A.E.T., Odos Panepistemiou.   ??, The Con-
                                        (see Summary
...stolides, P.O ??   of
                                        ?? known

MOST SECRET

ET

SECURITY INTELLIGENCE

(Based on Information from G.S.I.(b), G.H.Q., M.E.)

Egypt.

(a) George Ma'luf, a Syrian merchant with business interests in Egypt is reported to collect information here and pass it to German agents in Syria, and also to be a link between the Germans and Italians in Syria and Mohammed Subhi Shorbagi, a member of an Egyptian communist ..... that used to be in constant touch with ...... Italian propagandist.

..... the American Consul-General in Beirut has been ..... owledge of the presence of Karl Raswan (se .... for the mans ...2(b) of Security Appendix) in Syria. On the ot.. .... Govern-
.. confirmed report, that must be treated with reserve, say. Antonio Moroos, the Mexican Consul in Jerusalem, who is of Palestinian origin, recently met Raswan in Syria. It is known that Moroos was in Damascus and Beirut last month, and it is reported by another agent that he visited the Japanese Consul in Beirut, Yoriyoshi Sai.... (see Summary 405, para.4(f) of Security Appendix) and the President of the Lebanese Republic.

(b) ..... ein .... Saadi, the Spanish Consular agent at Beirut (see Summary ..., para.. of Annexure 1), arrived in Cairo on 8.2.41. Information from a usually reliable source states that he has been appointed Attache of the Spanish Legation here. Though he is a known Axis agent, his mental capacity is said to be such that he is likely to be of more use to us than to the enemy.

(c) The same source has reported as follows:-

(i) Paula Koch (see Summary 428, para.2(d) of Security Appendix) is said to have made contact with Mukhtar Mukayish, and Abdullah Mashru't, two German sympathisers in Beirut, on behalf of Rudolf Roser.

(ii) Riad Sulh (see Summary 433, para.2(a) of Security Appendix) and Omar Bayhum (see Summary 431, para.2(b) of Security Appendix) are reported to have met an Italian agent named Luigi Molinari. Another source states that members of a firm named Molinari in Aleppo are engaged in Italian espionage

(iii) Reference Summary 378, para.2(b) of Security Appendix and 4.., para.5(c)(vi) of Annexure 1 to Security Appendix. The information that Rudolf Roser and the Shami Pir secretly visited Transjordan last November is now denied.

(iv) Alois Moluth, a convinced German sympathiser, is said to be employed by the Shami Pir as tutor for his children

APPENDIX TO W.E.I.C. SUMMARY
No.450 DATED 12/3/41

SECURITY INTELLIGENCE

Based on Information from G.S.I.(b), G.H.Q., M.E.

1. **Egypt**

Further to Summary 447, paragraph 1(c) of Security Appendix A report states that Tahsin al Askari, the Iraqi Consul in Cairo, and Muhir-ul-Din Zarakli are allowing pan-Arab extremists in Egypt to use the Iraqi and Saudi-Arabian diplomatic ciphers.

2. **Syria**

(a) The Shami Pir (see Summary 440, paragraph 4(c)(ii), Annexure I of Security Appendix) is now reported to have assumed the role of chief German agent in Syria, possibly appointed by von Hentig. Several Arab leaders appear to be jealous of him on the grounds of his ignorance of Syrian politics and lack of standing in the country. Von Hentig is stated to have been disappointed with the political situation in Syria, as none of the heads of the various parties were prepared to subordinate themselves for the common cause.

(b) According to the Shami Pir, von Hentig intends to return to Syria soon.

(c) Reference Summary 435, paragraph 3(a) of Security Appendix, in spite of von Hentig's efforts to reconcile them, the Phalangist Christian Youth Movement is unwilling to come to any understanding with the Moslem Najada.

(d) Reference Summary 444, paragraph 2(a) of Security Appendix. is reported that when they visited Dair-Az-Zor, Colonel Falkenheim used the aliases of von Haner and Fritz Otto, and Rudolf Roser of Darmti.

Iraq

) It is reported that George Mansur, a comparatively moderate Arab propagandist (see Summary 257, paragraph (b) of Annexure I Security Appendix), who was formerly in touch with Lord Lloyd the formation of the Arab-British Association, arrived in Baghdad he end of February with money for the Mufti.

Mithir or Mazhar Ash-Shawi, an Iraqi tribesman was formed ted to be in touch with Dr. Grobba, to corr , the Arabic "Lord Haw-Haw" in Berlin Fawzi Qawukji (see Summary 441 r-Ruwaiha, who is aph 2(a)

SECURITY INTELLIGENCE.

(Based on information from G.S.I.(b), G.H.Q. M.E.)

EGYPT.

(a) Reference Summary No.495, paragraph 1(b) of Security Appen-
The Egyptian Government appear to be at last consenting to
action against the leaders of the Fifth Column. The Prime Minis-
has stated that the King has ordered Aly Maher to live on his
ate near Alexandria, and he is now under close surveillance; also
t Saleh Harb has been ordered to leave Cairo, and to stay either
h Aly Maher, which he has refused, or in Upper Egypt.

(b) Though the Japanese staff of the Japan Cotton Trading Co.,
l the Mitsui Bussan Kaisha, the most important Japanese concerns in
ypt, are preparing to leave, these offices are not closing down, but
e being left in charge of the local staff. On the other hand, it
reported by an unconfirmed source that the Yokohama Specie bank at
exandria is closing down. Its Japanese staff, together with those
the above mentioned firms, were proposing to leave for Japan vi-
.S.A. on 10.6.41. It is further stated that the Bank Manager
een receiving a number of cipher cables from Tokyo daily.
ome through normal channels, they would have been stopped   has
nip. It would appear, therefore, that they have come   Had these
ipher or some illicit means.   .d in Censor-
                                                            by diplomatic

(c) The members of the Guma'yat al Fidayi's
aragraph 1(a) of Security Appendix) appear to
nts, workers and young extremists. It is   n (see Summary No.523
note-books that Mohammed Rushdi al Uraibi   , have been chiefly stud-
in the society, who is one of those   learnt from one of his
age, when a student, for shoot   a young lawyer and leader
Makram Obeid Pash-   de plane some years
doned this ide-   ahas Pasha and
                                                         cently aban-

_STINE.

2.   It is learnt that enemy agents in Iraq were
        at the end of April of the strength and disp-
infor in Palestine. It is thought most likely that t-   ately
forc tely from Jewish sources, as the Jewish Agency is   r
ult informed about military dispositions in the country.   ine
wel

SYRIA.

(a)   source described as reliable reports as follows:-
        (i) Rudolf Roser (see Summary No.521, paragraph 3 of Security
        Appendix), Paula Koch (see Summary No.440, paragraph 2(c
        (i) of Security Appendix) and two other Germans went to
        Aleppo about 28.5.41, it is thought to supervise arrange-
        ments for the arrival of German aircraft and personnel,
        and to meet pro-German leaders from the Jazira. Roser
        re urned to Beirut on 1.6.41.

SECURITY INTELLIGENCE

sed on Information received from S.I.M.E.

.PT

It is expected that Angel Sanz-Briz, Spanish Chargé
-ires at Cairo and a Phalangist (see Summary 484, paragraph
of Security Appendix), will leave for Spain via Palestine,
-yria and Turkey towards the end of the month. His sympathies are
dubious, but he and other Spanish officials have been leniently
treated on account of transit facilities granted by the Spanish
Government in the Atlantic area. Information would be welcomed on
Sanz-Briz's activities and contacts during his journey.

2.   SYRIA.

Further to Summary 575, paragraph 3(b) of Security Appendix.
The same Turkish source reports that ten Germans are still at large
at Beirut, including Colonel Falkenheim (see Summary 459, paragraph
2(d) of Security Appendix), Major Lievonken, and Helmuth Linken.
This is partly confirmed by the fact that Linken has recently been
found at Beirut and interned (see Summary 611, paragraph 1(a) of
Security Appendix). The source goes on to state that the Brazilian
(see Summary 606, paragraph 3(a) of Security Appendix) and Swiss
(see Summary 472, paragraph 3(b) of Security Appendix) Consulates
have given the enemy considerable help in Syria and may have issued
false passports to enemy agents. He declares that the following
are prominent members of the Fifth Column intended to help the
Germans at such time as they may have disposed of Russia:-

Riad Sulh (see Summary 586, paragraph 2(b) of Security Appendix)
Jamil Bayhum (see Summary 521, paragraph 3(c) of Security
    Appendix)
Amin Arslan (last reported in Turkey, see Summary 579, p
    2(d) of Security Appendix, and to be an elderly man
    great importance)
Farid Zain ud-Din (see Summary 526, paragraph 4(c) of
    Appendix)
Shukri Quwatli (see Summary 592, paragraph 1(c) of Sec

of Armenia

Churchill Turkish sources, he concludes with a gene
ot encourage ns and Kurds, declaring that the Dashnak
ing this, howev Roosevelt declaration to mean that the
aming that Linken he formation of an independent Armenia
that this informati he report has definite value, all
                    been made a scapegoat by the
                    being "put over" by Germa.

IRAQ

Some 200 copies of an Ara
e rebellion were seized at the
.8.41, under protest (see Summ c pamphlet printed in
er Italian interests. The pamphlets contain lian Consulate at Da
    endix) ilian Consul, who i
                    606, paragraph 3(
                    a number of crude I'

                    :/ British ca

MIZA

ral denu
s inter-
Allies
Dis-
ys
Germans
n sources

Iraq dur
ascus or
looking
) of Sec
talian ant
rtoons

ESPIONAGE ORGANISATIONS IN SYRIA.

The establishing of a high degree of security from espionage is not easy in a newly-occupied country like Syria. In that country enemy agents were recently able to work unchecked; unfriendly elements abound among the natives of the country and among Vichy Frenchmen, who have been retained because they are essential for administration or commerce; and British Security authorities cannot work directly, but only through the Free French administration, which is lacking in trained personnel and does not favour the suggestion of British interference. On the other side of a long frontier, not easily controlled is Turkey, the nerve-centre of German Intelligence in the Middle East. German, Vichy French and Italian organisations exist there for the purpose of collecting information on British and Allied dispositions and troop movements, and on the activities of subversive organisation potential Fifth Columns, in Allied territory. This paper attempts to collect ....rise our knowledge on the activities of enemy

(Ahmad Abdul Qadir Ubaid.)

Maurice Hassad.	)		
Elias Dummar.	)	Wish to return to Syria.	longstan- ploit.
Najdat Wannes (Ohannes ?)	)	Reported to have been in Syria xand-	
Antoine Khayat.	)	past two months.	t

2. Colonel Falkenheim & Major Klevonken.

S.I.M.E. expressed the opinion that these men were probably non-existent, but recently their names have come up again in a fairl circumstantial context, and the possibility that they may have remai until recently in hiding in Syria cannot be entirely excluded. It has been reported that the organisation consits of some ten Germans who were recently in the neighbourhood of Beirut. It was stated on 22.9.41 that they have now withdrawn to the Anti-Lebanon, and that Klevonken himself has gone to Hatey.

/One report

One report coupled with them the name of Helmuth Linken, Sudeten-German who was employed by the Germans as a W/T operator before the Allied occupation. This man was recently interned i Syria, and S.I.M.E. has asked that he should be interrogated on knowledge of Falkenheim and Klevonken.

It was also stated that Artin Bagdassaroff (or Bagdessaria a Russo-Armenian of Beirut, belonged to this organisation. It h not so far been possible to trace him.

3. A French report stated that Dr. Grobba and the S ami Pir were at the head of an organisation of Moslem extremists with headquarters at Alexandretta. It has, however, since been that either Grobba or the Pir has recently been at Alexa that other well-known extremists, mentioned in the are there, and there is an increasing prob.... ....ed in fact.

propaganda in the Aleppo district was making p
paragraph 3(e) of Security Appendix) was a mistaken infe
ence from an ambiguous report. It now appears from thi
and other sources that Rifa'i escaped to Turkey when the
Allies occupied Syria and is now active in Hatay where h
has met his extremist Syria colleagues on the Syrian fro

(iii) A number of young Syrians who escaped from Syria with the
Germans are being trained as parachutists in Greece. Th
is supported by Summary 599, paragraph 2(d) of Security
Appendix.

(iv) The Arab Club (Nadi al Arabi) of Damascus (see Summary 59
paragraph 2(e) of Security Appendix) is stated to be a
small students' group which used to be directed by the
following:-

Dr. Said Fattah al Imam in Bagdad (see Summary 575,
paragraph 4(a) of Security Appendix) who, it is stated,
used to send £200 gold monthly to his colleagues in
Damascus until the collapse of the Iraq Rebellion.

Georges Charbein (see Summary 575, paragraph 3(a)
of Security Appendix) stated to be in Berlin.

Ihsan Bizri (see Summary 561, paragraph 1(a) of Security
Appendix) stated to be still at Damascus.

(v) Paula Koch (see Summary 615, paragraph 5(b) of Security
Appendix) is stated to have been seen with other Germans
at Antioch about 5.9.41.

(d)   Four Germans and sixty-seven Italians of military
age from Syria and the Lebanon have now been interned in
Palestine.

(e)   Further to Summary 616, paragraph 2 of Security
Appendix. A source of unknown reliability has reported
that some Germans of Major Klevonken's organisation are in
hiding in the Anti-Lebanon, and that Klevonken himself has
crossed the frontier to Alexandretta. It is stated that
the Surete Generale has arrested at Damascus a man who first
claimed to be Free French, then said he was Esthonian, and
finally admitted to being a German.

(f)   Further to Summary 611, paragraph 1(b) of Security
Appendix. It is stated that Anton Bishara Tayan has applied
for an exit permit to return to Turkey from Syria, and that
if this is not granted he will try to leave secretly, as he
has received urgent instructions to return to Istanbul.
If he should arrive in Turkey he should be kept under close
observation.

3. IRAQ.

Reports received from Iraq show that there is some disquiet
about the Security situation there. At the outset, however, it
must be recalled that as recently as last March, before the Rashid
Ali coup d'etat, the Italian Legation at Bagdad was still an active
centre of intrigue, the government was openly unfriendly to us, ther
was no censorship of mails and propaganda, no effective frontier con
trol to keep out our enemies, and no British troops in the country
except the R.A.F. staff and technicians as allowed by the Anglo-I
Treaty. In all these respects the situation has immeasurably
in these six months, and in addition our Security authorities
enjoy the ready co-operation of the Iraq C.I.D.

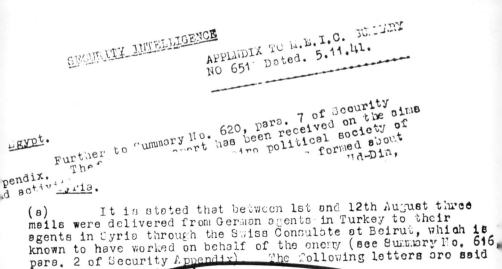

Egypt.

Further to Summary No. 620, para. 7 of Security
Appendix. The ....ort has been received on the aims
....d activi.... ..ro political society of ..... formed about
Syria. ..d-Din,

(a)   It is stated that between 1st and 12th August three
mails were delivered from German agents in Turkey to their
agents in Syria through the Swiss Consulate at Beirut, which is
known to have worked on behalf of the enemy (see Summary No. 616,
para. 2 of Security Appendix). The following letters are said
to have been identified:-

(i)   An envelope from Paula Koch (see Summary No. 635, para
I.1 of Annexe to Security Appendix) probably
addressed to Mohammed Tabara (see Summary No 458,
para. 4 (i) of Security Appendix) a Mufti-supporter,
who is stated by another source to have been hi.
former landlord and to be now chief of the public
Assistance Committee of Beirut.

(ii)/

German soldiers," Müller went on, "might depend on your mission. You are a German, and a man of honor. You want Germany to win this war. You must help us."

He went on speaking for a long time. Of the decisive battle in the desert that was to erupt so soon. Of the final victory. Of the camaraderie and mutual trust that characterized relations between Paul and the Abwehr officers he had met.

Fackenheim listened in silence. He could have objected. He could have argued that a German victory in the Middle East might be tantamount to a verdict of death for the Jewish community in Palestine, because a German victory wouldn't be only the victory of the army and the Abwehr, but also that of the Gestapo and the SS. He could have argued that by warring against the British he was also warring against the Jews of Palestine.

He didn't do it. Brainwashed by the Reich's propaganda, flattered by the confidence of the Abwehr, motivated by his faith in the good, decent, noble Germany, he finally let himself be convinced. He was neither a hero nor a martyr. He wasn't strong enough to persist in his refusal and rebel against his only friends, those who had liberated him, treated him with respect, protected him and taken care of his mother. He wasn't able to sacrifice his life as well as his mother's just to avoid being used by the Abwehr as a pawn. And he was sure, deep in his heart, that most men in his situation would feel the same.

He asked Müller for a few hours to be alone and make up his mind. In the evening, he let him know that he would carry out the mission. In two weeks he would return to the land of his ancestors—as a foreign spy.

September 30, 1941. That morning, the last stage of his training was to begin. Müller took Fackenheim to their favorite restaurant in Fallerum, where a young, blushing Greek waitress served them a frugal breakfast of strong black coffee, black olives, bread, and cheese. "We'll drop you in Palestine

by parachute," Müller said. "We considered for a while sending you over in a fisherman's boat, but lately the British sea
patrols have been intensified, and any boat is visited and
thoroughly checked long before it approaches the coast. That
leaves you practically no opportunities to reach Palestine.
Therefore we decided on the parachuting."

"I've never jumped before," Paul said. "I'll need some
training."

Müller shook his head. "We believe you don't need any
training. First, there is the matter of time. There is none.
Second, we don't have any training facilities here—there are
neither training installations nor paratrooper bases around
Athens. Our specialists believe that a few jumps wouldn't be
of any use to you; on the contrary, an accident might always
happen, you'll break a leg or a rib and the entire operation
will have to be called off. They say that the fear of jumping is
lesser before the first jump. You shall be dropped over a flat,
sandy terrain, and you'll run no danger of being hurt by landing on a tree or a roof. You'll be thoroughly briefed about
parachuting techniques. If you follow the instructions closely,
nothing will happen to you."

Fackenheim shrugged. Physical danger had never frightened him. "Good. But I'll need a set of forged papers, money,
and names of contacts in Palestine."

"No false papers. You're Jewish, aren't you? Your best
cover will be that of a German refugee who has illegally immigrated into the country. Palestine is full of such people. If
you're arrested, you'll say that you've recently disembarked
on the beach from a small Greek boat. Everybody will believe you."

"But I don't know a thing about Palestine. . . ."

"What would a refugee know? A refugee is a man on the
run who has escaped from his country and reached a land
that is virtually unknown to him. By the way, do you have
any relatives in Palestine?"

"Yes, an uncle. Karl Fackenheim. He is my father's brother. But I haven't seen him for more than twenty years."

Paul paused, then added thoughtfully, "I don't want to get him involved in this affair."

Müller shrugged. "That's for you to decide."

"And what about the language? I speak a very bad English."

"It doesn't matter. You can speak German without raising any suspicions. I told you and I repeat: Thousands of refugees have immigrated from Germany to Palestine during these last few years. Most, it seems, do not speak Hebrew or English."

Müller went on. "You'll have no contacts in Palestine. We don't want you to get in touch with anybody. If we feel the need to communicate, we'll send someone there. We'll give you early warning by radio and he'll know how to find you."

Fackenheim refrained from comment. But Müller's behavior made him suspect that the Abwehr didn't want to give the names of other agents in Palestine for the simple reason that there weren't any others. As illogical as it might seem, Paul Fackenheim was perhaps going to be the only Abwehr agent in the entire country.

Müller was busy fumbling with his wallet. He handed Paul a folded envelope containing a wad of bills. "This is your money. Fifty Palestinian pounds." Paul nodded and put the envelope in his pocket.

"Now, the contact routine," Müller said. "This is your call sign." He gave Paul a rectangular piece of paper on which a few letters and numerals were inscribed in capital letters: ORTM-37. Müller leaned over the table. "You'll learn that by heart, and you'll destroy it. It's easy to remember. Now, let's consider the worst. You might be captured and turned against us by the British. They'll order you to transmit false reports."

Fackenheim interrupted. "Why should they order me? They can transmit in my name whenever they want. They certainly have good operators."

Müller shook his head. "No way. We shall detect that at once. You see, each operator has his own personal touch. It's like his thumbprints. It can't be faked. Now, I know your touch. And I'll be able to tell if somebody else is transmitting in your name. The English know that too. So, if they want to play you against us, they must use you and nobody else. In such a case, you'll add to the call sign the letter F. That's how we shall know you've been burnt and you're in their hands. Remember, F. Everything could depend on that letter." He leaned closer, his face only inches from Fackenheim's. "And you'd better remember this. The English are as clever as we are. They know that a captured radio operator whom they're playing against us would most probably try to slip one or more letters into his message, to warn us that he has been caught and is run by them now. Give them all the letters and numbers you want, but don't forget to include the letter F in any message."

He stared fixedly at Paul until Paul nodded back. Then he took a book out of his leather briefcase. "This is your codebook."

Fackenheim leafed through the book and glared at Müller, astounded, It was a French novel that took place in the countryside of Avignon—*L'Âne Culotte* by Henri Bosco. It had been published in 1937.

Fackenheim protested. "Why the hell that book? It's totally senseless. A country novel, and in French! If they find it on me, they'll most certainly suspect something. Give me the Bible, or Goethe's Faust, or any other book that a refugee would take with him to Palestine. But that one?"

Müller took a deep breath. "Sorry, my friend. Unfortunately, I am not the one who decides in these matters. As you are fluent in French, our people have concluded that this book will suit our needs."

Fackenheim was about to say something, but finally gave up. Yet, he couldn't suppress his growing feeling that his superiors in the Abwehr were behaving like amateurs in his case.

Müller went on. "You know how to use the book for coding your messages. We went through that in Brussels already."

He suddenly got up, went to his car, and returned with a small suitcase. "I want to show you your Afu radio. That's what you'll be carrying with you on your mission."

Fackenheim whistled with admiration. The radio was compact and small, much smaller than the other sets he had used during his training here and in Brussels. A folding antenna fit snugly into two parallel grooves at the back of the transceiver.

"The handling is very easy. Plug it in any socket, and it will work perfectly. It is adapted to the electric current in Palestine—two hundred and twenty volts. And finally, for your better acquaintance with your operating zone, I've brought you this." He handed Paul a small book. "This is the Baedeker guide of Palestine. Here you'll find all you need to know about the country."

Fackenheim skeptically examined the travel guide and again felt a surge of anger. The Baedeker was a 1933 edition, outdated long ago. He couldn't believe that the prestigious Abwehr could be so sloppy in preparing an agent for his mission.

Paul Fackenheim was right, but he couldn't know he was hardly the only one in that situation. During the war, it was quite common for the Abwehr to dispatch agents into enemy territory who lacked adequate briefing, basic notions about the country, and contacts in place. This method brought disastrous results on the eve of Operation Sea Lion, the projected invasion of England, when many German agents were parachuted into southern England with nothing but Afu transmitters in their bags. They were supposed to spearhead an invasion that never came. When Sea Lion was finally called off, the great majority of those spies, who had no money, no contacts, and whose command of the English language was less than rudimentary, were easily unmasked and caught. Some of them were executed, others interned till the end of the war. Still, Canaris did not regard the operation as a failure. He preferred a poorly trained, totally unsupported agent in place on time to a well-prepared and well-protected spy who might reach his target too late. Except for a few master spies, most of the Abwehr field agents were coolly regarded as expendable. And Fackenheim was of that lot. He was going to be dropped in Palestine on the eve of Rommel's forthcoming offensive.

"Starting today," Müller told Fackenheim as they got back into the car, "we are entering the final stage of your training.

"The chief wishes you good luck."

IX

Point of No Return

THAT MORNING Fackenheim was busy shaving when suddenly the door of his room opened. A stranger stepped in.

He was a bizarre character—small, short-limbed, almost gnomish. He seemed to be dressed for a masked ball: a black and green Tyrolean jacket, elevated shoes, a hunter's hat ornated with chamois leather. Fackenheim's first impulse upon seeing that grotesque creature would have been to burst out laughing were it not for the pale, distorted face, the hateful eyes, the thin, evil mouth. The dwarfish Tyrolean had the visage of a monster. Something in that ugly, cruel face reminded Paul of Egon Zill, the commander of Dachau.

The man banged the door behind him. He coldly surveyed the room, taking in every small detail. Then, theatrically placing his hands on his hips, he smiled mockingly.

"Ach so! Here he is, then, the filthy Jewish bastard who fooled those suckers of the Wehrmacht!"

Fackenheim was dumbfounded. "Who the hell are you? What do you want?"

"Who am I? That's not your damned business, you stinking Jew, but I don't mind telling you. I'd even like telling you. I am Hauptsturmführer Kronberg, chief of the SD in Athens."

Fackenheim winced. The SD—Sicherheitsdienst—was the German security service, which had been founded as a section of the Nazi party, later to be attached to the headquarters of the security services of the Reich in close collaboration with the Gestapo.

"What do you want?" Paul repeated, taking a step toward Kronberg.

"I've been waiting for quite a while to get my hands on you," Kronberg said. "I just came to see how you looked, and to tell you that soon, quite soon, I'll have your hide."

Beside himself with fury, Fackenheim grabbed the nearest chair and brandished it over his head. "Raus!" he shouted. "Get out of here!"

The small man plunged his right hand in his pocket. Could he be armed? But at that very moment Paul heard the sound of steps outside. Somebody was coming up the stairs. It must be Müller, Fackenheim thought. He came every morning at that hour.

Kronberg had heard the footsteps too. He reached for the door's handle. As he was leaving the room, he turned back and hissed, "We'll meet again, believe me. And I'll get you at all costs. Do you hear? At all costs!"

A few moments later, Müller walked into the room. He did not say anything, but he seemed worried.

"Did you meet that son of a bitch on the stairs?" Fackenheim asked, still out of breath. He was trembling with fury and fear.

"Who?" Müller said, reaching for a cigarette. It was his favorite trick to gain time.

"Oh, come on, Müller. This is not the time to act like the village idiot. You surely know the Hauptsturmführer Kronberg better than me."

"He was here? In your room?" Gone was the studied indifference. Müller looked genuinely alarmed now.

"I almost broke a chair on his head." Paul stepped to the window and glanced quickly up and down the street. Kronberg was nowhere to be seen.

Müller sat down. "Calm down. Please. Tell me everything, in detail."

He listened, dismayed, to Paul's account. "I must warn you," Paul concluded, "that if this was to happen again, I'd refuse to undertake the mission, and I couldn't care less for the consequences."

Müller didn't seem to listen. He looked preoccupied and distressed. For once he didn't try to minimize the importance of the incident, as he always had before. He furiously stubbed his half-consumed cigarette in the ashtray.

"I have to go out," he finally said. "I'll be back in fifteen minutes. Lock the door and don't open it for anybody but me. Understand?"

Paul heard Müller run down the steps. He had never seen the big man so upset.

Less than fifteen minutes later, Müller was back. He came into the room, his breath shallow and his face red. "I spoke to the chief," he said. Fackenheim assumed that he had called the Abwehr headquarters on a safe phone. "The chief instructed me to tell you that you have nothing to fear from that maniac. You are officially under the protection of the Abwehr."

"Don't give me that," Paul said angrily. "Protection or not, the fact is that two Nazi agents found me and almost had me sent back to Dachau. And protection or not, the chief of the SD found me again in my new hotel."

Müller ignored his outburst. "We decided to step up the security measures. We have no time to transfer you to another hotel. Starting today, I'll be personally responsible for your safety. I'm moving into the room next to yours. You'll go out as little as possible. I don't want to make you a prisoner in your room, but I ask you not to leave unless it's absolutely necessary. Now, if anybody provokes you in the street, if anybody asks you delicate questions, tries to molest you or threaten you, you are to report immediately to any military patrol, or any German officer. You'll be safe that way."

Fackenheim was listening. Now he finally understood why those two strangers had accosted him in the street a few weeks before. They were also SD agents sent to ensnare him. They had probably submitted their report to Kronberg and he had relayed it to Berlin. The Nazi party knew of Paul's existence and of his employ. The Nazi police organizations knew who he was and what he was doing in Athens, and were shadowing each and every move he made. The SD chiefs seemed determined to prevent his departure by any means. They were certainly envisaging a different future for him, and Paul could guess exactly what they had in mind.

But Fackenheim didn't know all. He didn't know that he had become the helpless pawn in a battle between the Abwehr and the SS, the army and the party. For years now, an invisible but implacable war was being waged between Canaris and Himmler. It had started in 1935, shortly after Canaris's appointment as chief of the Abwehr, as a power struggle for the control of the Reich's secret services. The Abwehr of Wilhelm Canaris was the only nonpolitical organization in the German intelligence community. The other security services—SS, SD, and Gestapo—were connected to the Nazi party. The SS chief Heinrich Himmler, the young rising stars Reinhard Heydrich and Walter Schellenberg, and Heinrich Müller of the Gestapo—all craved to overtake the Abwehr as well. And this struggle was to go on throughout the war, until the tragic end of Canaris.

But since 1939 a new dimension had been added to the struggle, turning it into a confrontation between Nazis and anti-Nazis. Canaris, who was deeply attached to traditional conservative values and to the old-time German military ethos, was shocked by the monstrous new visage of Nazi Germany at war. On September 10, 1939, ten days after the invasion of Poland, Canaris traveled to the battlefield to see the Wehrmacht in action. He came back physically sick from the horrors he had seen perpetrated against the civilian population in the name of the Fuehrer. His faith in Hitler and Nazism was shattered forever.

Canaris became a dedicated anti-Nazi. He continued serving his country, but sabotaged several projects that were contrary to what he deemed worthy of German military honor. He sought secret contacts with the Allies in order to negotiate a separate peace after Hitler had been arrested by the army or killed. He transformed the Abwehr into a haven for anti-Nazi officers, offering them jobs and protection. Many of them would have certainly dangled on a piano cord or had their heads chopped with a medieval axe—Hitler's favorite execution instrument—if they had not been saved from the SD and the Gestapo by the fox of the Tirpitz Ufer. And all during the war, like hungry beasts of prey, the chiefs of the SD and the Gestapo would lie in wait, watching every step Canaris took, suspecting his anti-Nazi activities but unable to prove them, silently hoping that at the end he would trip and fall into their clutches.

In that context, it was only natural that the Nazi services hurled themselves onto the Fackenheim case with extraordinary zeal and soaring expectations. The liberation of a Jew from Dachau in itself was a scandalous initiative which they would have gladly aborted had it not been approved by the high command. If they could only induce Fackenheim into committing an error that might be qualified as a security breach, or if they could stop his mission before it got underway, they would have won another round in their long-term combat with Canaris.

That was how a Jewish prisoner from Dachau had become a pawn in a war raging at the highest levels of the Reich's power. And although shocked, infuriated, and distraught by Kronberg's appearance in his room, Fackenheim still underestimated the fanatical determination of the SD chief in Athens to hurt him in any possible way. If he had only suspected what the SD had in store for him, he would have undoubtedly broken that chair on the monstrous head of Haupsturmführer Kronberg.

But all he could do now was lie low and attend to his own security. He liked Müller and believed he would do his best to protect him. But his own experience had taught him not to entrust his life in anybody's hands. That very afternoon he sneaked out of the hotel and took a taxi to the nearby port of Piraeus. For once, his contacts with corrupt Wehrmacht officers and German civilian officials were to prove useful. After long negotiations he finally bought a Walther .08 pistol and fifty bullets. With the loaded gun in his pocket he felt a little more secure.

October 5, 1941. The events of the last few days, the threats of the SD, but most of all the excruciating torture of his own conscience had strung Paul's nerves to the limit. He couldn't listen to the radio, which was broadcasting triumphal marches and fanfares interspersed with dramatic announcements of Wehrmacht victories in its new offensive in Russia. He was unable to concentrate. He couldn't even memorize the radio call-sign. Finally, he copied it on two tiny strips of thin paper, which he carefully concealed in his clothing. He sewed one of the paper bits into the lining of his sleeve, and hid the other in the sole of his left shoe.

Müller and his assistant busied themselves around his room. They brought him large posters that had the insignia of various British units, and taught him how to identify planes, guns, and vehicles by their emblems. Other posters showed the different types of armor—tanks, half-tracks, armored desert cars—in use by the British army. And so forth— aircraft, cannon, machine guns and rifles, infantry, paratroops, commandos, overseas units. He was taught the names and shown grainy newspaper photographs of several high-ranking British generals, whose presence in Palestine might indicate the transfer of their divisions to the Middle East.

Early that morning, Müller had knocked on his door. Since he had moved into the room next to his, they were in each other's company most of the day. Müller was shaven, dressed, and apparently had been outside.

"Soon. All depends on weather conditions. Our Luftwaffe advisers have decided not to parachute your transmitter separately. We shall make a compact package of your radio, the book, and your personal effects, and strap it to your chest. You'll be more bulky and you might suffer some discomfort on landing, but on the other hand you will be spared the search for your second parachute in the fields in the middle of the night."

Fackenheim shrugged. He was rather apathetic about the technical details and accepted Müller's instructions without arguing. Still, he had a request to make. "I read in the Baedeker," he said, "that any immigrant into Palestine must prove that he has five hundred British pounds in his possession in order to be allowed to remain in the country. Can you provide me with that money?"

"That's a lot of money," Müller said thoughtfully, after having read the appropriate passage in the guidebook. "No other agent has ever received such a sum."

No other agent has ever been parachuted into Palestine, Fackenheim wanted to say, but he chose to keep silent.

"I'll check that," Müller promised. "Strangely enough, the chief likes you." He grinned. "Knowing you real well, I don't understand why. But he is quite a fan of yours, as I said, so I guess you've got a good chance of getting the money."

The following day, Müller brought him an envelope with 500 pounds in ten-pound bills.

Fackenheim was ready to depart. He had packed all his meager belongings into a suitcase that he would leave to the safeguard of the Abwehr, not knowing if he would ever get it back. In the evening, docilely following Müller's instructions, he removed the labels of the Belgian and Greek tailors from the clothes he would wear on his voyage.

The countdown had started. Any day could be D day now. He felt no urge to go out anymore and preferred to stay in his room. At night he couldn't sleep; and when he did, the old nightmares from Dachau and Brussels would mercilessly attack him as soon as he closed his eyes.

On October 10, Müller knocked on his door earlier than usual.

"It's for tonight. From now on, you're not allowed to leave the hotel. When everything is ready, I'll come for you."

For hours Fackenheim paced back and forth in his shabby hotel room, his heart torn by doubts and questions. The burden was too heavy for him. He was unable to decide if what he was doing was good or bad; if there existed any alternative; if he had any choice. What could he do in order not to betray his people? Perhaps, when he reached Palestine, he should go straight to the Jewish Agency, give himself up, and confess everything. Perhaps he should destroy his equipment, make his way to the farthest town, and start a new life under a new name as an illegal immigrant. But what about his mother? His word of honor? And could he betray his friends of the Abwehr? Didn't he owe them his life? The burden was too heavy, the decision too fateful for him to make. "What should I do?" he murmured in despair.

At the last moment he threw his gun in the suitcase he was leaving in Athens. He shouldn't carry a weapon on his mission. That could be too dangerous.

He didn't touch the trays of food an emaciated bellboy brought to his room. Late in the evening, Müller knocked on his door. He, too, was restless and high-strung. "The chief wanted to come in person to wish you good luck. But he had to leave town."

Fackenheim did not react. He didn't really care, not now.

"Your last instructions," Müller said, lighting another cigarette with quick, nervous gestures. "As soon as you land in Palestine, you must make your way to the city of Haifa. You have to find a room in a Jewish pension, or rent an apartment from a Jewish family. You'll tell them you're an illegal immigrant. They'll help you, they won't ask for papers, and they certainly won't report you to the authorities. Once you're organized, you'll call us by radio during our usual listening hours. Then you'll start your reconnaissance around Haifa. We know that the British army has built several large bases in the outskirts of the city. We want to know all about them: what kind of bases, exactly where they are located, how many men serve there, the quantities and types of vehicles, arms, and other equipment in each base, the names of the commanding officers, the numbers of the companies and regiments."

He paused a second. "Now, the roads. There are two main axes of military transportation from north to south, from the port of Haifa to Tel Aviv, and farther south to Cairo. There is the main highway starting at Haifa and going by Tel Aviv, Gaza, El Arish, and El Kantara, to Cairo; and the railroad, which follows approximately the same route. You must watch the traffic on the highway and the railroad daily, and report to us any movement of military units. Because it is impossible to be in two places at the same time, I am telling you already, before you ask: You're not to recruit any other agent. You'll work alone. I guess it will be easier and more efficient to watch the railway, since most of the British troops would be traveling south in special trains.

"At the beginning, you should concentrate on those objectives. Don't worry if you do not get a clear and complete picture immediately. It will take you some time to get your bearings. Later, when you will have gained experience and contacts, we'll ask you for more precise details about the British army over there."

At midnight, a military staff car stopped in front of the hotel. Fackenheim and Müller got into the vehicle, which smoothly drove away.

A half hour later, they reached the military airport of Phateron. Fackenheim drew back into the shadows as the car slowed down at the roadblocks and the air base gates. Müller had insisted that he conceal his face. No unauthorized people should get even a glimpse of him—not here and not tonight.

They got out of the car by the main runway. The night was cold, the sky clear and starry. A whispering wind gently swept the concrete runway. On a faraway hill loomed the black shape of the Parthenon.

On Paul's right, several mechanics were busy checking and refueling an aircraft under the dazzling glare of powerful floodlights. A cordon of armed German soldiers stood between the plane and the spot where the car had stopped. Nobody was allowed to pass near the car unless he carried a special pass. The plane was a Heinkel-111 bomber painted in black.

Paul saw several of the mechanics moving back; then the Heinkel engines coughed, caught, and, after an initial roar, droned. A sergeant of the Luftwaffe materialized beside him, carrying a parachute. "Will you come with me, mein Herr?" Paul followed him into a small hut, where the sergeant succinctly explained to him the functioning of the parachute. He was a young man, almost a boy, with candid brown eyes and a rebel forelock. A flight lieutenant, wearing air crew coveralls, crossed the room carrying a tray of sandwiches. Through the open door Paul saw him flash his pass, cross the army cordon, and climb into the plane.

"Any questions, sir?" He shook his head. The young sergeant bowed stiffly and was gone. Müller appeared at the door, beckoning him. They walked together on the runway, making a large detour in order not to be seen by the soldiers. Most of the mechanics had already left. By the glow of the floodlights Müller's face was pale and tense. He was chewing the tip of an unlit cigarette. "You'll be dropped over a sandy and deserted area, not far from the Haifa–Tel Aviv highway. You'll be able to reach the road in less than fifteen minutes." He tried to smile. "The weather report is good. Everything will work fine, you'll see."

The flight crew got into the plane. Paul was calm. He didn't feel any fear. In the Heinkel's shadow Müller shook his hand. His grip was vigorous, friendly.

"Good luck."

Paul leaned toward him. "My mother . . ."

"Count on us. She will be protected and taken care of."
The black aircraft took off into the night.

Deeply immersed in his thoughts, Fackenheim had lost
any notion of time. He was seated in a corner at the back
of the fuselage, wrapped in a blanket. His eyes closed, his
mind wandering, he was oblivious to what was going on
around him.

The gentle pressure of a hand on his shoulder made him
start and open his eyes. By the dim light inside the cabin he
could see the face of a young flight lieutenant. His face was
smooth and boyish. He looked like the sergeant at Phateron.
"Get ready," the lieutenant said.

He put on his parachute, checked the harness, snapped
the buckles shut. The lieutenant helped him, then thoroughly
checked the parachute. He nodded, satisfied. Paul raised his
hand to his shoulder and felt the handle that was supposed to
tear the parachute open. The leather straps dug into his flesh.
A sudden surge of panic stabbed his insides. What if the parachute didn't open?

He crawled clumsily to the middle of the cabin, where the
trap door was located. The lieutenant strapped to his chest
a voluminous canvas bag containing the radio, the codebook,
and some personal effects. The solid cord that the officer
had attached to the harness straps made him think of a hanging rope.

Suddenly there was silence. The pilot had cut off the engines and was gliding now in wide circles. The lieutenant
pointed toward a round porthole through which indistinct
shapes could be seen far below. "Haifa," he murmured.
"Here we are." Paul glimpsed the silvery reflection of the
moon in a gently rippling bay.

And all of a sudden they were at war. The Heinkel dived
and emptied its bays, releasing strings of bombs over Haifa.
Muted explosions thundered far below. A routine diversion.
The British were being led to believe that the black plane was

122 of the Almighty

on a bombing mission.

The anti-aircraft artillery responded immediately. Shells exploded around the plane, leaving white, wavering puffs of smoke hanging in the night sky. The pilot turned the engines on again, veered abruptly to the left, and dived southward. The young lieutenant ran down the cabin, squatted beside Paul, pulled a few bolts, and yanked at the trap door.

Fackenheim propped himself to sitting position on the edge of the black hole, his feet hanging in the void. A cold wind swirled around his ankles. He was numb and bewildered. He did not understand what was happening to him. But he suddenly realized that he had reached the point of no return. There was no way back for him now. He had to go ahead with his mission, come what may. The lieutenant stretched his hand toward him. Paul grabbed it with force, as if it were a lifebuoy.

The German slapped his shoulder.

"Raus!"

He jumped.

Part Two
NUMBER
64

X

Enter
SS General Koch

EIN UND ZWANZIG, zwei und zwanzig, drei und zwanzig . . ."

On his free fall from the plane, Fackenheim counted aloud as he had been instructed, then reached to his left shoulder and pulled the handle with all his strength. At once he felt as if some tremendous force, like a giant's hand, had grabbed him and stopped his fall. He was suspended in mid-air, his body swaying from side to side. Simultaneously he felt a sharp pull under his armpits and on the inner side of his thighs. He looked up. The beautiful, perfectly symmetrical canopy of the parachute floated above him, its round shape etched against a star-studded sky. The parachute had functioned flawlessly. A feeling of relief and elation overcame him.

Far to the north, the dazzling beams of the anti-aircraft searchlights were still sweeping the sky, and a couple of cannon were firing aimlessly. On the ground below, he noticed moving lights and a trailing wisp of smoke—probably a locomotive.

Paul felt a surge of triumph. He had been dropped successfully, the diversion had succeeded, nothing had gone wrong. He was about to land in a few seconds. Everything had worked according to plan.

Poor Paul Fackenheim! He could not know that his mission was doomed from its very beginning. He could not know that most units of the British army in the north of Palestine were on the alert, expecting his arrival. He could not know that he was the victim of a diabolic plot, a plot devised by the Nazi police in Berlin and Athens, and put in motion by Paul's new archenemy, the Hauptsturmführer Kronberg.

Kronberg was a ruthless fanatic. He had sworn to thwart Fackenheim's mission. In Athens he had tried to compromise Paul by sending agents to get him drunk and make him break the rules of secrecy. He had abruptly burst into Paul's room, hoping to scare him into backing away from his commitment and refusing to undertake his mission. Acting on instructions from his superiors, and with their wholehearted help, he had done all that he could to prevent Fackenheim's departure. He had failed. The Abwehr had foiled all his moves. Müller and the chief could both sigh with relief when the black Heinkel took off on its way to Palestine.

They had won a battle perhaps, but they had lost the war. Kronberg had been defeated in Athens, but he had not renounced his plans. "I'll get you at all costs!" he had screamed at Fackenheim in his hotel room. To get the damned Jew and the traitors of the Abwehr, Kronberg and his cronies hadn't hesitated to enlist the unwitting help of the enemy. They had decided to deliver "Herr Koch" to the British.

A few days before Fackenheim's flight to Palestine, a top-secret report reached British military intelligence in Cairo. It came from a mysterious informer in Athens and had been relayed by two agents, one in Greece and one in neutral Turkey. The report informed the chiefs of the MEIC—the Middle East Intelligence Center—that an important German spy was about to be parachuted near Haifa the first fortnight of October. The MEIC was the umbrella intelligence organization of the British army in the Middle East. The counter-espionage branch was the CSDIC—the Combined Services Detailed Interrogation Center. The report from Athens was analyzed meticulously and checked against other existing information. Army headquarters in Palestine was then instructed to take action.

The source in Athens was none other than Hauptsturm-

führer Kronberg.* Kronberg was determined to end an operation that would allow a Jew to escape unscathed from the
territory of the Reich. But such fanaticism played only a minor part in his motivation. Kronberg and his superiors were
sincerely convinced that the Abwehr was making a tragic
mistake, equivalent to an act of treason. They did not believe
for a single moment that Fackenheim really intended to spy
for Germany. They were certain that as soon as he reached
Palestine he would surrender to the British and reveal to them
all the details about his training, the names of his superiors,
the coding and decoding methods, the characteristics of the
equipment in use, and any other secrets he had learned about
the Abwehr. A Jew couldn't be trusted. Therefore, Kronberg
and his friends concluded that the best way to foil the operation would be to have the British arrest Fackenheim
immediately.

At first glance, that attitude seems inconsistent and utterly
contradictory. If Fackenheim were arrested following Kronberg's tip, he would talk anyway. He would disclose the
Abwehr secrets to the British. He would reveal his true identity. He would be thoroughly interrogated and then released,
or perhaps interned for only a few months.

Kronberg had thought of that, and had found a way of
killing two birds with one stone. He had figured out a way to
make Fackenheim's knowledge useless for the British while at
the same time making sure that he would be promptly
hanged as a dangerous enemy spy.

The plan of the gnomish SD chief was indeed worthy of
Machiavelli. It was a cunning ploy, based on devious logic.
The secret report that had been sent to British counterespionage in Cairo did not forecast the infiltration of an anonymous German spy. It gave his full name and position. It in-

*Some sources maintain that Kronberg not only delivered Fackenheim to the
British, but that he had been a British agent throughout the entire war. I could find
no evidence to support that theory.

formed the MEIC that the spy who would be dropped that night was the Obergruppenführer SS Koch, a general and a well-known dignitary of the Nazi regime in Germany.

Kronberg had made a shrewd use of Fackenheim's nom de guerre. An SS general named Koch did indeed exist: He was Erich Koch, who later became a Gauleiter and commissar of the Reich for the Ukraine. The British secret services were well aware of his existence. They knew of his strong Nazi convictions and his fanaticism. They knew that the Obergruppenführer Koch was reputed to maintain close links with the Gestapo in Berlin. By including the name and grade of General Koch in his tip to the British, Kronberg was throwing them a bait they were bound to swallow. He could anticipate that they wouldn't spare any effort to capture Koch.

SS generals weren't dropped every day over Palestine, or any other part of the British Empire. SS generals were not dispatched to carry out routine espionage missions either. For a general to be sent to enemy territory, the importance and the secrecy of the operation had to be of the highest order. General Koch could have been sent to Palestine for one of two reasons: to take control over an already established espionage and subversion network that could cause tremendous damage to the British in the Middle East; or to assume leadership over an Arab revolt that might be synchronized with simultaneous uprisings in the neighboring Arab countries.

The British knew well that the Arab cities and villages swarmed with Nazi sympathizers. Some well-known chieftains had escaped Palestine at the outbreak of the war and had made their way to Berlin, where they were trained in the hope they would rebel against the crown. At their head was the supreme religious leader of the Palestinian Muslims—Haj Amin el Husseini, Grand Mufti of Jerusalem. A fervent admirer of Germany and the Nazis, the Mufti had escaped from the British police dressed as a woman, crossed the border into Lebanon, taken part in the ill-fated pro-Nazi coup of Rashid

Ali in Iraq, then, disguised, sneaked across Iran and Turkey to Italy and finally reached Berlin. There he had solemnly promised the Fuehrer that the Arabs of the Middle East would soon revolt against England. His loyal supporters, who had followed him all the way to Germany, were preparing to infiltrate Palestine, assemble their followers, and rise up in arms with the help of German experts. Some of those experts were natives of Palestine, residents of the local German community who had fled to Berlin at the outbreak of the war. The rest were experienced officers who would assume command over the revolt.

The role of commander over the rebellion was one tailored for a Nazi and a general—and Obergruppenführer Koch could be the perfect choice. His mission, therefore, would seem logical from all viewpoints, and would confirm the worst fears of the British. Kronberg had every reason to expect that the British wouldn't rest before they had Koch securely behind bars.

Kronberg assumed that as soon as the British got hold of Koch, they would treat him as a general. They would question him about his contacts in Palestine, the projected uprising, the caches of weapons, the names of the Arab conspirators, the plans, the dates, the scale of the rebellion. The interrogators would concentrate on those matters, regarding them as a matter of life and death. Fackenheim, of course, would deny everything. The poor devil would claim he was Jewish, a former inmate of Dachau, with no contacts whatsoever in Palestine.

But who would believe him? And who would give credence to his confession and his "revelations" about the Abwehr, its codes and modus operandi? Who would ever believe he was small fry, sent to report on train movements? British intelligence would regard any such testimony by Paul Koch as phony, intended to divert them from the real goal of Erich Koch's mission. And Kronberg hoped that very soon the exasperated British counterespionage people would court-martial and hang Paul Ernst Fackenheim, convinced they were executing the SS General Koch, a fanatic Nazi, a master spy and a dangerous subversive leader.

Kronberg had hit the bull's-eye. British intelligence in Cairo behaved exactly as he had anticipated. Once the report about the imminent infiltration of Obergruppenführer Koch had reached the MEIC, a huge machinery was set in motion. Urgent measures were taken to apprehend Koch as soon as he touched ground. The military authorities in Palestine were immediately warned about the forthcoming drop. They were given no clue, however, about the identity of the German agent. Compartmentalization was of extreme necessity in this case. The identity of the German agent wasn't to be revealed before his interrogation and court-martial.

All over Palestine, infantry and armored units were placed on red alert. Reinforcements were hurriedly dispatched to the north of the country. Infantry companies were trucked to the Haifa region and directed to carefully selected positions. They were scattered on Mount Carmel, in the forests surrounding the city, along the coast, around the townships of Atlit and Zichron Ya'akov, and the Arab villages of Fureidis, Kurdani, and Tira. The areas northeast of Haifa were not covered, as they were hilly and strewn with rocks and therefore unfit for parachuting. Roadblocks were set up on the major highways and the entrances to Haifa were sealed.

Thousands of posters and tracts were distributed among the Arab population. They had been printed some time before to help stimulate the vigilance of the population against enemy spies and saboteurs. The illustrations on the tracts showed German paratroopers descending from the skies, on a background of Arab villages and mosques. In the picture, the paratroopers were wearing gloves and boots. They were armed with machine guns, and cartridge belts hung over their chests. On their backs they carried folding bicycles. The inscription under the picture was in Arabic and proclaimed:

> This is the fifth column.
> The life of the nation is in your hands.
> Hit them in their hearts!

It was signed "The Security Services." The British hadn't printed similar tracts in Hebrew. The Jewish population didn't need posters and tracts in order to increase its alert. It had its own account to settle with the Nazis.

On October 10, 1941, everything was ready. The huge trap was in place, ready to spring on the terrifying Nazi master spy who would fall from the sky. And straight into that trap, dangling from the shroud lines of his black parachute, came Paul Ernst Fackenheim, a wretched German Jew miraculously saved from the crematorium of Dachau.

Fackenheim's euphoria turned out to be premature. The first disaster struck him while he was still in the air. The rope that held the bag containing his personal effects and the Afu transmitter broke under the weight of the load. Paul frantically reached for it. Too late. The heavy bag slipped and disappeared in the darkness, crashing far below. In one second, Paul had lost everything—his belongings, his radio, the codebook, and even the small folding spade which was to help him bury his parachute.

He was about to land, going down at what seemed to him a terrifying speed. But even more terrifying was the landscape that took shape beneath him, bathed by a pale moonlight. He saw an asphalt road, congested with vehicles; a railroad, parallel to the highway; dark irregular shapes—trees and bushes—scattered on both sides of the road. He swore angrily. Was that the "flat, sandy terrain" that Müller had promised? Hadn't they reconnoitered the area before dispatching him?

He was a few feet from the ground now. He held his feet

together, raised his knees, and, as taught, pulled down the
two parachute risers. As his feet touched the ground, he
clumsily rolled to one side, but bumped against a hard obsta-
cle. He looked up. His roll had been stopped by a solid, sharp
rod planted in the ground. Around it snaked the stems of a
large-leafed plant. As his eyes got more used to the darkness,
he noticed similar bushes all around. And suddenly he realized what they were. He had landed in the very middle of a
vineyard. Were he less lucky, he might well have ended his
adventure impaled on one of those pointed stakes.

What really mattered, though, was that he was alive and
unharmed. He looked around him. He was still harnessed to
his parachute, which was entangled between the vines. A
light breeze billowed its canopy, making it look like a big
black sail. He released the master buckle of the parachute,
and gave some slack to the tight risers and lines. He collapsed
the chute, pulled the straps toward him, and managed to collect and fold the black silk fabric into a compact package.
The earth was moist. A small puddle had formed around the
vine, and some sticky mud had stained his trousers. He
couldn't tell if it had just rained or if the vineyard had been
irrigated.

When he started digging under the pole in order to bury
his parachute, he soon found that the moisture had stayed
only upon the ground. The soil was hard, dry, and unyielding. For more than an hour he clawed into it with his bare
hands, breaking his nails and sweating profusely. Finally he
buried the parachute, covering it with handfuls of mud and
leaves. On the nearby road, the heavy traffic of cars and
trucks did not stop. Once in a while, the piercing wail of a
siren could be heard in the distance. Much closer he could
hear shouts in English, and a few times he discerned shadows
moving at the vineyard's edge. There could be no doubt—the
British were looking for him. They must have seen the
parachute.

He knew it was useless and dangerous to go searching for

his bag in the dark. Even if he found it, the radio would have been shattered by the fall. His mission was therefore stillborn. He couldn't transmit a single message to Athens. A strange feeling of inner peace flooded his heart. He would not have to face the agonizing decision that had tortured him from the very start: Should he spy for the Abwehr? Should he collect military information and convey it to Athens? Until now he had been unable to make a clear decision, and had tried to bury the painful conflict in the farthest recesses of his mind. The accident that resulted in the loss of his radio might well have been a godsend, for he no longer had to make the hardest choice of his life.

But he had to get out of this mess. He was cold, hungry, and scared. He had lost everything. He had nothing left but the money. He had to hide now and in the morning try to reach Haifa. Carefully moving between the vine supports, he finally found a drier spot protected by a hillock. There he spent the rest of the night, his body jackknifed and shivering in the cold, his mind painfully aware of the symbolic way he, a Jew, was spending his first night as a free man, beyond Nazi reach, in the land of his ancestors. He was a hunted man again, pursued by armed soldiers, hiding like a beast, branded by the cursed fate of his people.

Shortly before dawn the traffic on the road ceased and a stillness descended upon the fields. He sank into an agitated, fitful sleep. When he woke up, the sun had risen in a vivid blue sky. He didn't budge, waiting for the right moment. After a while, he heard footsteps on the road. First it was a solitary figure, soon followed by small groups of people. They seemed to be Jewish, and were walking northward. Most of them were wearing khaki shirts and trousers. Some carried small parcels or shoulder bags. They appeared to be workers on their way to town.

Paul tried to make himself look more orderly. He cleaned his jacket, smoothed his shirt, and combed his hair. Among those khaki-clad men and women his suit would stick out rather conspicuously, but he had to try his luck. He waited till the highway was deserted again, then slipped out of the vineyard. When he got to the road he took the same direction as the others.

Some minutes later he was already in the middle of a thickening crowd that converged toward a big bus station beside the road. Nobody seemed to pay any attention to his haggard appearance. He felt more confident. Perhaps he could get to Haifa, change his money, and escape, across Syria and neutral Turkey, to Greece. If he managed to reach Athens and contact the Abwehr, his mother would be safe.

But all of a sudden he stopped in his tracks. A few hundred yards ahead a military roadblock had been set up. British military policemen, wearing red caps, brass-buckled chalk-white belts, and holstered guns, carefully examined the workers' papers. Some of them were watching the moving throng, stopping suspicious-looking men and taking them aside for a short interrogation. Paul hesitated. He couldn't go back now. It was too late.

On his left, he saw a young Jew with a frank, honest face. He looked reliable. Paul approached him. "Do you speak German?" he asked.

The young man smiled. "Yes, I do."

"I need help. I am a refugee from Germany. I landed on the coast last night. I came over in a boat."

The smile of the Palestinian broadened. He seemed well aware of these illegal immigrants who reached the shores of the Promised Land night after night, hoping to slip through the British net. He realized that getting past the British navy patrols and coastal guard was only a first step; the second was to evade the searches, the roadblocks, the dragnet operations of the British inside the country.

"What will they do to me if they capture me?" Fackenheim asked.

"If you're lucky, they'll intern you in a detention camp

right here in Palestine." The young man spoke an adequate German, but his accent was strong and hard. Paul assumed he must have immigrated from a central European country. "If you're not lucky, they'll send you to a camp out of the country. Quite a lot of people have been transferred to Cyprus lately."

They were approaching the line of buses and the road-block. "Listen, I have no papers," Paul said in a low voice. "Can you help me reach Haifa?"

"I can try."

The young man looked at him thoughtfully. "Do you carry any compromising papers or documents, anything pointing out that you're an illegal? The red caps might search you."

"Who?"

The Palestinian smiled nervously. "We call the military police 'red caps.' Did you hear my question?"

Paul shrugged. "I've got five hundred British pounds. I wanted to go to the bank and . . ."

"You must be out of your mind. You'll be arrested immediately. Didn't they tell you that in Palestine nobody is allowed to keep British currency? Give it to me, quick. They won't search me."

Fackenheim slipped the wad of bills into the Palestinian's hand. The young man placed his hand on Paul's shoulder and steered him toward the roadblock, animatedly speaking in Hebrew. Paul didn't understand a word, but kept nodding and smiling. The young man led Fackenheim confidently through the roadblock and toward the buses. The military policemen watched indifferently as the two friends walked by and didn't bother to check their papers.

The Palestinian bought two tickets from the bus driver. Then they walked to the rear of the vehicle. "You should know who I am," the young man said, and took out of his pocket an identity card which he showed Paul. The text was in English, Hebrew, and Arabic. Paul took a quick glance at the stranger's name—Rosenbaum or Rosenberg, he wasn't sure.

The bus set on its way. It was a crisp, sunny morning and the countryside looked pleasant and bright, the limpid Mediterranean air enhancing the sharp colors of the scenery. On the left, close to the road, blue waves lapped an unspoiled beach. On the right, Mount Carmel sloped gently toward the coast, its green forest still shrouded in morning shadow. They crossed a long narrow alleyway bordered by tall palm trees, and sped past a big Arab village whose round-domed houses clustered around a sturdy minaret. Many walls and fences were painted in blue. "Against the evil eye," the young man explained. After the bus made several stops, the road took a sharp turn and suddenly, in front of them, they saw Haifa. Its neat houses rose along the Carmel slopes, bathed in lush greenery, their immaculate whiteness gleaming in the rays of the rising sun. A magnificent golden dome sparkled in the sunshine high up in the mountain, topping a white temple surrounded by colorful gardens. "The Baha'i Temple," Paul's companion pointed out.

"We have to get off at the next stop," the young man said. "I am a male nurse in the hospital right here. You'll wait for me outside. I'll tell my boss that I am taking the day off. He'll let me go, I'm sure—he'd like me to assist you. Then we'll go downtown to the offices of the Jewish Agency. They'll help."

Paul followed the young man out of the bus and stayed in the street while the Palestinian hurried into the hospital building. Except for a few cars that drove up the street and into the parking lot of the hospital, the place was deserted. Very few pedestrians could be seen on the sidewalks.

Paul leaned on a wall in the shade, waiting. Ten minutes passed, then another ten, then another. The young man still had not come back. What if he doesn't return? he thought, slightly alarmed. He didn't know the boy. He could be a swindler who had taken off with his money. Five hundred pounds was a lot of money.

Two elderly people walked past him, speaking softly; then a young woman with a little boy. She wore a flowery dress and had long blond hair and a radiant smile. He heard her laughing, joined by the happy giggle of the child. Those were Jews, he suddenly realized. And the workers who had traveled on the bus with him were Jewish too. They didn't have to fear concentration camps and crematoriums. But they certainly didn't know what was happening to their brothers over there in Europe, otherwise they wouldn't be so calm. Once again he felt a frustrating sense of helplessness, an urgent need to tell, to warn, to scream aloud. But he couldn't tell anybody about Dachau, not yet. In an hour, maybe less, when he got to the Jewish Agency, he would finally be able to speak, and expose his horrid secret.

Two military policemen emerged at the street corner. They walked slowly, systematically stopping every passerby and checking his or her papers. The blond mother with the child had stopped laughing and was digging in her bag now, searching for her papers. Paul felt a surge of panic. He had to get away from here. He couldn't stand in the street, waiting for them to come. He turned the other way and casually started walking, leaving the hospital behind him. He could return there later and inquire about the young man. He kept walking for a few hundred yards, when he saw right in front of him three other red caps. They were walking toward him, also stopping everybody and checking papers.

He was trapped. The two military policemen behind him were quite close now, and the three in front would reach him in a moment. There seemed to be no way out.

On his right he saw a British military barracks. It was surrounded by a high fence topped with barbed wire. The large gate was quite close, its pillars decorated with the emblems of various army units. A guard wearing the insignia of a "corporal of horses" was walking back and forth in front of the entrance. He carried a stick topped with a silver ball. His sallow face was embellished by a huge, flamboyant red mustache.

Fackenheim threw a last look around. The street was totally deserted now, and he was caught between the two red caps' patrols. He couldn't wait any longer.

He suddenly had an idea. It might be crazy, but it could work. Anyway, it was his only chance. He turned sharply and hurried toward the gate of the British camp. The corporal of horses blocked his way, watching him with puzzled, pale blue eyes.

"I want to see your commander," Fackenheim stammered in English.

XI

The Spy with the Thousand Faces

CAPTAIN ARTHUR DOWDEN was a Scot. He was tall and slim, with broad shoulders, an open face, and sharp brown eyes. He sported a bushy mustache that always sheltered a crooked briar pipe. Before the war, Arthur Dowden had been pursuing a promising diplomatic career in the British Foreign Office. As a junior officer he had served in various European cities before being appointed to his last civilian job as vice-consul of Great Britain in Frankfurt. Along with his official functions, he had been entrusted with some discreet, less-publicized activities: rescuing persecuted German Jews, and collecting political and military intelligence.

At the outset of the war, Dowden had returned to England, enlisted in the army, and joined the MI-16, a special section of British counterespionage. He had spent more than a year and a half in London working at interrogation, research, and analysis. For the last three months he had been in Palestine, and had set up an MI-16 unit that worked in close contact with the CSDIC in Cairo. Dowden used as his official cover the position of recreation officer in the "Fun and Games" department of the army, but it could hardly fool anyone. The abundance of able, intelligent, and closemouthed officers in Fun and Games was such that their real occupation was a secret to no one. Every British officer realized those smart lads did not spend their time worrying about cricket tournaments and dart championships. Even the few genuine Fun and Games officers were thought to be masquerading spymasters.

That morning, standing by the large window of a beautiful villa at Stella Maris, on the very top of Mount Carmel, Dowden was contemplating a sight of breathtaking beauty. Before him lay the splendid Haifa bay, surrounded by gently sloping green hills. The port was full of supply ships, cruisers, and battleships. To the north he could see the giant shapes of the oil refineries, two concrete towers resembling colossal hourglasses. And far away, at the bay's edge, rose the impregnable ramparts of Acre, which had withstood the assaults of Napoleon's army.

Dowden was not stationed at Stella Maris. His office and the permanent base of his organization was in the Jewish village of Rehovot, south of Tel Aviv. Rehovot was a peaceful town, surrounded by orange orchards. It was close to the huge army base of Sarafand, a veritable military metropolis. But a few days earlier Dowden had been instructed to be ready to come to Haifa at immediate notice. He was told that according to certain information, the parachuting of one or several German agents was to be expected. They were to be dropped in the north of the country. Those reports had been given validity by a sudden increase of Luftwaffe flights in that area of the Mediterranean. For several nights now, unidentified planes—probably German—had overflown Haifa and its surroundings at low altitude. They had dropped bombs on only one occasion. The incursions had been rather short. It seemed that the Germans were building some routine pattern that would enable them to use one of those nightly flights for dropping their spies.

That morning the telephone had rang in his office at Rehovot. "Report to Stella Maris on the double," he had been told. "We got the German spy."

It had been a long trip—up to Tel Aviv, then along the coast, past the cities of Natanya and Hadera. He had just arrived, shortly before noon. Standing by a large window that offered a serene image of the city and its harbor, he was

listening absently to the detailed, tiresome report of a younger officer about the capture of the spy.

He turned around, slightly impatient. "Bring him over,"
he said.

The door opened and a man walked in, escorted by two
soldiers. He was of medium height, dressed in a crumpled,
mud-stained suit. He looked frightened.

"Guten Tag," Dowden said civilly. He was fluent in
German. "I was told a fantastic story about you, but my officers aren't sure they have really understood what you've told
them. So we shall have to start that conversation all over
again. But first of all I'd like to know: Who are you?"

"My name is . . . Koch, Paul Koch," the prisoner said
after a short hesitation. He raised his eyes and for the first
time examined Dowden's face. Dowden was taken aback
as he saw a look of immense surprise in the prisoner's brown
eyes.

"Lieber Gott!" the man said. "But that's you! How are
you, Mr. Dowden?"

Fackenheim's plan had almost worked. Almost.

Trying to get away from the red caps, he had decided to
throw himself straight into the devil's mouth: get into the military camp under some pretext and stay there till the disper-
sion of the military patrols combing the city for him. The idea
was brilliant; but to carry it out successfully, he had to know
how to bluff his way in and out of the camp. Fackenheim had
no such talent.

It had started well, though. He had been taken by the
corporal of horses to a junior officer, then transferred to
higher authorities till he had finally been put into the office of
the barracks' commander, a young captain. Paul had repeated to him the same story he had told the other officers.
He was Jewish, a refugee from Europe. He had disembarked
that very night on the beach, not far from Haifa. His name

was Paul Koch. But he had no papers and didn't want to be arrested by the police. Would the captain be so good as to tell him where he should register and get the appropriate identity papers?

The captain, flabbergasted, thought he was dealing with a madman. The real refugees knew, of course, that their one and only enemy in Palestine was the British army. If they were lucky enough to reach Palestine without being apprehended by British patrols, they would hide for months and maybe even years in the most remote corners of the land, fearing the sight of a British uniform. And here was this lunatic, who not only came to surrender to the British, but also politely asked them for an identity card. The man could not be a refugee. "Go to hell!" he had roared, and ordered him thrown out of the camp at once. Exactly as Fackenheim had hoped he would.

But after a moment the captain had had a second thought. Was the man really a lunatic? It was worth checking. He had picked up the telephone and called headquarters. Yes, they said, there was a dragnet operation going on in the city. Yes, they were looking for someone. Not a refugee. A spy, a German. He had parachuted last night south of Haifa from the same German plane that had bombed the city.

The captain had got up from his chair and buckled his belt. It carried a heavy revolver in its regulation holster. He approached Fackenheim. His eyes glittered with new interest.

"You say you're a refugee," he repeated thoughtfully. Fackenheim nodded.

"Tell me," the officer said. "How did you soil your clothes?" With his fingertips he rubbed the stains of dried mud spread all over his visitor's jacket.

"I told you that I came over in a fisherman's boat, and . . ."

"Yes, of course." The captain's voice was heavy with irony. "And that boat was apparently full of mud. But wouldn't you rather talk to me about the German aircraft that visited us last night? No ? What a pity."

He turned toward the corporal who stood by the door. "Get the car. We'll take this rare bird to headquarters. It seems that some people there would be delighted to make his acquaintance."

The staff car climbed to the top of Mount Carmel and stopped before a big house topped with an extraordinary array of antennae: the British army headquarters. The young captain disappeared into one of the offices, leaving Fackenheim in the middle of a large hall full of soldiers. It seemed to be the guardroom. Many British "Tommies" were sitting on their cots, talking, drinking, smoking. A few were cleaning their rifles. The news about Fackenheim must have traveled fast, because his entrance created quite a commotion. After the excited whispers had faded away, Fackenheim found refuge by the far wall. He felt the looks of the Tommies converging on him. Still, there was no hostility in their eyes, only curiosity.

One of the soldiers came to him, carrying a tall, steaming mug.

"Hello, Jerry, have a tea!" he said in English.

Another one slapped his back. "Hello, Jerry, have a cigarette!"

Jerry? Why that nickname? Fackenheim didn't know yet that the game was practically over. He had been unmasked by the British and they knew exactly who he was. "Jerry" was the familiar sobriquet by which the British used to designate their Teutonic enemies.

And now, a couple of hours later, he stood in the small office, facing Captain Dowden.

"I know you well!" Fackenheim exulted. He felt as if he had found a close old friend, and for a moment it seemed to him that all his troubles were over. "I know you from Frankfurt-on-Main, Mr. Dowden. You must remember. You were the British vice-consul, and I had come to apply for a visa. For my mother. Don't you recall?"

Dowden was watching him attentively, but didn't answer right away. He took some time lighting his pipe. His face was blank, impassive, but to Fackenheim he seemed puzzled.

"Now listen to me," he said. "I belong to the intelligence service. If you tell me the truth, I'll try to help you. I mean what I say. Therefore, before you start speaking, I ask you to give the matter some thought. Only the truth can save your life."

He lapsed into silence for a moment, then repeated his first question. "Who are you?"

"But Mr. Dowden," Fackenheim mumbled, "don't you remember me? From Frankfurt?"

Dowden shook his head. "I am afraid not," he said. "I was vice-consul in Frankfurt before the war, that's correct. But even if what you say is true, I couldn't possibly remember all the people who came to see me." He paused again. "You didn't answer me. Who are you?"

This time, Paul's answer was different from the one he had given the officer who had brought him over. "My name is Paul Ernst Fackenheim. I am Jewish, and my home is in Frankfurt. The Abwehr gave me the code name of Paul Koch."

He had decided to cooperate with Dowden and tell him the truth. After the tremendous tensions of the previous night and that morning, the sight of a familiar face triggered in him a sensation of overwhelming relief. He was determined to convince Dowden that he was telling the truth. Dowden could save him, he could vouch for him. Paul could remind him of quite a few details connected with their interview at the consulate, and Dowden wouldn't deny any longer that they had met in Frankfurt.

Fackenheim described in detail what happened in Dachau, his release, his recruitment by the Abwehr, his sojourn in Brussels, the visit to Berlin, and his departure from

Athens. But while he was speaking, gradually calming down, he felt a resurgence of loyalty toward his friends of the Abwehr. They had treated him as a comrade, they had trusted and protected him—he couldn't betray them. He held a few things back. He didn't breathe a word about his training in Brussels and Athens; he refrained from mentioning the codebook, *L'Âne Culotte,* which rested now somewhere in the Carmel vineyards; he abstained from revealing the code of his transmissions. "This is the newest and the most secret of the German radio codes," Müller had told him. He knew that by revealing the code he might endanger the lives of thousands of German soldiers. And he was a German. A Jew and an anti-Nazi, true, but still a German.

These voluntary omissions didn't escape Dowden's attention.

"What's your call-word?"

"I forgot it."

Dowden nodded his head pensively. "You forgot it, did you?"

The experts of MI-16 had no trouble remedying the unfortunate lapse of his memory. He was ordered to pass into another room, where he was told to undress. His body, his mouth, his hair, even his anus were meticulously examined, inch by inch. He was finally authorized to put on a khaki shirt and a pair of trousers. Dowden's assistants systematically went through his clothes and shoes. They found the two strips of paper with the code word "ORTM-37" sewn in the lining of his jacket sleeve and in his shoe.*

He was sent back to Dowden's office, where the captain and two other officers fired a hail of questions at him. "How were you trained? What was the purpose of your mission? What kind of information were you supposed to collect? Who

---

*Paul Fackenheim maintained in later statements that he had handed the two strips of paper to the British of his own will. But on this point I'd rather take the word of the intelligence service, according to Captain Dowden's testimony.

were your superiors in the Abwehr? Did they give you any
safe-house addresses in Palestine? Where are the Abwehr
headquarters in Brussels and Athens?"

To most of these questions, Fackenheim did not reply.
Partly because he did not want to betray his comrades, but
mostly because he did not know the answers. Except for
Müller, Braun, and the chief, he had not met any Abwehr
officials. He did not know if German espionage had other
agents in Palestine. He knew of no spy ring, no contacts, no
safe-house addresses. And he had never been admitted into
Abwehr headquarters, neither in Brussels nor in Athens.

The wretched prisoner was also torn between a desire to
come clean with the British and a desire to keep his word of
honor to the chief in Athens. He was determined to justify his
friends' trust, to prove that a Jew, even in that terrible situation, could still remain a loyal German. And he knew well
that his mother's life might depend on his behavior. If the
Germans found out in a day or a week that their newest radio
code had been broken, they would know that Fackenheim
had betrayed it. And Hedda Fackenheim would be sent to the
crematorium.

But Paul's silences only raised doubts in Dowden's mind
about the credibility of his story. Could he be who he said he
was? If the man didn't lie, if he was indeed Jewish, if he had
lived through the hell of Dachau, would he deliberately ab-
stain from delivering to Hitler's enemies the secrets of Nazi
espionage?

"You refuse to reveal certain matters," Dowden said to
Paul. "Perhaps you don't want to, but perhaps you really
can't. As far as your identity is concerned, we have no proof
whatsoever, except your word. You might indeed be Jewish,
and what you say about Frankfurt might be true, even if I do
not remember you. But you could just as well be a Nazi fanatic. There are a lot of Aryans who could be mistaken for
Jews. Like our friend Goebbels, for example. . . ."

Dowden ordered Fackenheim's clothes to be given back to

him. Then he drove him himself, escorted by another jeep, to the place where Fackenheim had landed and buried his parachute. They found the parachute but the bag that Fackenheim had lost during his fall was still missing. They searched the vineyard until late afternoon. Fackenheim was exhausted. Except for some tea and a handful of biscuits he hadn't eaten anything.

Dowden turned to him. "Listen, it's getting late. Come, let's go to my house. We'll talk later."

Amazed, Fackenheim followed Dowden to his jeep. Inviting a spy to one's own house, the very day of his capture, seemed to him a rather odd gesture, especially for a Scottish officer of the British army.

Paul was looked after almost as a guest in Dowden's villa in Rehovot. The house was surrounded by a tall fence, and an armed sentry kept permanent watch by the door to Paul's room. Nevertheless, he did not feel like a prisoner. He was well treated by Dowden and received the same food as him.

He spent three days in Dowden's house, and had several long conversations with the Scottish captain. He added no new details to his initial statement. Meanwhile, British special forces had carefully searched the area where he had been parachuted; in the vineyards they had finally found his personal belongings and the unusual codebook in French. They had not found the bag with the radio, however, and that made Dowden and his assistants even more suspicious of Fackenheim. Their logical assumption was that he had hidden the radio or that it had been collected by some local contact of his shortly after he had parachuted.

A team of MI-16 experts interrogated Paul over and over again, returning to the same questions: "What is your code? Where is the radio?" As Paul did not yield any new information, Dowden tried to reason with him. He patiently explained to his prisoner that he would run a great danger if he persisted in his silence. But his efforts were in vain. Paul stubbornly stuck to his first deposition, without changing a single word. In spite of his sympathy for Dowden, he was still deeply suspicious of the British. Not only were they the enemies of Germany, but their treatment of the Palestinian Jews and of the Jewish refugees from Europe revolted him. He knew that a Jewish underground was quite active against the British in Palestine. He had read about the discriminatory laws the British authorities were applying to smother Jewish immigration and settlement in Palestine. He considered the regulations forbidding Jews to buy land in many parts of Palestine to be similar to some of the anti-Jewish laws approved by the Nazi Reichstag. And if the Jews in Palestine staunchly opposed the British, how could he become a British informer, or a double agent?

But Arthur Dowden was a man of subtle and sharp perception. In spite of Fackenheim's silences and the lack of evidence, he quickly reached the conclusion that Fackenheim was indeed who he claimed to be—a second-rate spy, an agent of no real importance, and a Jew. During his work for MI-16 in England, Dowden had become familiar with the Abwehr practice of dropping badly trained agents in enemy territory, condemning them knowingly to capture, even death, but assuming that their short-lived activity was worth the sacrifice. Fackenheim was one of those, and Dowden quickly lost interest in him. Years later he would say to me, "Fackenheim wasn't important. Had he not been so stubborn and had he told me everything frankly and honestly, I would have released him in a fortnight. But he kept silent. And finally, Cairo got impatient."

Dowden was undoubtedly sincere. Still, in retrospect we can say that even if Fackenheim had fully cooperated with MI-16 and revealed all he knew, he wouldn't have been released. For Cairo was not motivated only by impatience, as Dowden thought. Unlike Dowden, Cairo didn't believe that Fackenheim was small fry. Cairo was convinced that Fackenheim was the SS General Koch. If Dowden could provide tangible proof that Fackenheim was only a desperate Jewish refugee from the Dachau crematorium, the CSDIC would have left him in peace. But Dowden could provide no such proof. At that particular moment nobody could. And the chiefs of British counterespionage in Cairo interpreted Fackenheim's behavior as confirming their suspicions and exposing his true identity: a Nazi master spy, a man of repugnant cynicism, who hadn't hesitated to arrogate the identity of a miserable Jewish prisoner.

That belief fit in with the shameful British propaganda in the United States that tried to justify the sealing of the gates of Palestine to Jewish refugees fleeing the Nazi hell. The British Information Services were diffusing pamphlets and brochures in government and press circles in America, claiming that the illegal immigration into Palestine was directed by the Gestapo. "Many of the German immigrants," the brochures said, "are disguised Nazis who intend to establish espionage networks in the Middle East." That accusation was base and revolting. Yet, Fackenheim seemed to be living proof that it wasn't totally false.

Three days after his capture, Fackenheim was summoned to Dowden's office. The captain seemed tense, sullen. "I've got bad news for you. Our Haifa headquarters did inform Cairo that we captured a spy. The Cairo Middle East headquarters just ordered us by cable to send you there. Tomorrow morning you're leaving with a special plane."

The next morning, when he was about to be driven to the airfield, Fackenheim turned to the captain. "Could you do something for me?"

Dowden was cautious. "If it's in my power, yes."

"Please have a news item released to the press. It should say that the British found the body of a German who had been parachuted near Haifa. That would make the Abwehr assume that I've been killed, and they would keep looking after my mother."

"I'll try," Dowden said, noncommittally.

Escorted by two armed guards and an officer, Paul Fackenheim was flown to Cairo. Had he revealed all he knew in spite of his concern for his mother and his pledge to the Abwehr, Dowden would have intervened in his favor.

Not that it would have helped. For Dowden didn't know that a most extraordinary coincidence had occurred, plunging the CSDIC in Cairo into a state of unprecedented turmoil. A strange, ironical whim of fate had metamorphosed Paul Fackenheim into an arch-villain—in the opinion of British intelligence. He was bound for a long and perilous ordeal that could lead him straight to the gallows.

Since the fall of France, the Middle East Intelligence Center, based in Cairo, had been closely watching the activities of German espionage in Syria and Lebanon. Under the Vichy government those two countries had become centers for Abwehr activity in the Middle East. British agents shadowed Rudolf Roser, who was the chief agent of the Abwehr in Syria and Lebanon. He operated mostly from Beirut. They also collected information about his most active agents.

On top of their list, since autumn of 1940, was a woman. She was a former matron of the Moslem Hospital in Beirut. A "Most Secret" intelligence summary, dated January 23, 1941, quoted an "independent source" as confirming that the mysterious woman "was working for Rudolf Roser." A second report, dated February 3, 1941, revealed that the woman was now employed in the Swiss consulate in Beirut. That made her even more suspicious, as the Swiss consul himself was believed to be an Abwehr agent. The woman in question was maintaining contact with the wife of a Paul Marcopoli, of Aleppo, a known Italian agent. A third intelligence summary, dated two weeks later, spoke again of the suspect woman. She had made contact with Mukhtar Mukayish and Abdullah Mashruk, "two German sympathizers in Beirut, on behalf of Rudolf Roser."

In May 1941, still another Most Secret report described the woman's visit to Aleppo together with Rudolf Roser and two other Germans "to supervise arrangements for the arrival of German aircraft and personnel, and to meet pro-German leaders from the Jazirah." In those days, Germany was engaged in a last-ditch effort to thwart the fall of the Levant to the Allies. Even after the conquest of Syria and Lebanon by the British and the Free French in June and July, the suspected woman continued to haunt British intelligence. In intelligence reports of September, October, and November of 1941, her movements were diligently reported but she could not be arrested, probably because of her official position at the Swiss consulate. Nevertheless, the British intelligence organizations regarded her as one of the main Abwehr agents in the Middle East.

The woman's name was . . . Paula Koch.

It was too much of a coincidence. According to certain espionage techniques, people belonging to the same spy ring are often identified by the same names. When British intelligence, which was stalking every move of the dangerous Paula Koch, learned of the capture of Paul Koch, they concluded that he was either Paula's chief or her immediate subordinate—in either case, a dangerous German spy.

But there was much more. Another enigmatic figure operating with Roser in Syria and Lebanon was a German colonel. The two men had visited the village of Dir as Zor, and according to a Most Secret MEIC report dated March 13, 1941, the colonel had used the aliases of Von Haner and Fritz Otto. The colonel and his close assistants continued to operate in Beirut after its liberation by the British. On September 25, 1941, an intelligence summary quoted a Turkish source reporting that ten German agents were still at large in Beirut. One of them was a Major Klevonken, and one Helmut Linken. The mort important, though, was the colonel who had been working with Roser. That colonel was supposedly very active in creating a fifth column in Syria and Lebanon, intended to help the Germans in their designs on the Middle East.

Klevonken and the colonel were even more slippery and mysterious than Paula Koch. They were reported in various locations in Syria and Lebanon but never captured. A top-secret document at the end of September quoted witnesses who had seen them in the Anti-Lebanon. Their presence was also reported in the Turkish port of Alexandretta. Actually their movements were so secret that at the beginning of October the analysts of the Staff Intelligence Middle East organization (SIME) reached the conclusion that those elusive Pimpernels might not even exist!

"These men are probably nonexistent," the SIME report said about Klevonken and the colonel, "but recently their names have come up again in a fairly circumstantial context, and the possibility that they may have remained until recently in hiding in Syria cannot be entirely excluded. It has been reported that the organization consists of some ten Germans who were recently in the neighborhood of Beirut. It was stated on 22.9.41 that they have now withdrawn to the Anti-Lebanon, and that Klevonken himself has gone to Hatay.

"One report coupled with them the name of Helmut Linken, a Sudeten German who was employed by the Germans as a W/T [wireless transmitter] operator before the Allied occupation. This man was recently interned in Syria, and SIME has asked that he should be interrogated on his knowledge of the colonel and Klevonken."

The report went on to detail the suspected activities of several other Germans, Arabs, and even a Russo-Armenian, who were all said to belong to the organization headed by the German colonel.

The name of the colonel was Falkenheim.

Could that be a coincidence too? Or was it proof of the

existence of an arch-villain, a spymaster with a thousand faces, who had fallen into the hands of the MI-16 by a lucky twist of fate? At the beginning of his interrogation that man had said his name was Paul Koch—a name almost identical to that of a most dangerous spy in Beirut. Questioned further, he had admitted that his true name was Fackenheim—almost identical to the name of a spooky colonel, considered extremely dangerous, who was so shrewd in covering his trail that a major branch of British intelligence had expressed doubts as to his very existence. A man bearing both names of two Abwehr spies seemed the personification of danger. And just to add more mystery, the Colonel Falkenheim was said to be linked with a wireless operator, Helmut Linken, who had worked for the Germans in Syria. And Paul Koch-Fackenheim had admitted parachuting with an Afu transmitter, which was nowhere to be found.

Those extraordinary coincidences were never revealed to Paul Fackenheim. He never knew during his interrogations that he was suspected of being the vanished Colonel Falkenheim or the right hand of the energetic Paula Koch. Only forty years later did the author of this book gain access to the secret reports and summaries of the SIME and the MEIC in London. And only then did he understand how that structure of suspicions, fears, and accusations had turned into a scaffold from which Paul Fackenheim could have easily tripped at the end of a hangman's rope.

XII

The Trap

THE SPECIAL PLANE, dispatched from Cairo, took off from a small airfield in the outskirts of Ramla, a picturesque Arab city not far from Rehovot. From the plane window Paul watched the extraordinary landscape through which his forefathers, led by Moses and Joshua, had made their way from Egypt three millenniums ago. The coastal plain of the Promised Land with the ancient Palestine cities of Ashdod, Ashkelon, and Gaza. The sandy wasteland of Sinai, its desertic monotony broken only by the palm groves along the seashore and the dark rocky mountains looming far in the south in a haze of smoldering air. Then the narrow waterway of Suez, which joined the Red Sea at the point where the Hebrews had presumably crossed and the Egyptians perished. The majestic river Nile, in whose reedy shallows Pharaoh's daughter had found the infant Moses. And finally the ageless pyramids dominating the teeming city of Cairo, the same pyramids the ancient Hebrews had seen dawn after dawn while they slaved for their Egyptian masters.

Paul was emotionally moved by this reverse journey into the past of his people. But he was brutally brought back to reality as he got off the plane at Cairo-West military airfield. A morose reception committee was waiting for him on the runway—a lieutenant and four tough-looking red caps. Their jeeps sped across Cairo, sirens screaming to clear a passage among the multitudes of fellaheen in turbans and long cotton robes. They stopped briefly at the British army headquarters, at the Semiramis Hotel, but Paul was gruffly ordered to stay in the jeep while the lieutenant dashed up the steps. Then they proceeded across the Nile to the Interrogation Center in the large prisoners' camp at Maadi, in the outskirts of Cairo. A gloomy sense of déjà vu pervaded Paul as the jeep went through several gates and barriers and he saw the armed sentries, the watchtowers, and the barbed-wire fences. Was it starting all over again?

"Get down! Quick march!" The moment he got out of the jeep, a towering sergeant materialized behind him and kicked him in the ass. Gone were the civil manners of Captain Dowden. He almost ran to the low administration building, escorted by two soldiers pointing their bayoneted rifles at him. Hunted by the sergeant, who took a sadistic pleasure in kicking him, he was pushed into an empty room.

"Take off your clothes." Once again the degrading examination. Hair, mouth, pubic hair, anus. Although he had been captured four days before, the British still suspected that he had concealed some papers or a minuscule device on his body.

His clothes were gone. A squat, freckled corporal threw at his feet a khaki shirt, shorts, a pair of socks, and canvas shoes. In the neighboring room he was photographed and his thumbprints were taken.

"Quick march!"

His cell was quite spacious, furnished with a bed, a table, a couple of chairs. There were bars on the window, and an armed guard kept watch by his door. The sergeant who had shown such enthusiasm for kicking his behind now carefully placed a tray on his table. The food was copious and excellent.

He had barely finished his meal when the sergeant was back, roaring again. "Get up! Quick march!" He was shoved into a big, dark room. In front of him, on a two-foot high platform, stood a desk covered with papers and documents. Behind the desk was seated an officer with red-blond hair. He was freshly shaven, clad in an impeccable uniform; he threw a fierce look at Fackenheim, while absently playing with his officer's stick. His revolver had been placed beside his elbow. Paul noticed a huge Union Jack flag pinned to the wall. A lamp hanging directly over Paul blinded him with its powerful light. The lighting, the platform, the flag, the gun, the ferocious eyes of the officer—Paul thought this a well-staged theater scene, intended to make him feel small, exposed, and defenseless.

"Wie heissen Sie? What is your name?" the officer shouted in German. His accent was excellent.

"Paul Fackenheim."

"Don't lie to me. I know well who you are. Lying won't get you anywhere."

"If you know," Paul retorted, also losing his cool, "why do you ask?"

"You'll be sorry for your insolence." The officer slapped his stick on the table. "You're going to tell the truth, or else it's curtains for you. People like you should be liquidated, and the sooner the better!"

He pressed a button. The guards burst into the room. Shouting, waving their weapons, they drove Fackenheim back to his cell, kicking him en route.

Barely a minute had passed when the door of the cell opened again. An orderly entered and put a big mug of strong, sweet tea on the table. He was followed by a young, slim officer with bushy blond hair and a frank, blushing face.

"My name is Lieutenant Hull," he said to Paul. "I am a sort of social assistant to the prisoners and I am in charge of their welfare and their rights. I must make sure that you are treated correctly. May I do something for you?"

Fackenheim was at a loss. He had trouble adjusting to this abrupt change in the behavior of his jailers. "May I have some cigarettes?" he finally asked.

Hull handed him a package of Players. "Keep it. You are also entitled to a daily ration of bananas and other fruit. I'll come to see you every day."

A few minutes later another visitor entered Fackenheim's

cell. It was the red-haired officer who had interrogated him. One of the sentries had told Paul that his name was Major Tilly. Paul could hardly recognize him: The man was suave, affable. He sat on the cot beside Fackenheim and smiled at him.

"Let's have a gentleman's talk. You cannot deny, after all, that you've been sent over here as a German spy. How long have you been in Palestine?"

"A few days. I surrendered to the British army because I didn't want to serve the Germans." That was a lie, but Paul knew it couldn't be easily dismissed.

"That's what you're saying, but how can you prove it? I believe that you've been in Palestine for quite a while now. You're lying to us. Last week you scattered your affairs in the fields and you dug out your parachute from its hiding place to make us believe that you've just arrived in the country. But you made a mistake. You gave your radio to another agent. If not, we would have found it. Believe me, we searched the area thoroughly. We explored the vineyards inch by inch. Your radio cannot be found. For a very simple reason—it never was there."

Tilly paused, then continued in the same civil, patient tone. "There is more than that. You pretend to have parachuted from a German plane. But you should know that when your parachute opens, the harness straps dig into your flesh and leave visible marks on your skin. Our doctors have examined your body in Haifa, in Rehovot, and here. You don't carry any marks. As for myself, I believe that you were dropped here quite a while ago, and now you have decided to surrender for a reason known only by you."

Tilly wasn't bluffing. The report about Paula Koch and the mysterious Falkenheim had made him assume, logically, that Paul had been spying in the north of Palestine for a long time. One possibility was that he had obtained and transmitted vital information about the counteroffensive against Rommel that was to start in November. Then, by destroying or concealing his radio and surrendering to the British troops as if he had just landed, he could lull them into assuming that their secrets were safe and the only spy who could get access to their plans was behind bars. Slowly, cautiously, Tilly was trying to break his prisoner by pointing at the inconsistencies in his story. "And then there is the money," he went on. "I can't believe that they sent you over with fifty Palestinian pounds in your pocket. Didn't you have any other funds?"

Fackenheim had fallen into his own trap. He hadn't told Dowden about the 500 pounds he had entrusted to the young Palestinian. Now he couldn't retract his initial statement. He doubted if the British would believe him. On the other hand, 500 pounds was a lot of money. The British might be led to believe that he was indeed a very important spy, as they were repeating time after time.

"That's all I had," he said. "I had been told in Athens that when . . . when I'd run out of money, I shall be contacted by somebody who'll get me some more."

Tilly got up, shaking his head. "You're lying. And I know well that you're not the man you pretend to be, Herr . . . Koch!"

If the Maadi investigators needed proof that Fackenheim was actually a Nazi, they were soon to get it. That very evening, Tilly returned to Paul's cell, accompanied by a captain—a pale, fat, middle-aged officer who looked awkward in his ill-fitting uniform. They greeted Fackenheim like old friends and started an informal conversation. Bit by bit, the captain steered the discussion toward the war and its real causes.

"The whole thing is Germany's fault," he said. "She is ruthless and bloodthirsty. She simulated the Polish attack on the Gleiwitz radio station in order to have a pretext for the aggression against Poland."

The very mention of Gleiwitz made Paul shiver. Yet, his Prussian upbringing made him protest. "You can't deny that the real cause of the conflict was the humiliation of Germany at the end of the First World War. When the war ended you shoved that accursed treaty of Versailles down our throats. You took Danzig away from us. And Danzig is a German city. You gave the Danzig corridor to the Poles, to cut our access to the city. And you also robbed us of Alsace-Lorraine. Alsace-Lorraine isn't French. Even its population doesn't speak French, but their own dialect."

He continued. "And even the First World War—was it our fault? Of course not. Those crazy Serbian terrorists started a campaign of murder and sabotage, and ended up assassinating the crown prince of Austria. Now, how do you think Austria should have reacted? Should she have tolerated such barbaric crimes? Naturally, she demanded from Serbia formal guarantees that such outrages would never happen again. Austria-Hungary was absolutely justified to behave the way she did. And now Germany, with her rights on Danzig . . ."

The two officers exchanged looks. Everything seemed clear now. They had succeeded in irritating this Nazi, and here he was, expounding his imperialistic nonsense. A Jew would never speak that way.

Thus, gradually, inexorably, the grotesque misapprehension was taking shape. Fackenheim had refrained from revealing his code, his contacts, the addresses of the Abwehr centers in Europe, the secrets of his training. His radio set had disappeared. He preached expansionist German theories. He had first admitted that his name was Paul Koch. Therefore he could be the chief or assistant of Paula Koch. He could be the elusive Falkenheim. And most likely of all, he could be the elusive General Koch. He had popped up in Haifa while winds of upheaval were sweeping the Arab nations, as sheiks and chieftains flocked to Berlin, begging for help and arms for their rebellion against Britain. He had emerged in the open a few weeks before the largest counteroffensive against Rommel was about to be launched. What more proof did

Tilly and his colleagues need to become convinced that they were indeed holding a high-ranking Nazi?

The interrogations went on and on. Every day Paul's British captors would devise a new method to make him talk. One morning the guards would take away all his clothes, remove the furniture, take down even the glass panes of the windows, and leave him nude in the cell, shivering with cold and humiliation. The next morning everything would shift back to normal. He would receive laundered and freshly pressed clothes. The guards would talk to him respectfully and would rush to his cell special trays of food from the officers' mess.

It was the stick and carrot, from early morning till late night. A new day would start with "Quick march!" and kicks in the ass; at lunchtime, smiles, jokes, and fine food; in the afternoon, Tilly's black room, blinding lights in Paul's eyes, the major threatening, yelling, swishing his stick and brandishing his gun, then the guards pushing and shoving with their bayoneted rifles; and in the evening the same Tilly knocking on his cell door, asking permission to visit him, coming in with a big bottle of Chianti wine. They would spend the night drinking as if they were the best of buddies—and jolly old Tilly would narrate nostalgic tales from Berlin, or describe the glorious times when he was spying against the Nazis, posing as a textile importer.

But all that ended in failure. Days, then weeks passed by, and Fackenheim didn't talk. On the contrary, exasperated by the threats, the humiliations, and the blows, Paul grew more stubborn. *Those Englishmen,* he said to himself, *aren't better than the Nazis after all. Let them do to me whatever they want. I shall not give them the satisfaction of breaking down.*

His attitude infuriated the superior officers of the Combined Services Detailed Interrogation Center. A main function of this branch of British intelligence was the interrogation of secret agents and prisoners of war who were captured and dispatched to Maadi from all over the Middle East.

The D day for their upcoming November offensive against Rommel approaching, the British felt they had to crack Fackenheim's silence without delay.

But they chose the wrong approach. If only once they had shown Fackenheim some trust and compassion; if only once they had treated him as a lonely man, afflicted by a cruel destiny—a wretched, desperate Jew, shaken by the Dachau nightmare, trembling for his mother's life; if only once they had behaved toward him with a little warmth and understanding, he would have surrendered, he would have told them all he knew. That was how he felt, and many times, when he was alone at night, he made up his mind to present a full confession. But as the new day came, and the brutal sergeant savagely kicked his ass all the way to the black room, and Tilly started yelling and rattling his revolver, he would grind his teeth and glare back, unyielding. He wouldn't bow to threats and degradation. He wouldn't talk to them.

Still, Major Tilly would not admit defeat. He was as stubborn and as determined as his prisoner. He firmly believed that sooner or later, Fackenheim would slip and make a mistake. And then he would crush him.

Tilly was right. An old hand in that devious game, he knew how to outsmart his prisoner. He only needed the proper timing and the right bait—and Fackenheim would go for it.

In Maadi, Fackenheim was isolated from the other prisoners. Only rarely did he catch a glimpse of another inmate of the camp. One of the guards had told him that quite a few prisoners of war were kept in Maadi. They had been captured in Libya and Cyrenaica during the last few months. But Fackenheim was unable to communicate with them. Even when he went out for his daily stroll in the open air, he would be taken into a small inner court, surrounded by barbed wire. The British were determined to keep their super-spy totally cut from the outside world.

Yet on an early November morning, his guard told him, while escorting him to his "private" court, "Today you have company. We've got too many prisoners in the camp and not enough guards. You'll have to share your private domain with another fellow. He is a Jerry like you. Enjoy yourself."

The German was a likeable blond man in his mid-thirties. He was wearing the khaki uniform of the camp prisoners. Paul recognized in his speech the thick accent of Cologne. "My name is Rudolf," the man said.

Fackenheim was exhilarated by this opportunity to talk to somebody. "How did you get here?" he asked.

"I was a sergeant in the reconnaissance unit of the Afrika Korps. We were on a long-range patrol and drove straight into a British ambush. I was badly wounded and taken prisoner. I woke up in the hospital, surrounded by doctors and armed guards." He chuckled. "They were certain that I knew all of Rommel's secrets, and right away transferred me to this stable. You might have noticed that the camp is exclusively reserved for spies and special agents. Then they started getting nasty."

"The black room?"

The sergeant nodded. "The whip and the gun of his red-haired excellence," he said mockingly. "After a while, though, they realized that I wasn't such a big shot after all, and I couldn't be of much use to them. So they decided to get rid of me. They had nothing to lose, you see—I am not fit to fight anymore because of my wounds. So I am going to be repatriated via Switzerland in exchange for a British POW. You can't imagine how happy I am to be going home. The war is over for me."

Fackenheim sighed. "I envy you." He had heard of this method of exchanging prisoners, and the sincere joy of the young sergeant inspired confidence.

Back in his cell, his thoughts kept returning to his meeting with Rudolf. An idea slowly took shape in his mind. His new German friend could be of invaluable service to him, and relieve him of the obsession that had haunted him since his capture. Having received no sign of life from him, the Abwehr might assume that he had betrayed his mission, and that could mean a death warrant for Hedda Fackenheim. Dowden had promised to try to insert an item about his death in the papers. But that hadn't been done, as far as he knew. For weeks now he had been raking his brains to find a way of communicating with the Abwehr and informing his superiors that he hadn't betrayed them.

And here was a German on his way back home. Wasn't that a godsend?

Thus Fackenheim walked straight into the trap set by Tilly.

The next morning, he again met Sergeant Rudolf in the court. "I must ask you for a service," he said in low voice. "As soon as you're back in Germany, you must get in touch with the Abwehr in Berlin, on Tirpitz Quay. Ask to speak to any officer who deals with the Middle East. Tell them that you've met me at Maadi. Tell them also that you talked to me, and that I had been captured by the British but it hadn't been my fault. They must know that I'll try to escape at the first opportunity. Tell them you've been entrusted with this message by a man named Koch."

The sergeant listened, frowning. He seemed to hesitate, but after having given it some thought, he nodded approval. "All right. I'll be back in Germany in four weeks. You can rest assured. I'll deliver your message."

They continued pacing in silence, but Rudolf suddenly stopped, shaking his head. "No," he said. "It won't work. Your message doesn't prove anything. As far as the Abwehr is concerned, you might have gone over to the British, and you're using me to dispel their doubts while you actually work hand in hand with the British. I have a better idea. Can you give me a password or a written letter, something only they can understand, so that those gentlemen from Berlin wouldn't doubt the authenticity of the message?"

Fackenheim took his time before answering. "No," he finally said. "That would be too dangerous. For me and for you as well. If somebody intercepted that letter we'd both be in big trouble."

But later in his cell he had an idea. He grabbed a sheet of paper and a pencil. His guards were supplying him with stationery, perhaps on explicit orders of their superiors. Then he plunged into a pile of soldiers' magazines, full of photographs of naked girls. The guards were slipping him some of these publications once in a while, doubtlessly trying to cater to his spiritual needs.

He put himself to work. A couple of hours later, he put down his pencil and allowed himself to admire the results of his travail. He had before him a rather amateurish drawing of a naked girl playing with a poodle. The girl, whose voluptuous curves he had copied shamelessly from the magazine, was seated on an oriental sofa. By the open window behind her one could see a few houses and a mosque. The window carried an inscription in capital letters: KAIRO.

Two diaphanous curtains hung from the ceiling in the background of the drawing. At first sight, they seemed to be ordinary lace curtains. The effect of lace was created by tiny points and dashes forming intermittent lines that descended from the ceiling downward. Only after a minute examination of the drawing would an observer see that the lines were drawn in such a way as to form signs of the Morse alphabet. Once decoded, the signs would become a garbled, completely unintelligible jumble of letters. But after they were cut down in blocks and arranged according to the grille Paul had learned to design, they would produce a clear message:

"Bin erwischt Hoffe wegzukommen Koch."

Which meant, "I was caught, I hope to escape, Koch."

The next morning, Paul slipped the paper in the hand of his new friend. "That's a drawing," he murmured. "Don't conceal it. Carry it openly between the papers in your wallet.

There is nothing more natural than a war prisoner carrying sketches of nude women in his pockets."

"Good," Rudolf said, adding cheerfully, "I'm leaving tomorrow." They shook hands warmly. As they parted, Rudolf turned back and called, "I wish you a successful escape, comrade!"

Fackenheim went to his cell, his spirits soaring. In the hall, he passed Major Tilly. The red-haired officer cast him a strange look, a mixture of such hatred and triumph that he felt a sudden tremor run through his body.

At four A.M. somebody brutally shook him awake.

"Get up!" Armed soldiers stood around his bed.

"Get dressed, on the double!" the sergeant barked. Paul buttoned his shirt with trembling fingers, under a stream of shouts and insults.

Outside the cell, Major Tilly was waiting. His face was sealed and cold.

"This way."

In the deserted courtyard, a jeep was parked, its engine humming, the driver at the wheel.

"Get in!"

The jeep dashed across the sleeping camp, crossing several barriers and leaving the prison compound behind. Soon they were alone on a narrow road, heading into the desert. A little while later they were swallowed by a sea of yellow sand stretching in all directions. No living soul could be seen. They drove in silence for about a half hour.

"Stop here!" Tilly ordered. He got out of the jeep. Fackenheim followed. Tilly left the road and walked straight into the sand. Fackenheim mopped his brow. Dark premonitions filled his head.

"Over here. Turn back!" Tilly said.

Behind a dune stood six British soldiers, clasping their rifles. An NCO jumped to attention and saluted the major.

"All is ready, sir."

Fackenheim blanched. Now he finally understood. He had been betrayed. The German sergeant, the good friendly Rudolf, was nothing but a stool pigeon, planted by the British with the purpose of gaining his confidence and making him slip. Rudolf had succeeded. The British undoubtedly had intercepted his message to the Abwehr. That was the proof they needed against him. And now they must have decided to eliminate him, swiftly and discreetly.

Fackenheim stood alone before the soldiers. Tilly stepped aside. As he turned to face the squad, Paul noticed a rock about fifty yards behind him. Its surface glowed with an eerie golden light, as the sun rose slowly over the desert.

The NCO gave an order. The soldiers raised their rifles. This was the end, he thought, and straightened up.

At least, he said to himself, *die like a man.*

XIII

The Night of the General

AT LEAST die like a man.

Trying to conceal his trembling, he straightened up, sticking his chin forward. His mouth was dry, and a lump had settled in his throat, almost choking him. But as he stood in the sand, facing the firing squad, feeling Tilly's eyes boring into his face, he was overcome by a single desire: not to break down, not to give them the pleasure of seeing him beg for his life.

Bracing himself, he turned toward Tilly and said in a cool, stable voice, "If you have decided to shoot me, I would have preferred to be told in advance. I don't appreciate surprises."

There was a second of silence. Maybe his last, he thought.

And then, unexpectedly, Tilly burst out laughing. His laughter was loud, forced, artificial.

"What the hell are you talking about?" Tilly feigned amused indignation. "I brought you over here to show you the pyramids at sunrise. From this place the view is splendid, absolutely splendid, old boy."

He nonchalantly dismissed the armed squad. The NCO froze, straight as a ramrod. "Left turn! Quick march!"

And all of a sudden they were alone. Fackenheim felt dizzy and off balance. His knees seemed made of cotton. The specter of death had vanished as if dispelled by a magic wand. He clumsily waded in the sand after Tilly, who was again his most affable best, the perfect English gentleman, proud to show a distinguished guest the marvels of his domain. He offered his arm to Paul to help him climb on top of the dune. Paul refused his help and worked his way up alone. Sweat was running down his face. If Tilly's intention had been to submit him to shock treatment by means of the mock execution in the desert, he had fully succeeded.

From the top of the dune, the view was breathtaking. But the prisoner had no breath left. He kept seeing the six soldiers pointing their rifles at him. Never before, not even in Dachau, had he felt death so near, so immediate.

They rode back to Maadi in silence. In his cell, Fackenheim devoured his breakfast with a ferocious appetite. He couldn't remember ever enjoying a meal so much as this morning.

His troubles weren't over, though. The interrogations went on, Tilly becoming more and more impatient. Finally, after all other means had failed, the CSDIC experts decided to bring Fackenheim's case before the highest authority.

"Get up!"

This time he was awakened in the middle of the night. In the crude light of the bare electric bulb hanging from the ceiling, he made out the puffy features and the bloodshot eyes of the huge guard sergeant. Behind him stood the two sentries, carrying rifles and bayonets. He dressed hurriedly. The tall sergeant, whom the soldiers had nicknamed Lofty because of his height and width, seemed particularly tense. The kick in the ass arrived with the punctuality of a Swiss clock. Then the quick march through the dimly lit corridors, toward the black room. The door opened, and he was shoved forward to the center of the vast chamber.

The black room wasn't black tonight. It was brightly lit, and almost unrecognizable. He was taken aback by the multitude of khaki uniforms, some of them adorned with insignia of high rank. Major Tilly wasn't seated at his usual place on the platform. He stood among the crowd of officers forming a half circle around their commander, a tall, meager soldier whose cap was adorned with a general's red band. He was wearing khaki shorts and a short-sleeved shirt, with brand-new leather belts as straps. Paul noticed his thin legs and bony knees. He recognized him at once, as his photograph often made the front page of the newspapers. The man was the highest ranking British officer in Egypt: General Sir Claude John Auchinleck, commander in chief of the British forces in the Middle East.

The general took one step toward him. Paul discerned deep hostility in his cold blue eyes. They really did believe he was a master spy, Paul concluded, otherwise why would they honor him with such a visit?

There was a minute of tense silence, then Tilly spoke. "The general will ask you a few questions. Till now, you have lied to us. In your interest, I advise you to tell us the whole truth."

General Auchinleck had a hard voice with a metallic ring. "Who is the chief of the German espionage network in Palestine?" He paused briefly, then went on. "What is his address? Where are the secret airfields behind our lines, used for the transport of German agents?"

"I don't know," Paul said. Major Tilly had spoken about the absence of marks, made by parachute straps, on his body. Perhaps they believed that he hadn't jumped, but landed in a secret airfield in Palestine.

Auchinleck was watching him with a deep frown. Paul saw the anger building in the tightly pressed lips and the slit eyes.

After more silence, Auchinleck said, "I give you six days. If you don't talk by then, you will be shot. As a spy, you're not under the protection of the law."

Before Paul even opened his mouth, Tilly motioned to the guards, and they were upon him. "Quick march!" Lofty bellowed. The two soldiers pushed him toward the door. The kick in the bottom signified that his audience with the commander in chief was over.

In his cell, Paul undressed quickly and fell asleep almost at once. He had grown used to these threats. Even the well-staged, dramatic appearance of Auchinleck left him cold.

He could not tell how long he'd been asleep. It could have been five minutes or an hour. He awoke again to the sound of Lofty's shouting "Get up! Quick!"

They chased him again to the interrogation room. The generals and colonels were still there. Paul had the impression that nobody had budged since he had left the room.

Auchinleck, too, had kept the same position. Watching Paul closely, he repeated the questions he had asked before, then added, "I give you three days." His voice trembled with fury.

"If you decide not to talk, in three days we'll kill you." He didn't say "execute," but "kill."

"Okay," Fackenheim murmured, but the guards were already dragging him toward the door. Lofty yelled at him all along the way to his cell, but Fackenheim failed to understand. Auchinleck's words still rang in his ears: "We'll kill you."

This time in bed, he didn't even manage to close his eyes. The guards were all over him again, shouting and kicking. Third act. The corridor, the room, the blinding lights, the Union Jack on the wall, the superior officers, the furious face of the commander in chief of the British army in the Middle East.

"It's three o'clock in the morning," Auchinleck roared. "That's your last chance. I give you three hours. At six o'clock you will be shot!"

Fackenheim couldn't take it anymore. He knew he was lost anyway, and nothing could save him. He shouted back at the general, "Why don't you bring the bloody firing squad immediately?"

Auchinleck started. His face colored with anger. "Out!" he yelled.

When the door of the cell finally clanged behind him, he

collapsed on his cot. He was desperate. Those people would never believe he was really the Jew Paul Fackenheim. They would gladly shoot him as the Nazi Koch. And there was nothing he could do.

He hadn't even noticed that the door had opened again. His good Samaritan, Lieutenant Hull, sat down beside him. His face looked grave. He touched Paul's forearm and said softly, "You should know that in the British army we never execute a man without a trial and a verdict according to the law."

Fackenheim didn't answer. But he felt a surge of immense relief. It had all been a game, then. Tilly's promenade in the desert, and Auchinleck's dramatic appearance. They were just trying to make him break down and talk.

"Take a cigarette," Hull said. There was something shy, almost apologetic in his smile. "I believe that tonight you also deserve a nightcap."

He took a silver-colored flask from his back pocket and left it on the table. "I'll come for it tomorrow."

Fackenheim didn't sleep anymore that night. But nobody came for him at six o'clock.

Major Tilly did not capitulate. He made one last try.

He had left Fackenheim in peace for a couple of days, following the memorable night of the general. Now he peeked into the cell, concern painted all over his face. "Tell me, Koch, were you vaccinated before coming over?"

"Yes. Against yellow fever, cholera, smallpox . . ."

"And what about black fever?"

"Is that a disease? I've never heard about it."

"Of course it is a disease, and a pretty deadly one, too. We just got a new serum against it. It works miracles. We decided to inoculate you, just to be on the safe side."

Fackenheim didn't believe a word. The very mention of a vaccination rang an alarm bell in his mind. In Dachau he had heard the rumors about the Gestapo using injections of poison to discreetly eliminate political dissidents. Maybe the British had chosen that way to get rid of him, without bothering about a trial. Hull wouldn't even know.

The next morning, Tilly made a brief appearance in the cell. "In a half hour the doctor will come over to give you your shot."

Fackenheim erupted. "Now listen to me. If you have decided to liquidate me that way, tell me. I want to at least write a few words to my mother before I die."

Tilly stared at him blankly. "If I were you," he finally said, "I would have written that letter long ago. One can never know."

He went out. A few minutes later, a corporal he had never seen before brought him some paper and an envelope. Was this another trick? Another ploy to make him talk? Or maybe Tilly was serious this time?

Tense and nervous, he barely managed to scribble a few lines:

Dear Mother,
When you receive this letter, I shall probably be dead. Be strong.
This had to happen sooner or later. You must know that I love you dearly and wish you well.
Paul.

The doctor was a handsome young man, wearing an officer's uniform. He was escorted by an elderly sergeant who carried a medical kit.

Lying on his cot, Fackenheim watched the sergeant prepare the injection. He broke a vial and plunged the hypodermic needle inside. The syringe filled with a transparent, colorless liquid.

Fackenheim turned to the physician. "I must ask you something. You are a doctor. Are you going to give me a shot of poison?"

The young officer looked at him, stupefied. He seemed about to say something, but changed his mind. Silently, he rolled up his patient's sleeve and felt for his vein. He finally shrugged, and looked up. "I am a doctor, not a murderer. This injection will make you talk. And tell the truth."

It was not poison, therefore, but a truth serum. After all other means had failed, Tilly had turned to drugs.

The needle penetrated his flesh. A strange warmth spread all over his body. He felt himself sinking, drowning, and finally collapsed into heavy sleep.

He woke up after a half hour. A guard had just entered the cell, and was quietly placing a mug of scented tea on the table beside him.

Had he talked? And what had he said? Tilly stood at the door, sullen, furious. The English had failed to learn anything new.

Tilly was quitting.

"Get ready. Tomorrow you're leaving."

"Where to?"

"You'll know when you get there."

The Maadi ordeal was over.

The next morning, the Eighth British Army, 100,000 men strong, supported by 1,000 aircraft and 800 tanks, thrust into Libya under the command of Lieutenant General Sir Alan Cunningham. Operation "Crusader" was to disengage Tobruk from Rommel's siege and inflict heavy casualties upon the Afrika Korps. Some of the bloodiest fighting took place on Totensonntag, the Sunday of the Dead—November 23. That day Cunningham was replaced in his command by General Sir Neil Ritchie, on orders of Auchinleck.

In spite of some brilliant fighting by his armor, Rommel finally had to abandon Tobruk and order a general retreat, which took him back more than 300 miles in one month. One of the main reasons for Rommel's failure to repel the British offensive was the lack of reliable intelligence about the enemy. Rommel had returned to his Libyan headquarters the very day of the British attack, after a two-week vacation with his wife in Rome and a pleasant meeting with Mussolini on November 15, the day of Rommel's fiftieth birthday.

Till the last moment, British headquarters in Cairo feared that Rommel might be tipped off by the Abwehr intelligence network in Egypt and Palestien.

But the Abwehr failed, and in spite of some fragmentary reports that filtered through the border, Crusader came to Rommel as a complete surprise.

Fackenheim's silence, therefore, did not conceal advance knowledge of British plans. Once his interrogators in Maadi realized that, their immediate interest in him waned and he was cast on the next leg of his grim odyssey.

XIV

Kennen Sie Dieser Mann?

AT EMMAUS, in the Jerusalem foothills, Jesus Christ appeared before his disciples for the first time after his resurrection. Here assembled the huge Seleucid armies of Antiochus before their defeat by the legendary Jewish rebel Judah Maccabee in 165 B.C. Here camped the Fifth Roman legion before storming Jerusalem and drowning in blood the Jewish rebellion against Caesar in 70 A.D. Here converged the Arab tribes that had set out to conquer Palestine in 639 A.D. And at that same emplacement the British army had now established one of its camps and shrouded it in a veil of secrecy. The compound consisted of a few long, low wooden barracks, several small houses of rough Jerusalem stone, a score of large khaki-colored tents—all protected by sentries, watchtowers, and barbed-wire fences.

Less than two miles away, amid olive groves and vineyards, the peaceful Trappist monastery of Latrun offered its immaculate walls to the sun. On the gently sloping pasturelands of the fertile Ayalon valley the flocks of sheep seemed to have emerged straight from the Song of Solomon. Joshua had stood on one of those hills during the battle for the conquest of Israel by the Hebrews, and had ordered, "Sun stand thou still upon Gibeon; and thou, Moon, in the valley of Ayalon." And he had routed the five kings who had fought against the twelve tribes of Israel, and liberated the Promised Land.

This landscape of lush hills and shaded valleys, unspoiled heartland of the Bible, was the view that Paul Fackenheim would contemplate during the entire winter. He might have even enjoyed it in other circumstances. But between insults, kicks in the ass, rifles pointed at him night and day, a fence of barbed wire, and a wall of hatred, he was hardly inclined to savor the beauty of his ancient homeland.

On arriving, he had discovered that he was the only prisoner in the camp. That special honor was certainly due to the unshaken faith of his captors that he was indeed an important Nazi spy. That was also the firm belief of the camp staff. He was received with a mixture of apprehension, caution, and curiosity, as if he were a captive wild beast. And like a wild beast he was locked in a cage made of barbed wire that formed an enclosure of nine by eighteen feet. In one corner, the soldiers had put up a tiny scout's tent where he was supposed to sleep.

During the day, he was free to walk in his domain. Facing his cage, and only a few yards away, stood a watchtower that had been built specially for him. An armed sentry watched him round the clock. Other guards patrolled around his cage. He had been formally ordered to keep away from the barbed-wire fence. "If you come closer than one yard, we'll shoot without warning." At night, an entire platoon would be positioned around the enclosure, and powerful floodlights would converge on his tiny tent. No effort was spared, and no precaution neglected, to thwart any escape attempt of the dangerous spymaster.

Paul spent three months at the Latrun camp. He was totally isolated from the outside world. The interrogation was over: Nobody asked him any more questions, threatened him with death, or even tried to induce him to talk. He didn't see any other prisoners in the camp except when half a dozen Luftwaffe pilots and paratroops, captured in Libya, were transferred temporarily to Latrun. Even then, he saw them every morning from afar, and was forbidden to exchange a word with them.

His only friend was Strauss. Strauss was the camp's interpreter and had the right to move, unrestricted, around the compound. He was a German Jew who had immigrated to Palestine before the war. Strauss was twenty-five years old, he lived in Tel Aviv, and he sincerely believed that Fackenheim was a Jew like him. Often, Strauss would come to see his fellow Jew and talk to him about the Zionist ideas, the pioneers, the return of the Jews to the land, the determination of the Jewish community to establish an independent state in the land of Israel. He would explain, somewhat apologetically, that he had joined the British in order to combat Hitler. But once the war was over, the Jews would drive the British out of the country. Several resistance movements already existed, he confided to Paul, and they awaited the right time to start their combat. The Hagana, the biggest, was one of them. But Strauss was more fascinated by the extremists, the Stern terrorist organization. "Those guys are real heroes," Strauss said.

Strauss might have been less enthralled by the Stern heroes had he known what was to become public many years later. Driven by their fanatical hatred of the British and their determination to chase them out of the country, the leaders of the Stern group had gone as far as offering to establish an alliance with Nazi Germany. In January 1941 they had even dispatched to Beirut a secret envoy, Naftali Lubinchik, who met the Abwehr agent Roser (the same Roser who was the case officer of Paula Koch and Colonel Falkenheim) and the representative of the German Foreign Ministry, von Hentig. Lubinchik brought with him a draft proposal for an agreement between the Stern group and the Third Reich. According to official German records, the Stern organization declared that it was disposed to help the Reich conquer Palestine by launching an armed revolt against Great Britain. Germany, then, had to lend its assistance to the establishment of a Jewish state in Palestine and facilitate the transfer of European Jews to that state. The Stern chiefs went as far as to emphasize that the accord had an ideological basis, since both

movements, the Stern and the Nazi party, had similar views
on nationalism and totalitarianism.

Roser and von Hentig had listened attentively to Lubinchik's proposals and had conveyed them to the Reich's em-
bassy in Ankara. One of them, however, told the Jewish emissary that his project was quite interesting, but that for the
moment Germany hadn't decided yet what its policy toward
the Jews was going to be: expulsion from its Lebensraum or
total annihilation. The stunned emissary was arrested by the
Vichy authorities, expelled from Lebanon to Palestine, and
incarcerated by the British in the fortress of Acre. The sorry
episode at least proved that as far as the Third Reich was
concerned, Fackenheim wasn't the only one who was naive.

In the middle of December 1941, Fackenheim's living
conditions improved drastically. Without being given any explanation, he was transferred to a stone house where he had
his own toilet and shower. Once again, trays laden with excellent food started arriving from the officers' mess. At
Christmas Eve, a gargantuan dinner was served to him: roast
turkey, a huge bowl of pudding, a bottle of whiskey.

One morning in February 1942, his friend Strauss shook
him awake. "You're leaving today. For Jerusalem."

Handcuffed, escorted by an impressive outfit of red caps,
he was driven to the military prison of the Holy City: the
52nd Detention Barracks, a compound of tawny buildings
sprawled on the crest of a barren hill overlooking Jerusalem.
The guards led him through narrow corridors smelling of dis-
infectant and into a spacious cell.

"This is our guest suite," the lance corporal of the guard
chuckled. He was a clear-eyed, heavy-boned Scot.

"What do you mean?"

"This cell is reserved for choice prisoners—inveterate
criminals, assassins, and spies like you."

"Thanks for the compliment," Paul said wearily.

The lunch was delicious. "You should know that you're

getting your food from the staff kitchen," the lance corporal said. "The other prisoners aren't as spoiled as you."

"Whom should I thank for this special attention?"

"Come on, don't try to be a wise guy. You are being treated according to your military rank."

What rank were they talking about? Fackenheim knew nobody believed he was Jewish. But no one had told him, till now, that for the intelligence service he was SS General Koch.

That same afternoon, the prison sergeant major brought him a typewritten document.

"Sign the receipt, down here."

The document was an indictment. It was drawn over the name of Koch. The man named Koch was informed that he was going to be court-martialed. The charges: war crimes and espionage. The indictment was rather laconic. It stated that Koch had been parachuted in British territory on a mission of espionage for Germany. He had falsely claimed he was a Jewish illegal immigrant and had surrendered only with the purpose of gaining the confidence of high-placed officials. He had intended to escape after having achieved access to secret documents and maps.

The next morning an unknown man entered Paul's cell. He was an officer, but he wasn't wearing the insignia of his rank on his worn-out, crumpled trench coat. Paul was told later by one of the guards that his name was O'Shaughnessy. He had piercing blue eyes, an open face, a stubborn chin. He shook Paul's hand and smiled.

"I am going to be your attorney," he said. He had a strong Irish accent. "I have been appointed to assume your defense. Tell me your story."

He took off his trench coat. Under it he was wearing an impeccable uniform adorned with captain's bars. He was about forty years old. Fackenheim watched him suspiciously.

"How can I know this is not another ruse you're using to make me talk?"

The Irishman shrugged, unruffled by the question. "I can give you my word of honor of a British officer. I can add that in civil life I am an attorney, and for a long time I have served as a public prosecutor. I believe that you're in good hands." He grinned. "I don't think you know our laws well enough. I can promise you that you will be treated with equity and without prejudice. You'll get a fair trial."

Fackenheim told him his story, sticking to the basic points of his first deposition.

"I saw your file," the attorney said. "There is a primary point that we should make clear. The intelligence service doesn't believe that you are the Jew Paul Fackenheim. The prosecutor doesn't believe it either. They are convinced that you are somebody else, and they are confident they can prove it. We must destroy that accusation. The only way we can do that is by establishing your identity beyond any possible doubt. We need somebody who could formally identify you. Do you have in Palestine any friends or relatives who can swear in court that they know you, and that you are indeed Fackenheim?"

"Yes, I have an uncle, Karl Fackenheim. I don't know where he lives. I haven't seen him for more than twenty years. I don't even know if he is still alive."

The captain noted the name in a small, leather-bound notebook. "Any others?"

Paul shrugged. "I know several German Jews who have immigrated to Palestine during these last few years. They know me well. But how shall we find them? I don't have their addresses. The investigators of your military intelligence told me they were going to get in touch with them, but it seems that they failed."

The captain smiled. His eyes twinkled. "Military intelligence and the military prosecutor are not very keen to look for those people. Their very existence might prove that they have made a tremendous mistake."

His face turned grave. "You must make an effort to remember names and details. This might be a question of life and death."

There was something ominous in his voice, and Paul, sitting down, scribbled seven more names in the captain's notebook.

Barely three days had passed since Paul had given the list of his acquaintances in Palestine to Captain O'Shaughnessy. This morning he was sitting on his cot, reading a thick volume—the complete works of William Shakespeare—that one of his jailers, a young, bespectacled soldier, had lent him. The door of the cell opened and the guard corporal stuck his head in.

"You, to the warden's office. On the double!"

The warden, a stocky, red-faced officer with a splendid mustache, was standing behind his desk, beside the ubiquitous Union Jack. Beside him, Fackenheim saw a familiar face: Major Tilly, his interrogator from Maadi. In ordinary circumstances, Fackenheim would have been surprised by his presence. But today's circumstances were not ordinary. Fackenheim's attention focused on the third man in the room. He was a very old man. He was seated, immobile, by the window. He was wearing a dark-brown jacket, a white, open-collared shirt, tan riding breeches, and long woolen socks that ended below the knee. An abundant shock of snow-white hair crowned an emaciated, wax-colored face. The old man was seated by the open window, which let in the sunshine of a bright, crisp winter morning.

Paul skipped a heartbeat. He had recognized the old man at once. "Uncle Karl!"

They had found his uncle. He was saved.

"Uncle Karl. I am so happy that you're here."

He spontaneously darted toward him, but the guard restrained him, gripping his arms.

Major Tilly bent toward the old man. "Kennen Sie dieser Mann?" he asked deferentially in German. "Do you know this man?"

Karl Fackenheim remained immobile for a moment, staring at Paul. Finally he shook his head in a slow, definite movement.

"Nein," he said. "I've never seen him before."

Paul was stunned. He recoiled, as if he had been hit in the face. "Good God, Uncle Karl. It's me, Paul."

The old man didn't move.

Paul started trembling uncontrollably. He had the sensation that he was living a grotesque, absurd nightmare.

"Uncle Karl, please try to remember. It's me, Paul. Paul Fackenheim from Frankfurt. The son of your brother, Wolf. And of Hedda. Remember Hedda? Don't you remember me, Paul, your nephew? I was often visiting you in Mühlhausen, at grandmother's house. We often had breakfast together. We would go out for walks, visit the store . . ."

He had managed to regain control over himself. He started describing episodes and details of family life that only a Fackenheim could know of. He spoke of the vacations he used to spend with his grandparents at Mühlhausen. The famous breakfasts at Grandmother Fackenheim's—the old lady was always seated next to her youngest daughter, Anna. Anna, the sister of his father and of Uncle Karl. Everybody was in love with that bubbly, mischievous girl. "Do you remember, Uncle Karl, how she loved the white of an egg, and the stories she would make up every morning while removing the yolks?"

But Tilly, bending over the old man, softly observed, "They must have done very thorough research about your family, and this spy has learned everything by heart. Secret services do that, you know."

"Uncle Karl," Paul started again, but a sense of defeat and hopelessness was already choking him, strangling his voice. "It's me. Try to remember. Please. I beg you, Uncle Karl."

The old man turned his head toward Tilly.

"Nein!" he said firmly, his voice carrying a ring of finality. "Ich kenne diesen Menschen nicht."

I do not know this man.

XV

Coup de Théâtre

THE COURT."

The courtroom was half empty. On the three rows of long wooden benches sat about a dozen officers and civilians, all of them members of the various branches of military intelligence. Major Tilly was sitting in the front row. The public was not admitted. It was an espionage trial, held in March 1942 before a court-martial, and it was going to take place in utmost secrecy.

In front of the benches stood two tables, strewn with papers and law books, one table for the prosecution and one for the defense. The prosecutor was a tall, plump captain. Paul was seated beside Captain O'Shaughnessy. Paul had made a great effort to look respectable. He had been given a haircut by the prison barber and had polished his black shoes. He had spent a long time cleaning and brushing his old gray suit.

The two armed sentries who had escorted him from the prison had taken their place behind him. On the way, his face glued to the tiny porthole in the prisoners' van, Fackenheim had caught a glimpse of the majestic ramparts of the Old City Wall, and the towering, gold-roofed Dome of the Rock. On the green flanks of a hill beyond the Old City, he had noticed the onion-shaped domes of the Church of Maria Magdalene. Down in the Arab city, throngs of people moved between sleek, needle-shaped minarets. The morning wind brought to him the pure, whispering sound of church bells, carrying a forgotten sensation of peace and serenity. And he felt a pang, knowing that so close, almost at hand's reach, an entirely different world existed, but that his accursed path would always lead him away.

Facing him, on an elevated platform, was a long rectangular table covered with a green cloth. A British flag was fastened to the back wall.

His judges entered the courtroom. There were five of them, all officers. The president of the court was a white-haired old general. A small square mustache bestowed some virility to his rosy-cheeked, chubby face. Paul noticed the wrinkled skin of his hands and the dense network of tiny blue veins.

He felt a strange melancholy, and even indifference, about the forthcoming events in which he was the main protagonist. It could have been because of the overflowing glass of gin which his guard had offered him that morning, before he left for the court, or because of the rain that swept Jerusalem, pouring from a carpet of black clouds creeping low over the city.

But in his heart he knew the real reason for his dejection. He had reached the limits of despair. Nobody believed him. His closest relative in Palestine had rejected him. He had disappointed his friends of the Abwehr who had saved his life, but by agreeing to work for them he had become unworthy of his people. He had been unable to choose between his sense of German patriotism and the need to fight the Nazis—but did he ever really have that choice? He had no news from his mother. He did not have even one single friend to reach for. And he was going to die for crimes he hadn't committed, bearing the name of a man he had never seen.

The indictment and the testimony of the first witnesses who were called to the stand had a distant, muted sound. He absentmindedly identified the two tiny strips of paper carrying his call-word, and admitted that they had been concealed in his clothes. But he suddenly became alert after the first unpleasant surprise of the trial found him totally unprepared.

He had just identified the French book, *L'Âne Culotte,* that the British soldiers had found in the fields. He vigorously denied that it was a codebook. "I liked it," he said. "I had started reading it in Athens, and I took it with me because I wanted to finish it."

"You like it?" the prosecutor said mockingly. "A children's book? Come on, Mr. Koch, why don't you admit that you were to use it for coding your messages?"

"No, definitely not," he said stubbornly. They can never prove that, he thought.

"If that is so, will you then tell the court what these documents mean?" The prosecutor waved two sheets of paper, which he dramatically threw on the green-clothed table.

"I'd like to inform the court that we found these papers inside the book, the same book that the accused pretends he had been reading for his pleasure. These papers are covered with ciphered messages, written with invisible ink. We examined them with roentgen rays and photographed them. I ask the court to examine these exhibits."

Fackenheim's attorney threw him an astonished look. He swiftly scooped the two documents and spread them before his client. "Do you recognize them?"

Fackenheim bit his lower lip. Did he recognize them? Of course, those were the exercises in code and invisible ink that he had practiced in Athens, on Müller's instructions. But why the hell were those papers in the book? He didn't remember leaving them there. Maybe Müller, by negligence?

"I don't recognize those papers," he said in a wavering voice, striving to regain his poise. "I already told you that it was not me, but the Germans who packed my affairs. They might have put them inside."

"Exactly!" Fackenheim's counsel exclaimed, turning to the president. "Exactly, Your Honor. Those papers were certainly destined for another German agent who was supposed to come for them. The accused had no knowledge of their presence among his affairs. That's further proof that . . ."

Fackenheim wasn't listening. O'Shaughnessy could say what he wanted, the truth was that they had suffered a devastating blow. The court was going to interpret the ciphered scribblings on those papers as proof that the *Âne Culotte* was a codebook indeed. His firm denials had turned against him, undermining his credibility.

The prosecutor stormed through the open breach.

"Your name is Koch."

It was not a question. It was a statement of fact.

Fackenheim jumped to his feet. "No, I told you that already. My name is Fackenheim. I am 'Koch' by hobby and by profession." Noticing the puzzled look on the face of the president, he added hurriedly, "Koch means cook in German."

"Yes, of course," the prosecutor said mockingly. "Listen, we've had enough of your lies."

"I am ready to prepare lunch for the members of the tribunal to prove it," Paul said.

"Your Honor, this man is mad. He wants to . . ."

But the old general seemed intrigued by the culinary fervor of the accused. "Will you approach the bench?" he said to Paul with a thin smile. "You claim to be a professional cook. I believe we can verify your statement without necessarily asking you to concoct all kinds of delicacies for my colleagues and myself." He seemed quite amused by his own sense of humor. "I believe that I know of a way to find out if you're telling the truth. Tell me, how do you prepare a Madeira cake?"

A few smiles flourished throughout the courtroom. The prosecutor looked furious and Tilly was shaking his head angrily, but the president of the court seemed delighted.

Paul was too tense to grasp the comic absurdity of the situation. He stood up, stiff and solemn, and recited:

"You take a half pound of butter, a half pound of sugar, you add vanilla and lemon juice, you stir for a few minutes. Then you add five eggs and continue stirring till the blend becomes as thick as cream. You add a quarter of a pound of flour and a quarter of a pound of ground malt. But beware! This is a very rich cake. You must keep stirring for quite a while."

The general frowned and seemed sunk in thought.

"That's right," he announced, beaming. "That's exactly my wife's recipe."

This time the whole courtroom burst into laughter. Fackenheim joined the crowd. The whole thing was stupid, he conceded, but it brought him a moment of relief.

His laughter died down as the prosecutor stood. He had kept another trump up his sleeve.

"You said in your depositions"—he put a pair of wire-rimmed glasses on the edge of his nose and made believe that he was perusing a sheaf of papers that lay on his desk—"that your radio had disappeared when you were parachuted. You said that the rope had broken and your bag, including your affairs and the transmitter, had slipped and vanished in the darkness. You couldn't find them later."

"Yes, that's right."

"Was the radio protected by a special material, a case or some other wrapping, for the parachuting?"

"Yes. The radio was packed separately into a bag made of very thick canvas."

The prosecutor turned to the president of the court. "Well, you heard that, Your Honor. The accused said, 'into a bag made of canvas.' Now, I can prove that a week after the capture of the accused, our services finally discovered the radio."

A hum of excitement rippled through the audience. The prosecutor paused to let the dramatic effect of his disclosure sink in, then went on. "The radio was indeed broken in pieces. But it wasn't discovered somewhere in a field, as the accused wants you to believe. It was hidden in the hollow trunk of an olive tree. And no sign whatsoever of a canvas bag."

Fackenheim was stunned. This time he truly failed to understand. He had never seen the radio once he had landed in that vineyard.

O'Shaughnessy was on his feet.

"My learned colleague is mistaken," he said calmly. "I am sure that the accused is telling the truth. The transmitter had fallen from a considerable height and had broken inside the bag. I believe this is the most logical and simple answer, which my learned friend seems to overlook. It probably was found by an Arab, who got rid of the pieces of the radio and kept only the canvas bag."*

The prosecutor, however, continued his offensive.

"Now, with your permission, I'll unmask the accused and furnish you the proof of his real identity."

He turned toward the door. Two men stood there, side by side. They were dressed in British uniforms and were wearing lieutenants' bars.

Fackenheim paled. He had recognized one of them. The last time he had seen him, he wasn't wearing an army uniform, but prisoners' clothes.

It was "Sergeant Rudolf of the Afrika Korps," his companion in captivity whom he had met in Maadi, the stool pigeon who had delivered to the English Fackenheim's drawing containing his coded message to the Abwehr.

"Do you know the accused?"

"Yes, I do know him."

"Where did you meet him?"

"Rudolf" was speaking good English, but his German accent was quite strong. He described their meeting in the prison yard and their conversations about the war.

"Following our talks," Rudolf said, "I became certain that

---

*This point was never fully clarified. But it is likely that Captain O'Shaughnessy's version was the closest to the truth. Fackenheim maintains that he never saw the radio after the drop. And it has been established that he never radioed any message to the Abwehr.

Koch was a big shot in the SS. He hinted to me that he had made himself prisoner with the purpose of winning the trust of the British and gaining access to the secrets of the military intelligence."

Fackenheim did not even try to protest. It was clear that the witness had memorized a statement that he had been ordered to deliver. It could be the work of Tilly. The secret services, convinced of his guilt, would use any means, including lies, to get him convicted.

"Do you recognize this exhibit?" The prosecutor held in his hand the ill-fated drawing of the naked girl.

"Of course. The accused gave it to me on the eve of my pretended departure. He asked me to deliver it to the headquarters of the SD in Berlin."

"Your Honor," the prosecutor said to the president of the court. "Would you care to examine this drawing? You'll notice Morse symbols that have been dissimulated in the folds of the curtains. We immediately discovered that the drawing was a cover for a coded message. According to our experts, it seems that the message is the following: 'Everything progresses according to plan. Hope to return soon with necessary information.' "

Fackenheim jumped up, trembling with anger and frustration. "This isn't true. That's a lie."

His attorney joined him and assailed the prosecutor with questions. He asked for explanations and demanded to hear the testimony of the experts who had deciphered the code of the drawing. "I want to know how your experts have cracked the code," he shouted, for the first time losing his cool. "I want them to tell the court how the code works. I want them to reconstruct the grille used by the accused. I don't believe any court can accept your declarations without substantiation by tangible evidence."

The prosecutor, ill at ease, tried to defend his accusations, but his answers were confused. No, he couldn't bring over the experts. No, he couldn't provide a reconstruction of the grille.

No, he hadn't assisted in the deciphering of the code.

The old general turned to Fackenheim.

"Is that the text of the message that you tried to send?"

"No, Your Honor." He tried in vain to control himself. His face was burning and his heart was hopping madly in his chest.

"You certainly could reveal to us the real contents of the message.'"

"Yes, Your Honor. I mean . . . I don't remember the exact wording, but I remember the essence." He closed his eyes and quoted: " 'I have been captured by the English. I'll try to escape. Koch.' Yes, I think that was it, Your Honor."

The general leaned toward him over the table. His voice was soft, reasonable. "So show us how you coded that message."

Somebody gave him a sheet of paper and a pencil. O'Shaughnessy placed the drawing beside his elbow. With a trembling hand Paul drew the grille. He started to fill the small squares, inscribing in them the letters of the code. He failed. He was unable to concentrate. He started again, then again. He was sweating profusely. He could feel everybody's eyes trained on him.

"Well?" the general asked.

"I haven't succeeded yet. But if you allow me, Your Honor . . ."

"That's enough." The general's voice was cold and sharp. The brief experiment had convinced him that he couldn't trust the protestations of the accused.

The prosecutor, confident again, was ready for the coup de grâce. He called the second officer to the witness stand. Fackenheim had never seen the man before.

"Do you know the accused?"

"Yes, sir." Again, the strong German accent.

"Who is he?"

"I was told that he was a high official of the Gestapo and an Obergruppenführer in the SS."

"What is his name?"

"Koch."

"Where did you see him?"

"In Berlin. At the headquarters of the Gestapo, on Ferdinandstrasse."

"In what circumstances?"

"I had been summoned for an interrogation on a certain matter. The accused was present in the room where the interrogation was held. With him were four other high officials of the Gestapo."

"Did he speak with you?"

"No, sir."

"But you're sure he is the same man?"

"Yes, sir."

Paul glanced about him. In the silence that had descended upon the courtroom, he became the center of a new kind of attention. He felt himself naked, crucified by those looks of surprise, triumph, and hatred. *An Obergruppenführer in the SS.* He was living another nightmare, worse than those terrible dreams that were haunting him at night. Was it possible? Was this the reason for everything they had done to him? The nocturnal interrogations, the threats, the insults; and also the fine meals, the spacious cells, the tight guard . . . "according to your rank." This time he knew he was lost. The nightmare had become reality. The Jew Fackenheim didn't exist anymore. He had disappeared long ago, somewhere between Dachau and Jerusalem. It was the SS general whom they were trying today, it was the SS general whom they were going to escort to the gallows. Whether he wanted to or not, he was going to die for Hitler.

O'Shaughnessy, obstinate as a bulldog, wouldn't let go. He went for the witness with a meager hope of discrediting his monstrous testimony.

"Don't forget that you're testifying under oath. When did you say that you met the accused?"

"In nineteen thirty-nine."

"And you claim to have seen him in the company of other Gestapo officials."

"Yes."

"How long did that meeting last?"

"At least five minutes."

O'Shaughnessy approached the witness, speaking softly, conversationally. "And you certainly had a good reason to keep the face of this man in your memory."

The witness hesitated, throwing a quick look around him. "No," he finally said. "Not at that time."

"That's it, then. If I understand you properly, one day you happened to be, by pure chance, in the same room with five other men. That happened three years ago. You remained together for five minutes. And today"—the Irishman raised his voice—"today you testify under oath that you can identify one of those five men beyond the shadow of a doubt. And even remember that this particular man—and not anyone in that room whom you had seen for five minutes—is the SS General Koch. Isn't that somewhat strange?"

"Objection, Your Honor." The prosecutor's face had turned crimson.

Fackenheim's attorney went on. "And there is another point, Your Honor. I believe it is of the utmost importance. Those two witnesses"—he pointed with disgust at the two Germans—"are here in the uniform of British officers. We don't know their names. We haven't seen their credentials. I demand that the two witnesses disclose their identity."

Fackenheim heard murmuring in the room. One of the civilians got up from his seat, crossed the courtroom in large, quick strides, and slipped a hastily scribbled note in the prosecutor's hand. The prosecutor read it, then caught the eyes of the German witness and shook his head.

"I am sorry," "Sergeant Rudolf" said. "We don't have the right to reveal our names."

"I order you to state your names," the general snapped.

The civilian who had given the note to the prosecutor now crossed the room again, approached the platform, and exchanged some comments in low voice with one of the judges. The officer, in turn, whispered in the general's ear. The general whispered back furiously, but the younger officer seemed firm. Finally, the president of the court surrendered with a sigh.

"All right," he said to the two lieutenants. "You are free to go."

He kept silent for a moment. Finally he raised his head and surveyed the courtroom. His voice was weary, and he sounded as if he were speaking to himself.

"I am sorry that such people have got to be used."

Then he added, "The hearing of the witnesses is over."

That night Fackenheim didn't sleep.

He knew he was going to die.

He had grown somewhat used to the idea. Dachau and Maadi had instilled a dark fatalism in his soul. How many times had he seen people die around him, how many times had he heard people yelling in his face, "We'll kill you. You'll be shot"? Tonight, tomorrow, at dawn. . . . He had learned to live with death, to expect it and to accept it as inevitable. An early death seemed to be his destiny, and he could do nothing about it.

Tomorrow he would hear his sentence.

The hours crept by in silence. All the noises had faded away, even the usual sounds of a prison, the squeaking of the heavy iron doors, the heavy steps of the sentries in the wards, the clatter of arms, the muffled cries of the prisoners in their restless sleep.

He lay still in his bed, resigned, till the new dawn bathed his cell with a pale gray light.

He was unable to touch his breakfast. He refused the glass of gin that the lance corporal brought over with a roguish smile. Handcuffs attached to his wrists, he was taken away in the military van. It was raining again this morning, a gray, noiseless drizzle that gave Jerusalem an air of melancholy and solitude.

Paul sat down behind the table of the defense in the courtroom. One by one, the civilians and the officers who had assisted in the trial walked in, each one heading for the place he had occupied before. The prosecutor was all smiles.

"The Court!"

The five judges walked into the room.

Fackenheim realized that the seat beside him was empty. Captain O'Shaughnessy was not there. The general, visibly annoyed, beckoned to the clerk of the court, who seemed at a loss as well. Nobody knew where the attorney was. Time passed and the irritation in the courtroom grew. In the absence of the counsel for the defense, the court was paralyzed. The prosecutor whispered angrily in the ear of the president, the civilians stirred on the benches, the judges grunted in discontent.

A half hour had passed when suddenly the Irishman burst into the room. He was barely recognizable. His face was soiled, unshaven. His trench coat, his clothes, and his shoes were wet and stained with mud. He rushed toward the bench.

"Your Honor, I beg you to forgive my being late." His voice was tired, hoarse, but Fackenheim discerned in it a note of joy.

"I succeeded," he went on, his voice growing louder, "in finding a certain person whose testimony might be of capital importance for the outcome of this trial. I request the right to hear that witness."

The prosecutor was angrily waving some papers. "I object," he shouted, removing his glasses and putting them on again. "I object, Your Honor. The hearing of the witnesses was concluded yesterday."

The general pondered for a moment.

"The request is highly irregular," he said, speaking directly to O'Shaughnessy, "as well as the liberties you afford yourself concerning the proper conduct of this court-martial. But you know all that. Still, the court will hear the witness. The life of the accused is in question, and the court cannot ignore testimony in his favor."

"Thank you, Your Honor." O'Shaughnessy threw his cap and trench coat on a chair and darted out of the courtroom.

He reappeared a moment later. He held the hand of a small woman wearing a heavy winter coat. She had hesitantly started to unbutton it with her free hand, revealing a dark gray shirt and a blue sweater. She had abundant auburn hair and large green eyes. She seemed lost and frightened amid all those British officers.

Fackenheim stared at her with fascination. A spark exploded in his memory, and suddenly he felt the room swaying around him. He gripped the table's edge with both hands, to keep his balance. Could this be possible?

The woman had seen him too. She hurried toward him across the room, extending both her hands to him, as an uncertain smile spread across her face.

"Good Lord, Paul Fackenheim. What are you doing here?"

XVI

The Verdict

IRMA KOBLINER had woken up early that morning. She hadn't slept well the previous night because of the thunderstorm that had raged for hours in the coastal plain. At dawn the storm had rolled east, toward the Samaria mountains. But heavy rain was still pouring from a dark low sky. The north wind lashed on the roofs, bent the young orange trees, howled in the closed window shutters. The courtyard of Irma's small house in the township of Petach Tikva, about fifty miles north of Jerusalem, had turned into a big puddle, and the street was covered with mud. Later, when the rain stopped, she would pull on her old boots and go visit her good friend Martha Rosenzweig on Shapira Street. That decision made, the petite Irma Kobliner, bursting with vitality, sailed into the kitchen to get breakfast ready. Her older daughter, Ruth, was still asleep in her room. The younger one, Marion, was spending a few days with friends.

Somebody knocked on the front door. "I'm coming," she chirped, but the impatient visitor pounded on the door with his fists. As she hurried through the living room she heard somebody calling in English, "Open the door!" She did, and found herself facing a British officer and two soldiers, who stood in the rain. A jeep of the military police was parked by the entrance to the courtyard.

"Mrs. Irma Kobliner?"

"Yes, that's me. Did something happen?"

The officer, huddled in an old trench coat, glanced at a crumpled sheet of paper he held in his hand. "You're Mrs. Kobliner, originally from Frankfurt, Germany?"

"Yes."

"I must ask you to come with us. At once."

She turned pale. "Why? What do you want from me?"

"I can't tell you. But rest assured, you've nothing to fear."

Frightened all the same, she hurried to her bedroom to dress. While she was brushing her hair and putting on her coat, scary thoughts flashed through her mind. When the military police knocks at your door at this hour of the morning, it must be for something very serious. But she had done nothing. It was a mistake, no doubt.

Ruth, trembling with anxiety, watched her mother depart in the military car with the officer and the two soldiers. Those days, Jews were being arrested by the British for two main reasons: membership in an underground organization, or involvement with illegal immigration. But her mother? She had never had anything to do with these things.

The journey to Jerusalem took place in total silence. Her fears kept growing, but the officer, who also seemed nervous and tense, didn't talk to her; he kept looking at his watch and rubbing the back of his hand on his unshaven face. His eyes were bloodshot, as if he hadn't slept. The car climbed at a dizzying speed up the narrow, winding road to Jerusalem, darted across the city, and stopped before a building surrounded with barbed wire and sandbags. Armed sentries and military vehicles full of soldiers protected the entrance. The officer left her with the two soldiers and disappeared in the maze of corridors. A short time later he was back, his cap and trench coat gone. He took her by the hand and dragged her behind him into a vast room full of Englishmen.

She stood there totally bewildered, failing to understand what it was all about, why she was here among all those men. And then, in front of her, behind a wooden table, she spotted a familiar face. That dear Paul, the son of Hedda. And she ran to him.

"Your full name, please," the officer said. The interpreter, a middle-aged, stocky man with a round face, smiled at her.

"Kobliner, Irma."

She was standing in a witness box. On her right, several officers were seated on a platform. She understood now that she was a witness in a trial. A fat captain with wire-rimmed glasses was glowering at her from across the courtroom.

"Your address?"

"27, Mohliver Street, Petach Tikva."

"Do you know this man?"

"But of course."

"Who is he?"

"Paul Fackenheim, the son of Hedda Fackenheim, from Frankfurt-on-Main, in Germany."

"Are you absolutely sure?"

"What a question! Of course I am absolutely sure. For three years, I had been seeing him every day."

"Tell the court in what circumstances."

"I knew Hedda Fackenheim in Frankfurt. We were very close friends. After the death of my husband, Dr. Kobliner, I rented a room in Hedda Fackenheim's apartment. Her husband had died too, a few years before. I was taking my meals with her and we were spending our afternoons together. In her house I met her son, Paul, who also became a good friend of my family. My daughter, Marion, went to his cooking school. But I don't understand, really, what he is doing here. How did he manage to escape from Germany?"

Paul was elated. Irma Kobliner had identified him. Her testimony destroyed the most devastating charges and so-called proof that the prosecution had brought before the court. The Obergruppenführer Koch had disintegrated like a bad dream and vanished from the courtroom.

He felt deep gratitude toward his attorney. Day after day, the stubborn Irishman must have been crisscrossing the country, looking for the witnesses whose names were on Paul's list: a handful of men and women whose addresses Paul didn't know.

And finally he had discovered Irma Kobliner. Paul remembered her well, of course, along with the young Marion, who had been his pupil in his cooking school for Jewish women. He had been fascinated by the lovely Marion at the time, and had courted her for a while. He had even helped her and her family to escape from Germany to England barely three weeks before the outbreak of the war. He had often thought of Marion and wondered what would have happened if the war hadn't thrown them apart. But how could he ever imagine that one day Marion's mother would appear out of the blue and save his life?

Irma Kobliner completed her testimony. Captain O'Shaughnessy thanked her warmly, and the white-haired officer on the platform nodded at her encouragingly. The sullen prosecutor glared at her from behind his desk, but didn't question her.

Irma Kobliner left the courtroom in the best of moods. She wanted to ask Paul about his mother, but she was politely escorted out. She still didn't understand what was the matter, and why did they have to bring her all the way over from Petach Tikva just to tell the judges that Paul Fackenheim was indeed Paul Fackenheim. But judging by Paul's beaming face, she realized that she had accomplished a good deed.

Outside, the military jeep was waiting to drive her back home. She settled inside comfortably. She would have some story to tell Martha Rosenzweig later.

Still, Paul's troubles were not over yet. As the trial neared its conclusion, O'Shaughnessy asked the court to hear Fackenheim's testimony. Under British law the accused can defend himself with his own testimony. Paul's first mistake was to take the stand. Very soon, he became confused. The old contradictions between the findings of the investigators and Paul's deposition emerged again, rekindling the court's suspicions.

Second mistake. Paul tried to impress the court by volunteering information and revealed that when he parachuted he had in his possession 500 pounds sterling. He described in detail how he had entrusted his money to the young Palestinian, who had disappeared at the hospital in Haifa.

They didn't believe him. "That story of a mysterious Palestinian who ran away with your money is an insult to our intelligence," the prosecutor said, and turned to the court. "What really matters in the new testimony of the accused is his admission that he had so much money in his possession. That proves that he was an important Abwehr agent. Five hundred pounds is a lot of money. I believe that he hid that money, or delivered it to another agent who was waiting for him near the drop zone. It confirms what we said from the start. One does not dispatch a spy in enemy territory with fifty Palestinian pounds in his pocket."

Captain O'Shaughnessy lost some of his confidence. The effect of Irma Kobliner's *coup de théâtre* was quickly fading away.

The prosecutor arose and slowly adjusted his glasses, preparing for his final remarks. He seemed to have regained his arrogance as well as his self-control. "It is true," he conceded, "that the accused has given this court proof of his identity. He is not Koch, but the Jew Paul Fackenheim. So what? It doesn't change the basic fact that he is a very important spy who has been sent to this country, equipped with an ultra-modern transmitter and loaded with money, to spy against the British army in Palestine in the service of Nazi Germany. The fact that Paul Fackenheim is a Jew does not change the other facts either, namely that he refused to make a full confession, to reveal his code, the purpose of his mission, the secrets he knows about the Abwehr. We have succeeded in

proving—and the accused admitted it of his own free will—
that while imprisoned in Maadi he tried to smuggle a message
to his superiors. You have all seen the drawing and the concealed signals, which by some strange forgetfulness he failed
to decipher yesterday. But I am satisfied with his testimony.
He was informing his Abwehr chiefs that he intended to escape. That admission by itself is grave enough to have him
condemned."

But the worst was yet to come. The prosecutor had also
kept a trump card for the last moment. And now, enjoying its
dramatic effect, he tossed it before the court.

"I am authorized to reveal to you now a capital element
that I had no right to mention before. The accused was indeed dropped from a German aircraft on the night of October tenth, nineteen forty-one. Our services had advance
knowledge of that operation. We had received, a few days
before, a report informing us of the imminent parachuting of
a spy named Koch."

The audience held its breath. The prosecutor paused and
turned to face Fackenheim. He then turned back to the president of the court.

"We, too, have our informers. The one who warned us of
the forthcoming parachuting of the so-called Koch is based in
Athens and has access to highly placed sources. We knew
quite a few days in advance what was going to happen that
particular night at that particular place. Even if Koch hadn't
come to us, we would have got him. It was a question of
hours at the most. And if he did surrender, it was not by
choice but by lack of choice. It was his only way to escape the
net that was closing in on him."

His last words were received in silence. O'Shaughnessy
got up to speak, but his arguments sounded worn out. It
seemed that the prosecutor's revelations had tipped the
scales again.

Paul was unable to follow the summation of his counsel.
His mind was elsewhere, on the morning of October elev-

enth. Only now did he understand the real reason for all those roadblocks and police patrols, the army vehicles on the highway, the packs of red caps in the cities. They hadn't been alerted at the last moment. They knew. They had been expecting him.

"The court will retire for deliberation," the president announced.

Flanked by two guards, Fackenheim walked into the adjacent room. His legs felt wooden, senseless, and he moved like an automaton. He was convinced now that he had lost. He would be found guilty. His guards apparently thought the same—they treated him gently, speaking to him with soft, solicitous voices, the way one talks to a terminal cancer patient. They gave him a cigarette, poured him some tea. He let them serve him. The burning liquid had no taste. The cigarette seemed to be made out of straw.

He was sitting, immobile, on the only chair in that empty chamber. His eyes were focused on a vague spot on the opposite wall. It would be a death sentence. He tried to convince himself to be brave. Hundreds of thousands of soldiers had died in battle. He would die too. One of the guards had told him yesterday that spies were shot. He had told him a British execution squad numbered nine soldiers. The rifles of five of them were loaded with real ammunition, the four others were loaded with blanks. The soldiers themselves didn't know who had received the blanks and who was given the real bullets. That way nobody would ever know who fired the fatal shots.

What an irony of fate, he said to himself. The only Jew to be released from Dachau; the only one to be spared the crematorium; one of the very few to leave the territory of Nazi Germany and reach the land of the Jews; he, the lucky one, would die in Jerusalem by the hand of Hitler's enemies.

In his cell he read and reread an old copy of the Bible. A verse from the book of Job came to his mind: "For the arrows of the Almighty are within me, the poison whereof drinketh up my spirit: the terrors of God do set themselves in array against me."

"The accused to the Court!"

He got up. The door opened. They placed him, standing, in the middle of the vast courtroom. Like that morning in Dachau, at the Appelplatz. Alone, defenseless, without a single friend, waiting for the voice that would decree his destiny.

The general was looking at him. He said something. Fackenheim had become more fluent in English, but he failed to understand what the old man was saying.

The interpreter approached him.

"The president of the court just announced that the tribunal has reached a verdict. The verdict is 'Not Guilty.' "

Not Guilty!

The room turned black and he collapsed, unconscious, under the bright colors of the Union Jack.

XVII

The Circle Closes

THE MENU of the 1942 Christmas dinner served at the 52nd Detention Barracks in Jerusalem included the traditional Christmas dessert: a plum pudding. For the first time since the outbreak of the war, the 136 prisoners and guards of the prison could enjoy that delicacy, as typically English as tea, smoked haddocks, and bowler hats. Unanimous praise converged upon the man who had conceived and concocted the treat, Paul Fackenheim.

Paul had become a "Koch" again. Even though he had been acquitted by the court-martial, the British authorities had decided to keep him in prison as an "enemy alien." It was only natural that he would settle in the kitchen and devote himself to his favorite hobby. Still, the intelligence investigators hadn't given up. For months to come, they would devise and carry out countless sophisticated ploys to provoke the "master spy," obtain his confession, learn his secrets. They still firmly believed he was more important than he pretended to be; they were still puzzled by his strange mission, by the tip they had received from Athens, by the names of Paula Koch and Colonel Falkenheim. They continued sending informers and stool pigeons to Paul. The most ingenious of them was a perfidious Pole, the Count Manshinski, who became Paul's closest friend and who did not spare any effort to make him confess or write down the secrets he was supposed to know.

Manshinski failed, like all the others before him. Paul's experience in the English prisons had developed in him a sixth sense for spotting informers and keeping clear of them. He had also resigned himself to the idea that he would have to spend many more years in His Majesty's prisons. He didn't fear death anymore. Nevertheless, one incident was to shake him deeply and again bring to life the terrors of the past.

In early 1943 he was transferred for a few days to the cell of a South African. Suspecting another scheme to make him talk, he kept in his corner, responding in monosyllables to the young man's overtures. Forty-eight hours later, he was allowed to return to his cell. He found it in a piteous state. The "Khamsin," the desert wind that had been blowing over Jerusalem those last few days, had brought from the south thin, dry dust that had settled on the floor tiles. Marked deeply in that carpet of sand were hundreds, perhaps thousands of footprints. They all belonged to the same man, who had been turning round, in endless circles. The bed was still warm, and Paul could discern the impression of a body on the blankets. The tin can, used as a garbage container, was overflowing with cigarette butts.

"What happened here?" Paul asked his old friend, the Scottish lance corporal who had escorted him to that cell on the eve of his court-martial.

The Scot lowered his voice. "You know that your cell is the one reserved to criminals. The chap who passed the night here was in jail since last year. He tried to escape and killed one of the guards. This morning, at dawn, he was hanged."

Paul winced, terrified. He closed his eyes, and saw all the grim details of the man's last night of life. The man who was going to die, frightened, restless, walking in circles in his cell, counting the minutes he had left to live; lying on the cot, chain-smoking, throwing himself on the heavy iron door and hammering it with his fists, then starting again to walk in circles, a journey that could lead nowhere. True, he was an assassin and he had to die. But death, which he hadn't feared in Dachau or Maadi, had turned into something he could no longer confront. Its very passage through his cell left him trembling with fear.

Perhaps it was a delayed reaction to all the misfortunes

that had befallen him. And now neither logic nor reason could help him overcome this surge of despair, this feeling that he was falling apart. For the first time in his life, he sought refuge in prayer. Kneeling in the dust among the dead man's footprints, he tried to pray. Phrases forgotten since his early childhood slowly surfaced in his memory, ancient Hebrew words whose meaning he didn't even understand. "Shma Israel, Adonai Eloheinu . . ." *I want to be left in peace*, he murmured. *Do I not have that right? I have not wronged anyone. Why do I deserve such a miserable fate?*

The next morning, the Scottish lance corporal escorted him to a military pickup truck waiting in the inner court of the prison. He was being transferred.

Pulling back the canvas top covering the back of the truck, Paul contemplated the scenery along the narrow road. The sight seemed familiar. He had seen those hills, those fields and olive groves. He suddenly remembered. This was the region of Latrun, where he had been imprisoned before his court-martial. The recollection worried him. Were they going to throw him back into his barbed-wire cage and again treat him like a wild beast in that forgotten camp?

But the pickup bypassed the camp and descended toward the Trappist monastery. The truck slowed down as it approached the large iron gates. Inside the convent's enclosure stood a big stone house, decorated with columns and arabesques, surrounded by barbed wire. It must have been a beautiful house once, but had been ravaged by neglect. The walls were dirty and peeling, the roof rotting, the windows barred and sealed with wooden boards, the porticos falling.

"You're home," scoffed his escort, a short corporal named Jacobson. "Welcome to the Latrun internment camp."

In the small office near the entrance, Paul went through the usual procedure: undressing, meticulous search, interrogation. A huge captain appeared at the door. "Starting now," he boomed in a deep, cavernous voice, "you'll be called

Mister X. He chuckled mockingly. If you don't like your new name, you can use your number. You are Number 64."

Number 64. In Dachau he was Number 26336. History was repeating itself.

He was led across a large filthy hall and up a dark staircase. Furtive shadows moved in the badly lit corridors. He was not yet aware that he was entering a strange, absurd universe, a world of untouchables. This new prison was a dreary backwater, where the crown had shoved all the undesirables and the banished of the Middle East—a unique mixture of repulsive underworld scum side by side with maverick national leaders revered by millions of their countrymen. Here he was to meet scores of men from fifteen different nationalities—princes and spies, traitors and ministers, swindlers and warriors, Nazis and Communists. Most of them had been suspected of espionage, subversion, agitation, resistance against the British. Because of insufficient evidence, or in certain cases because of the danger of mass riots and national turmoil, they had not been condemned. They had been imprisoned in the former Latrun hostel, under the guard of 200 Bedouins of the Arab legion, twenty English soldiers, and a Welsh captain whose main concerns were how to steal the internees' rations, fatten his pigs that reigned in the courtyard, and spoil his capricious mistress living in Haifa.

As Fackenheim walked down the corridor, he passed the open doors of several cells. Actually, these weren't cells, but rooms. Some of them looked repugnant—dirty, fetid, full of ramshackle wooden beds and straw mattresses; others were clean and furnished with taste. Two or three privileged prisoners even had the right to lock their rooms and hang paintings and photographs on their walls. They were not prisoners in the real sense of the word. They had the right to take walks, to meet one another in their rooms, and to buy provisions at the camp canteen.

In the corners of the refectory and on the staircase steps, various ethnic groups gathered daily. There were Yugoslavs,

Russians, Poles, Arabs, Germans. The largest community consisted of fifteen Greeks—a few fishermen, two brothel owners, a notorious assassin, a sculptor, some well-known political figures named Papandreou, Papadopulos, Coralides, Kanelopulos; and presiding over that peculiar assembly, the huge mayor of Crete, fat, illiterate, proud of his booming voice and the thick head of hair that made him look like a mythological deity.

In the corridor, Fackenheim ran into an old acquaintance, Count Manshinski, the informer who had tried to make him talk in the Jerusalem prison. Manshinski was sharing his room with two other Poles, a young homosexual named Pitzush and an elderly colonel from Warsaw. With a remarkable lack of shame, the count warmly hugged his "old and dear friend Koch." With the same impudence he revealed to Paul that he was a professional spy. He had spied for Soviet Russia against the Germans, for Nazi Germany against the Russians, for Russia and Germany together against Poland. Dispatched to the Balkans by Canaris, he had been kidnapped by the British and flown to Palestine.

What he didn't disclose, however, was that since his capture he spied for the British against his fellow prisoners. In all the prisons where he had been jailed, he had spied, provoked, and informed. Latrun was no exception. But he was stretching his luck too far. The furious prisoners had decided to take revenge. The very night of Fackenheim's arrival, the inhabitants of the big house were awakened by Manshinski's terrified screams. Several prisoners had waited until darkness had fallen, then slipped into his room, rolled him in a blanket, and beaten him savagely. The English guards kept prudently away. They used informers, but they didn't protect them.

The next morning, another fantastic spectacle. A military staff car stopped in the monastery courtyard; escorted by two armed guards, a curious personage got out. He was dressed in a splendid uniform of white silk, loaded with colorful ribbons, medals, golden buttons, and epaulets. In one arm he clutched a magnificent helmet decorated with ostrich feathers. His head, however, was hooded in a crumpled jute bag. He stood still for a while in the middle of the courtyard, then started to feel his way blindly. The British soldiers kept laughing at him and pushing him around; they didn't allow him to remove his hood until he had reached his room. Only then did the man so ridiculed by the English reveal his identity to his companions in captivity. He was General Zahedi, strong man of Iran and former minister of war to the deposed Shah Reza Pahlavi.

How had he got there? After the occupation of Iran by the British and the Soviets, the Germans had fomented a revolt of the Qashqai tribes in the region of Shiraz. Zahedi, who was worshiped like a god by the fierce Qashqai, had been urgently dispatched by the British to Shiraz, to bring the tribes to reason. It soon became clear, however, that Zahedi did not show excessive zeal in his assignment. Zahedi turned into a liability, and the British acted swiftly. They threw a sumptuous party in Teheran, and Zahedi was invited as the guest of honor. He arrived in his parade uniform, resplendent with all his medals. At the end of the dinner he was served coffee, brandy, and a cigar; and as he was relaxing among his British friends, some heavyweight agents jumped him, slipped a bag on his head, and threw him in a car that then sped to the airport. The next morning Zahedi disembarked in Palestine, still wearing his hood. To the worried inquiries of the Iranian royal family, the British officers seemed astonished. General Zahedi? They hadn't seen the gentleman for quite a while. Disappeared? How ghastly indeed.

Every day now, Fackenheim was meeting new friends. For the first time since Dachau, he was among people with whom he could mix and talk freely. And for the first time he was to discover that his experiences, as unhappy and unusual as they had been, were not unique. The adventures of some other Latrun internees were quite amazing too. One man, Erwin Weissrock, was a German Jew arrested in Teheran for having sheltered a fanatic Nazi spy, the Austrian Dr. Kummel. Kummel himself, arrested and brought to Latrun together with Weissrock, would jump to attention, raise his right hand, and bark "Heil Hitler" whenever he was summoned to the commanding officer. Another picturesque character was a bearded Dutch sailor, Mynheer Rosenblad, a man of gargantuan dimensions and appetite, who had been arrested on board a ship in Haifa and accused of espionage. Only two or three people in Latrun knew that his real name was Myaceslaw Rosenblatt, a Jew from Lodz, in Poland.

And so many others: the former Syrian minister Asslan, who night after night tried to commit suicide; Elmas, the former privy counselor to King Zog I of Albania; a mysterious Ukrainian botanist who had served as political adviser to the Nazis in Yugoslavia; Dr. Gotz, suspected to have been one of the principal Abwehr agents in the Balkans and Turkey; and the Druze sheik, Ibrahim Ali, magnificent with his white turban, long embroidered galabia, drooping mustache, and ardent black eyes. A fierce man, full of hatred for the British, he had tattooed the swastika on his right arm and would stick it in the commander's face at any possible occasion, completing his gesture by some contemptuous remarks about the deplorable sexual capacities of Winston Churchill. Ali's two sons, who shared his cell, claimed that during his tumultuous life he had killed in battle more than a hundred enemy warriors.

Only a few months after his arrival, Paul Fackenheim met a small, fat man who pompously introduced himself: Fritz Edler von Fialla, a noble Austrian. And only after the war was over would Fackenheim learn that Fialla was the Nazi journalist who, in October 1942, published in his Slovakian newspaper *Der Grenzbote* misleading articles about Auschwitz, describing that factory of death as a "paradise on earth." "I saw around me only smiling faces in Auschwitz," he had written before turning up, by an absurd chain of developments, at the Latrun monastery.

In the room next to Fialla's, Fackenheim met a Hungarian, Bandi Grosz, who had been charged with an extraordinary mission by the Nazi lieutenant colonel Adolf Eichmann, the man responsible for the extermination of the Jews in the territories occupied by the Third Reich. Grosz, an agent of the Nazi counterespoinage, had been sent by Eichmann to Istanbul, together with the Jewish leader Joel Brand, to negotiate with the British the exchange of one million Jews, condemned to die in the gas chambers, for ten thousand trucks. The British, hostile to the idea of absorbing a million Jewish refugees, preferred to lock Joel Brand in a Cairo prison as "enemy alien"; on the other hand, they accused Grosz of being a spy—which he was—and interned him in Latrun. Thus they managed to make both emissaries, who knew of the embarrassing Eichmann offer, disappear until the end of the war.

In the attic, which in the summer turned into a steaming inferno, Paul discovered a group of eight Germans. They were kept apart from the other prisoners. Most of them were members of the SS, and all of them were fervent Nazis. A year earlier they had landed in secret airfields in the south of Iran, loaded with arms, explosives, and gold sovereigns, to raise the troublesome Qashqai tribes against the British. The Qashqai had cooperated with them as long as they generously distributed their sovereigns. But once their gold treasure had been exhausted, the rebels delivered them to the British. At Latrun, they maintained their military routine: uniforms, discipline, heel clicking, Heil Hitler, Nazi songs. Only after the Fuehrer's death would they metamorphose in twenty-four hours and become dedicated anti-Nazis.

Often Fackenheim would wonder how his superiors in the Abwehr had reacted to his disappearance. Had they tried to find out what had happened to him? Had they unmasked the British agent in Athens who had betrayed him? And had the Abwehr ever tried to infiltrate another spy behind Brisith lines after the failure of his mission? He finally got a partial answer to those questions from a German prisoner, recently transferred from Maadi. Yes, Canaris had sent another spy after Fackenheim had vanished. He had been the last—and probably the best—the Abwehr ever had in the Middle East. The German had seen him once, in the Maadi Interrogation Center, after his capture that had shaken the high-society circles of Cairo.

The man's name was Hussein Gaafar, an Egyptian, son of a high-ranking magistrate. But he had another name and another allegiance. His mother was German; he also called himself John Eppler. Under that name he had sneaked into Germany at the outbreak of the war, had volunteered to the Z.-b.-V.-800 unit of the Brandenburg regiment, and after proving his skills in Turkey, Iran, and Iraq had been dispatched to Egypt. According to certain rumors he had spent several weeks with Rommel himself, in his headquarters in Libya, preparing for his mission; Canaris had flown to Libya to see him off. He had set on his way at the end of April 1942, a month before Rommel's attack on Tobruk. Together with his radio operator, Peter Monkaster, Eppler had crossed the desert by car, outflanking the British positions, and reached Cairo. There he had established his residence in a fancy boathouse anchored in the Nile, renewed his prewar contacts, and started his operation.

The story of Eppler's exploits sounded like a tale from the *Arabian Nights*. The clever, handsome young man had become a close friend of the voluptuous Hekmath Fahmi, the best belly dancer of Egypt, who became his accomplice; he had made friends with high-ranking British officers, played golf with Major Dunstan, the chief of British counterespionage in Cairo; met with Masri Pasha, the former commander in chief of the Egyptian army; established contact with

Anwar Sadat and the Free Officers. At times, disguised as a British officer, he would visit the various officers' clubs in Cairo. Other nights, wearing his Arab fez and posing as a spoiled, rich young Egyptian, he would drop in at the Kit-Kat and other famous nightclubs, and spend long hours drinking and chatting with English civilian and military personalities. He became involved with a local Jewish girl, Edith. But another Jewish name, Rebecca, had been the key to his activity. Indeed, the novel *Rebecca* by Daphne du Maurier had been the codebook which his radio operator had used for transmitting their reports to Rommel. Ken Follett's bestselling novel, *The Key to Rebecca*, was based on Eppler's exploits.

Eppler and Monkaster had been arrested in the fall of 1942, and interrogated by an old acquaintance of Paul Fackenheim: Major Tilly. Fackenheim's interlocutor said they had been sentenced to death.

He could not say if their broadcasts had helped Rommel. In June 1942 Rommel had taken Tobruk and crossed the Egyptian border. But he had been defeated by Montgomery at El Alamein, and after a 2,000-mile retreat to Tunisia had abandoned his dream of entering Cairo and planting the German flag on the banks of the Suez Canal.

In December 1944, two new prisoners were brought to Latrun after spending a few weeks in the Interrogation Center in Maadi. They told Paul that Eppler and Monkaster were still alive, that their execution had been suspended. The two newcomers were German officers, captured after parachuting into the Jordan valley. They were the first German agents to infiltrate into Palestine from the air after Paul Fackenheim. The two men, a captain and a major, had been parachuted near Jericho in the early morning of November 5. They had been dropped from a Heinkel-111 together with three other men—a German born in Palestine, Friedrich Deininger-Schaeffer, and two local Arab chieftains who had escaped to Berlin at the outbreak of the war, Kiffel Abdul Latif and Sheik Hassan Salameh. They had been entrusted with a satanic mission, which was to be the ultimate revenge of the Mufti of Jerusalem on the Jews of Palestine.

The Mufti, that devoted ally of Nazi Germany, had fled to Berlin in 1941, and had established his headquarters in the sumptuous Bellevue Palace. There, with the help of dozens of Palestinian exiles, he had planned a grandiose Arab revolt in the Middle East. His men, now training in Wehrmacht installations, were to return to Palestine and the neighboring countries, and incite the population against the British. An Arab liberation army, 10,000 strong, would defeat the 40,000 British troops in the Middle East and found a new order with the help of Nazi Germany. The plan was indeed inspiring, but after a while the German high command had to bow to the facts: The mighty Arab army of the Mufti existed only in his imagination. There weren't even one hundred Arabs in the whole Middle East willing to risk their lives for the Mufti by rebelling against the British Empire. The "Lawrence of Arabia" dream of Canaris was shattered.

Still, in the autumn of 1944, when Hitler was planning his last desperate offensive against the Allies in Belgium, the German high command tried to divert British troops to the Middle East by triggering an Arab uprising in Palestine. To put the plan in motion, two German agents, members of the famous Brandenburg Regiment, were to be parachuted into the Jordan valley. They were to be accompanied in their mission by a Palestine-born German and two Arab chieftains.

When the plan was presented to the Mufti, he agreed to cooperate, but on one condition. The commando had to carry out the Mufti's personal vengeance against the Jews: He had to poison the wells of Tel Aviv.

The next morning, a dashing colonel of the Brandenburg Regiment had clicked his heels in the audience room of the Bellevue Palace and informed the Mufti that the high command had agreed to his project. And on November 5, 1944, when the five agents were parachuted in the region of Jericho, they carried in their bags, besides weapons, maps, provisions, and gold, several cardboard containers filled with poison.

The results of the mission could have been disastrous. Had the commando reached the wells of Ras el Ein, which supplied Tel Aviv with drinking water, 160,000 people might have died in terrible agony.

But the operation was doomed to failure. Bedouin children playing in the rocky Wadi Kelt canyon found one of the paratroopers' bags soon after the drop and brought it to their sheik. It contained handfuls of gold coins—British sovereigns, Maria Theresa thalers, Turkish lira. The Palestinian police found out about the sudden windfall, and quickly learned about the parachuting.

One of the most extensive manhunts in the history of Palestine was organized under the expert command of the chief of police for the country district of Jerusalem, Fayiz Bey Idrissi. The ingenious Idrissi succeeded in tracking down the enemy agents to a cave in the Judea mountains. He stormed the cave at the head of his men, and captured two German officers and one of the Arabs. The third German escaped and turned up in Australia years later, while Sheik Hassan Salameh, who had broken his leg during the drop, found refuge in a little hamlet close to Latrun. A prize was put on his head, but his traces had vanished.

Neither the British nor their German prisoners who had ended up at the Latrun hostel ever guessed that Salameh, the most wanted man in Palestine, spent the rest of the war hiding in a house barely a few miles away from the Trappist convent.

The day of Hitler's death, Fackenheim was still in Latrun. He had become the hostel's cook. Helped by the Jew Weissrock, the Nazi Fialla, the Italian Communist Martino, he fed the prisoners and their guards, making miracles out of the monotonous rations of soybeans, growing his own vegetables and spices in the backyard of the convent. He became the main spokesman of the prisoners vis-à-vis the camp authorities, and would often engage in crusades to defend internees' rights. The higher authorities in Jerusalem and Cairo learned to respect the tough, outspoken cook. Following his repeated protests they finally dismissed the corrupt commander of the camp.

May 8, 1945. V-day. Officially, the end of the war did not change the daily routine at Latrun. But a few weeks later, the British discreetly began preparing for the future. The first notable change concerned General Zahedi. The Iranian was suddenly authorized to transfer money into Palestine, buy new furniture, and have gourmet food served in his quarters. The crown already anticipated his return to Teheran, where he was bound to become one of the most influential political leaders. The other political internees also became objects of special attention. The Nazis and the spies, however, weren't as fortunate. The Ukrainian botanist was extradited to Yugoslavia, to be hanged by Tito. The Albanian, Elmas, was executed in Tirana. The old Polish colonel encountered the same fate in Warsaw. The Jew Rosenblatt, an innocent victim of circumstances, was also extradited to Poland and hanged. The Austrian journalist Fialla, though, was lucky: Flown to Czechoslovakia, he got away with only ten years of hard labor. The Druze sheik addressed a last colorful curse to the British Empire and returned to his tribe on his splendid Arab mare.

In March 1946, Fackenheim and Weissrock were transferred to Cairo and imprisoned in Maadi. The regime was milder than before, and the guards, even some of the officers, would freely chat with the prisoners. Here Fackenheim heard for the first time about the unsuccessful attempt on Hitler's life on July 20, 1944. Among the officers connected with the conspiracy, two names were familiar to him: Field Marshal Erwin Rommel and and Admiral Wilhelm Canaris. Rommel had been forced to commit suicide by taking poison. Canaris had been hanged at the concentration camp of Flossenburg. The SS had got their last revenge on the man they had hated and fought for so many years: They had used a piano cord for Canaris's hanging, to prolong his agony.

After a few weeks in Egypt, Fackenheim and Weissrock took off in a transport Douglas bound for Europe. The plane was full of German agents and spies. "Do you know this bloke?" Weissrock asked, pointing at a passenger across the aisle.

Fackenheim shook his head. "Who is he?"

"John Eppler." Alias Hussein Gaafar, the famous spy of Rommel.

The aircraft flew across Europe, landing at Athens, Bari, Vienna, and finally Frankfurt. An American officer in full combat gear was waiting on the runway. "Who are those guys?" he asked their British escorts.

"German spies."

"Why the hell didn't you shoot the damn pigs?"

They spent the night in the Frankfurt prison. Paul Fackenheim couldn't close his eyes. He was beside himself with anger and frustration. His mother was so near, yet he couldn't see or inquire about her. Nobody would even talk to him.

The next morning, at dawn, they left aboard a convoy of military jeeps for Hamburg. As they approached the city, they took a turn and drove straight into a huge camp.

A sign formed an arch over the main gate.

"Arbeit macht Frei."

The sight was so familiar. Barbed-wire fences. Watchtowers. Machine-gun nests. Gallows.

This was the Nazi concentration camp of Neuengamme. Here the SS had massacred thousands upon thousands of Jews, freedom fighters, political dissidents. Now the camp had been transformed into a prison for the same Nazis. Seven thousand SS, Gestapo officials, notorious assassins, and Nazi fanatics from all over Germany were now assigned to the same barracks where they had tortured and murdered their victims.

At Neuengamme Paul Ernst Fackenheim's odyssey had ended. It had started at Dachau, the crown gem of the murderous Nazi enterprise. The former 26336 now found himself in the same concentration camp with his former jailers and torturers.

The absurd had no limits.

XVIII

Coming Home

PAUL ERNST FACKENHEIM, Number 26336, alias Paul Koch, alias Mister X, Number 64, was released from Neuengamme on June 23, 1946.

The same day, in the Hamburg railway station, he boarded a train for Frankfurt. He ran through the ruins and the piles of rubble to his house, to his mother.

His mother wasn't there.

He was told that in February 1943, she had been arrested by the Gestapo, together with many other Frankfurt Jews.

He was told that on March 16, 1943, she had been deported to the death camp of Theresienstadt.

He was told she had died there.

The Abwehr hadn't kept its word. It hadn't protected Hedda Fackenheim.

All he had done had been for nothing.

That night, in a drab hotel room in Frankfurt, a broken man, prematurely aged, cried for a long time.

His neighbors knocked on his door and asked him to be quiet.

He wasn't letting them sleep in peace, they said.

Author's Note

I first heard of "our Jewish spy" from a former officer of the Abwehr in a crowded Bierhalle in Hamburg. He knew vaguely that a Jew had been sent to Palestine; he didn't know his name. A year later, at a party in Paris, a former Abwehr general gave me his name: Paul Ernst Fackenheim. I started my research, contacting experts, historians, writers. I spent a long time in archives and libraries. Nobody had heard about Paul Fackenheim. No record of his mission existed. But finally, two years after I had started my quest, I found a bundle of handwritten papers in a private archive.

The story those papers told hardly seemed credible. I had to find the man himself, if he was still alive. All my other efforts having failed, I finally hired a German student and instructed him to scan all the phone books of Germany, looking for Fackenheim's name. As it was a quite unusual name, I doubted that there would be many people carrying it. About a month later, the student called me. He had found Fackenheim in a small town in West Germany: Ulzburg, in the Land of Holstein, about fifteen miles north of Hamburg. I wrote him a letter, and informed him I was researching a book on his life. He replied by cable, agreeing to cooperate with me. He sent me his diary, written after the war ended, in which he had described his extraordinary adventures. I traveled to Germany and spent several weeks with him, interviewing him at length on every stage of his tumultuous life. He told me his story in detail, stating names, places, and dates. He reconstituted, word by word, his feelings, his impressions, his conversations with his superiors and his interrogators. He reconstructed for me the grilles, the codewords, the drawings mentioned in his story.

After I finished writing down and recording the interviews, I asked for proof. Neither the documents I had in my possession nor Fackenheim's monologues were enough to convince me of the accuracy of the story. Fackenheim started telephoning and writing all over Germany, and soon we began receiving letters and affidavits from his former companions and mentors, who confirmed his story. Colonel Dieschler, the former station chief of the Abwehr in Athens, wrote to me about Fackenheim's departure to Palestine. Another former Abwehr official, Heinrich Berzeviczy, addressed to Paul Fackenheim a sworn affidavit confirming the main points of his story. Several former inmates of the detention camp in Latrun sent to me detailed statements about their common life in the convent.

I left Ulzburg and proceeded with my research. Several British officers, who had served in military intelligence in Cairo, confirmed by writing their knowledge of the capture and court-martial of "Koch." In England I located and interviewed Arthur Dowden, the MI-16 captain who had captured and interrogated Fackenheim in Palestine, the same Dowden who had been vice consul of Great Britain in Frankfurt before the war. Dowden had been discharged from the British army with the grade of general and had become a businessman in London. He also gave me a written statement on the Fackenheim affair.

In the Public Record Office in London, I found the "Most Secret" reports of the SIME and the MEIC describing the search for Paula Koch and Colonel Falkenheim. Other documents relating to the Fackenheim affair are still classified for a great many years to come.

In Israel I found Ruth and Marion Kobliner, the daughters of the deceased Mrs. Irma Kobliner, who had saved Fackenheim's life. They remembered that dear Paul Fackenheim and his mother, and the day when their mother had been "abducted" by the British captain in order to identify Paul Fackenheim at his court-martial.

One question, though, remained unanswered. Why did Karl Fackenheim, Paul Fackenheim's uncle, fail to recognize his nephew when they met at the 52nd Detention Barracks? Karl Fackenheim had been dead for a long time, and I couldn't obtain any testimony on that particular subject.

I got the answer in a most unexpected way. An Israeli reporter, who had heard about my research, interviewed me on a live talk show on the national radio. While I was describing the story of Paul Fackenheim, we got a dramatic phone call from a kibbutz in the north of the country. On the other end of the line was Karl Fackenheim's daughter. She remembered the event vividly. "My father recognized Paul, of course," she said, "but he was so ashamed that his nephew had become a Nazi spy that he decided to deny any connection with him."

That phone call solved the last mystery of the Fackenheim case.

After his liberation, Paul Ernst Fackenheim married again, but his wife died a year later of a disease contracted during the bombing of Hamburg. He remarried for the fourth time and settled in Ulzburg, where he lived until his death. In Ulzburg he finally realized his boyhood dream— writing. Under the pseudonym of Paul Ernst, he published quite a few novels.

"On what subject?" I had asked him, when we met for the first time.

He had smiled. "After all that happened to me, I could write on one and only subject. Espionage, of course."

The real Koch—Oberpraesident of East Prussia and later Reichs Kommissar for the Ukraine Erich Koch—was sentenced to death in Warsaw in 1959, and his appeal was rejected. His execution was deferred, however, and he was incarcerated in Mokossov Prison.

It was established that while Paul Fackenheim, "Koch," was on trial in Jerusalem, suspected to be an Obergruppenführer SS, Erich Koch was busy carrying out mass executions in Kiev.

Index

Fackenheim, Luzi Schiller (wife), 29-30, 62
  death of, 31-32
Fackenheim, Paul:
  meets Abwehr "chief" in Athens, 89-92; acquitted at espionage trial, 204; trip to Athens, 72-79; in Athens, 76-79, 80-94, 95-110; last day in Athens, 116-22; in Berlin, 67-74; biography of, 23-37; attitude towards British in Palestine, 148; taken to Brussels, 39-46; stay in Brussels, 48-58, 59-66; strange dream in Brussels, 48-50; discovers Jewish quarter in Brussels, 63-65; cooking and, 36, 42; in Dachau hospital, 8-9; released from Dachau, 3-22; death of first wife, 31-32; held as "enemy alien" after trial, 205-19; inquires about English visa, 33-34; espionage trial of, 184-96, 197-204; final release and freedom of, 220; applies for service in German Army, 37; identified as Gestapo agent, 191-92; enters Haifa, 133-38; as hardware company representative, 27-28; initial interrogation by British in Haifa, 143-47, 147-50; in Jerusalem, 178-83; and Jewish community meetings in September 1933, 34-35; given "Paul Koch" papers and identity, 42-43; at the Latrun camp, 175-78, 207-19; interrogated at Maadi, 154-66; first marriage of, 27-28, 61-62; marriage to Luzi Schiller, 29-30; MEIC interest in, 150-53; MEIC trap set for,

154-66; mock execution in desert, 167-68; instructed in Morse code and radio transmissions, 52-53, 55; transferred to camp at Neuengamme, 218-19; briefed for Palestine mission, 104-10; convinced about Palestine mission, 104-05; final preparation for Palestine mission, 116-22; parachutes into Palestine, 121-22, 125, 131-33; in post-World War I Germany, 26; pro-German feelings of, 34-35, 37, 38; incident with two SS guards in Berlin, 67-70; in Sofia (stopover), 75-76; sugar warehouse in Athens and, 80-82; "surrenders" to British in Haifa, 139-47; testifies at his trial, 200-02; Major Tilly's trap for, 162-66; truth serum used on, 171-73; and uncle Karl, 181-83; in World War I, 24-26
Fackenheim, Willy (son), 30, 32
Fahmi, Hekmath, 213
Falkenheim, Colonel, 157, 159, 205, 222
  confused with Paul Fackenheim, 152-53
Fialla, Fritz Edler von, 211-12, 216, 217
Flo (Brussels girlfriend), 60, 65
Follett, Ken, 214
Frankfurter Allgemeine Zeitung, 26

"G-Tinten" (secret ink), 85
Galland, Adolf, 57
Gleiwitz episode, 11-12
Goebbels, Joseph, 146
Goering, Hermann, 3, 25, 30
Gotz (doctor-prisoner), 211
Graziani, Marshal Rodolfo, 95